D1530129

20217802R10148

Made in the USA
Middletown, DE
20 May 2015

Data Mining
for the Masses

Dr. Matthew North

A Global Text Project Book

This book is available on Amazon.com.

ISBN: 0615684378

ISBN-13: 978-0615684376

DEDICATION

This book is gratefully dedicated to Dr. Charles Hannon, who gave me the chance to become a college professor and then challenged me to learn how to teach data mining to the masses.

Table of Contents

ACKNOWLEDGEMENTS

I would not have had the expertise to write this book if not for the assistance of many colleagues at various institutions. I would like to acknowledge Drs. Thomas Hilton and Jean Pratt, formerly of Utah State University and now of University of Wisconsin—Eau Claire who served as my Master's degree advisors. I would also like to acknowledge Drs. Terence Ahern and Sebastian Diaz of West Virginia University, who served as doctoral advisors to me.

I express my sincere and heartfelt gratitude for the assistance of Dr. Simon Fischer and the rest of the team at Rapid-I. I thank them for their excellent work on the RapidMiner software product and for their willingness to share their time and expertise with me on my visit to Dortmund.

Finally, I am grateful to the Kenneth M. Mason, Sr. Faculty Research Fund and Washington & Jefferson College, for providing financial support for my work on this text.

SECTION ONE: DATA MINING BASICS

CHAPTER ONE:
INTRODUCTION TO DATA MINING AND CRISP-DM

INTRODUCTION

Data mining as a discipline is largely transparent to the world. Most of the time, we never even notice that it's happening. But whenever we sign up for a grocery store shopping card, place a purchase using a credit card, or surf the Web, we are creating data. These **data** are stored in large sets on powerful computers owned by the companies we deal with every day. Lying within those data sets are patterns—indicators of our interests, our habits, and our behaviors. Data mining allows people to locate and interpret those patterns, helping them make better informed decisions and better serve their customers. That being said, there are also concerns about the practice of data mining. Privacy watchdog groups in particular are vocal about organizations that amass vast quantities of data, some of which can be very personal in nature.

The intent of this book is to introduce you to concepts and practices common in data mining. It is intended primarily for undergraduate college students and for business professionals who may be interested in using information systems and technologies to solve business problems by mining data, but who likely do not have a formal background or education in computer science. Although data mining is the fusion of applied statistics, logic, artificial intelligence, machine learning and data management systems, you are not required to have a strong background in these fields to use this book. While having taken introductory college-level courses in statistics and databases will be helpful, care has been taken to explain within this book, the necessary concepts and techniques required to successfully learn how to mine data.

Each chapter in this book will explain a data mining concept or technique. You should understand that the book is not designed to be an instruction manual or tutorial for the tools we will use (RapidMiner and OpenOffice Base and Calc). These software packages are capable of many types of **data analysis**, and this text is not intended to cover all of their capabilities, but rather, to illustrate how these software tools can be used to perform certain kinds of data mining. The book is also not exhaustive; it includes a variety of common data mining techniques, but RapidMiner in particular is capable of many, many data mining tasks that are not covered in the book.

The chapters will all follow a common format. First, chapters will present a scenario referred to as *Context and Perspective*. This section will help you to gain a real-world idea about a certain kind of problem that data mining can help solve. It is intended to help you think of ways that the data mining technique in that given chapter can be applied to organizational problems you might face. Following *Context and Perspective,* a set of *Learning Objectives* is offered. The idea behind this section is that each chapter is designed to teach you something new about data mining. By listing the objectives at the beginning of the chapter, you will have a better idea of what you should expect to learn by reading it. The chapter will follow with several sections addressing the chapter's topic. In these sections, step-by-step examples will frequently be given to enable you to work alongside an actual data mining task. Finally, after the main concepts of the chapter have been delivered, each chapter will conclude with a *Chapter Summary*, a set of *Review Questions* to help reinforce the main points of the chapter, and one or more *Exercise* to allow you to try your hand at applying what was taught in the chapter.

A NOTE ABOUT TOOLS

There are many software tools designed to facilitate data mining, however many of these are often expensive and complicated to install, configure and use. Simply put, they're not a good fit for learning the basics of data mining. This book will use OpenOffice Calc and Base in conjunction with an open source software product called RapidMiner, developed by Rapid-I, GmbH of Dortmund, Germany. Because OpenOffice is widely available and very intuitive, it is a logical place to begin teaching introductory level data mining concepts. However, it lacks some of the tools data miners like to use. RapidMiner is an ideal complement to OpenOffice, and was selected for this book for several reasons:

- RapidMiner provides specific data mining functions not currently found in OpenOffice, such as decision trees and association rules, which you will learn to use later in this book.
- RapidMiner is easy to install and will run on just about any computer.
- RapidMiner's maker provides a Community Edition of its software, making it free for readers to obtain and use.

- Both RapidMiner and OpenOffice provide intuitive graphical user interface environments which make it easier for general computer-using audiences to the experience the power of data mining.

All examples using OpenOffice or RapidMiner in this book will be illustrated in a Microsoft Windows environment, although it should be noted that these software packages will work on a variety of computing platforms. It is recommended that you download and install these two software packages on your computer now, so that you can work along with the examples in the book if you would like.

- OpenOffice can be downloaded from: http://www.openoffice.org/
- RapidMiner Community Edition can be downloaded from:
  http://rapid-i.com/content/view/26/84/

THE DATA MINING PROCESS

Although data mining's roots can be traced back to the late 1980s, for most of the 1990s the field was still in its infancy. Data mining was still being defined, and refined. It was largely a loose conglomeration of data models, analysis algorithms, and ad hoc outputs. In 1999, several sizeable companies including auto maker Daimler-Benz, insurance provider OHRA, hardware and software manufacturer NCR Corp. and statistical software maker SPSS, Inc. began working together to formalize and standardize an approach to data mining. The result of their work was **CRISP-DM**, the CRoss-Industry Standard Process for Data Mining. Although

the participants in the creation of CRISP-DM certainly had vested interests in certain software and hardware tools, the process was designed independent of any specific tool. It was written in such a way as to be conceptual in nature—something that could be applied independent of any certain tool or kind of data. The process consists of six steps or phases, as illustrated in Figure 1-1.

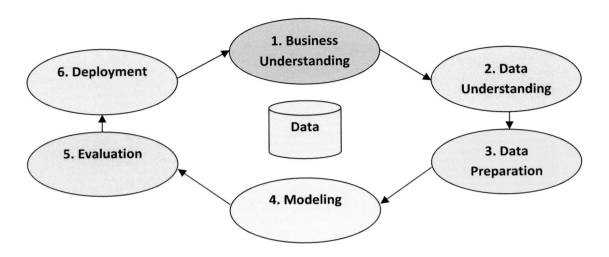

Figure 1-1: CRISP-DM Conceptual Model.

CRISP-DM Step 1: Business (Organizational) Understanding

The first step in CRISP-DM is **Business Understanding**, or what will be referred to in this text as **Organizational Understanding**, since organizations of all kinds, not just businesses, can use data mining to answer questions and solve problems. This step is crucial to a successful data mining outcome, yet is often overlooked as folks try to dive right into mining their data. This is natural of course—we are often anxious to generate some interesting output; we want to find answers. But you wouldn't begin building a car without first defining what you want the vehicle to do, and without first *designing* what you are going to *build*. Consider these oft-quoted lines from Lewis Carroll's *Alice's Adventures in Wonderland*:

"Would you tell me, please, which way I ought to go from here?"

"That depends a good deal on where you want to get to," said the Cat.

"I don't much care where--" said Alice.

"Then it doesn't matter which way you go," said the Cat.

"--so long as I get SOMEWHERE," Alice added as an explanation.

"Oh, you're sure to do that," said the Cat, "if you only walk long enough."

Indeed. You can mine data all day long and into the night, but if you don't know what you want to know, if you haven't defined any questions to answer, then the efforts of your data mining are less likely to be fruitful. Start with high level ideas: What is making my customers complain so much?

How can I increase my per-unit profit margin? How can I anticipate and fix manufacturing flaws and thus avoid shipping a defective product? From there, you can begin to develop the more specific questions you want to answer, and this will enable you to proceed to …

CRISP-DM Step 2: Data Understanding

As with Organizational Understanding, **Data Understanding** is a preparatory activity, and sometimes, its value is lost on people. Don't let its value be lost on you! Years ago when workers did not have their own computer (or multiple computers) sitting on their desk (or lap, or in their pocket), data were centralized. If you needed information from a company's data store, you could request a report from someone who could query that information from a central database (or fetch it from a company filing cabinet) and provide the results to you. The inventions of the personal computer, workstation, laptop, tablet computer and even smartphone have each triggered moves away from data centralization. As hard drives became simultaneously larger *and* cheaper, and as software like Microsoft Excel and Access became increasingly more accessible and easier to use, data began to disperse across the enterprise. Over time, valuable data stores became strewn across hundred and even thousands of devices, sequestered in marketing managers' spreadsheets, customer support databases, and human resources file systems.

As you can imagine, this has created a multi-faceted data problem. Marketing may have wonderful data that could be a valuable asset to senior management, but senior management may not be aware of the data's existence—either because of territorialism on the part of the marketing department, or because the marketing folks simply haven't thought to tell the executives about the data they've gathered. The same could be said of the information sharing, or lack thereof, between almost any two business units in an organization. In Corporate America lingo, the term 'silos' is often invoked to describe the separation of units to the point where interdepartmental sharing and communication is almost non-existent. It is unlikely that effective organizational data mining can occur when employees do not know *what* data they have (or could have) at their disposal or *where* those data are currently located. In chapter two we will take a closer look at some mechanisms that organizations are using to try bring all their data into a common location. These include databases, data marts and data warehouses.

Simply centralizing data is not enough however. There are plenty of question that arise once an organization's data have been corralled. Where did the data come from? Who collected them and was there a standard method of collection? What do the various columns and rows of data mean? Are there acronyms or abbreviations that are unknown or unclear? You may need to do some research in the Data Preparation phase of your data mining activities. Sometimes you will need to meet with subject matter experts in various departments to unravel where certain data came from, how they were collected, and how they have been coded and stored. It is critically important that you verify the accuracy and reliability of the data as well. The old adage "It's better than nothing" does not apply in data mining. Inaccurate or incomplete data could be worse than nothing in a data mining activity, because decisions based upon partial or wrong data are likely to be partial or wrong decisions. Once you have gathered, identified and understood your data assets, then you may engage in…

CRISP-DM Step 3: Data Preparation

Data come in many shapes and formats. Some data are numeric, some are in paragraphs of text, and others are in picture form such as charts, graphs and maps. Some data are anecdotal or narrative, such as comments on a customer satisfaction survey or the transcript of a witness's testimony. Data that aren't in rows or columns of numbers shouldn't be dismissed though—sometimes non-traditional data formats can be the most information rich. We'll talk in this book about approaches to formatting data, beginning in Chapter 2. Although rows and columns will be one of our most common layouts, we'll also get into text mining where paragraphs can be fed into RapidMiner and analyzed for patterns as well.

Data Preparation involves a number of activities. These may include joining two or more data sets together, reducing data sets to only those variables that are interesting in a given data mining exercise, scrubbing data clean of anomalies such as outlier observations or missing data, or re-formatting data for consistency purposes. For example, you may have seen a spreadsheet or database that held phone numbers in many different formats:

(555) 555-5555	555/555-5555
555-555-5555	555.555.5555
555 555 5555	5555555555

Each of these offers the same phone number, but stored in different formats. The results of a data mining exercise are most likely to yield good, useful results when the underlying data are as consistent as possible. Data preparation can help to ensure that you improve your chances of a successful outcome when you begin…

CRISP-DM Step 4: Modeling

A **model**, in data mining at least, is a computerized representation of real-world observations. Models are the application of algorithms to seek out, identify, and display any patterns or messages in your data. There are two basic kinds or types of models in data mining: those that **classify** and those that **predict**.

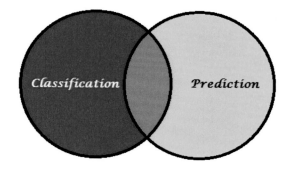

Figure 1-2: Types of Data Mining Models.

As you can see in Figure 1-2, there is some overlap between the types of models data mining uses. For example, this book will teaching you about **decision trees**. Decision Trees are a predictive model used to determine which attributes of a given data set are the strongest indicators of a given outcome. The outcome is usually expressed as the likelihood that an observation will fall into a certain category. Thus, Decision Trees are predictive in nature, but they also help us to classify our data. This will probably make more sense when we get to the chapter on Decision Trees, but for now, it's important just to understand that models help us to classify and predict based on patterns the models find in our data.

Models may be simple or complex. They may contain only a single process, or stream, or they may contain sub-processes. Regardless of their layout, models are where data mining moves from preparation and understanding to development and interpretation. We will build a number of example models in this text. Once a model has been built, it is time for…

CRISP-DM Step 5: Evaluation

All analyses of data have the potential for false positives. Even if a model doesn't yield false positives however, the model may not find any interesting patterns in your data. This may be because the model isn't set up well to find the patterns, you could be using the wrong technique, or there simply may not be anything interesting in your data for the model to find. The Evaluation phase of CRISP-DM is there specifically to help you determine how valuable your model is, and what you might want to do with it.

Evaluation can be accomplished using a number of techniques, both mathematical and logical in nature. This book will examine techniques for cross-validation and testing for false positives using RapidMiner. For some models, the power or strength indicated by certain test statistics will also be discussed. Beyond these measures however, model evaluation must also include a human aspect. As individuals gain experience and expertise in their field, they will have operational knowledge which may not be measurable in a mathematical sense, but is nonetheless indispensable in determining the value of a data mining model. This human element will also be discussed throughout the book. Using both data-driven and instinctive evaluation techniques to determine a model's usefulness, we can then decide how to move on to…

CRISP-DM Step 6: Deployment

If you have successfully identified your questions, prepared data that can answer those questions, and created a model that passes the test of being interesting and useful, then you have arrived at the point of *actually using your results*. This is **deployment**, and it is a happy and busy time for a data miner. Activities in this phase include setting up automating your model, meeting with consumers of your model's outputs, integrating with existing management or operational information systems, feeding new learning from model use back into the model to improve its accuracy and performance, and monitoring and measuring the outcomes of model use. Be prepared for a bit of distrust of your model at first—you may even face pushback from groups who may feel their jobs are threatened by this new tool, or who may not trust the reliability or accuracy of the outputs. But don't let this discourage you! Remember that CBS did not trust the initial predictions of the UNIVAC, one of the first commercial computer systems, when the network used it to predict the eventual outcome of the 1952 presidential election on election night. With only 5% of the votes counted, UNIVAC predicted Dwight D. Eisenhower would defeat Adlai Stevenson in a landslide;

something no pollster or election insider consider likely, or even possible. In fact, most 'experts' expected Stevenson to win by a narrow margin, with some acknowledging that because they expected it to be close, Eisenhower might also prevail in a tight vote. It was only late that night, when human vote counts confirmed that Eisenhower was running away with the election, that CBS went on the air to acknowledge first that Eisenhower had won, and second, that UNIVAC had predicted this very outcome hours earlier, but network brass had refused to trust the computer's prediction. UNIVAC was further vindicated later, when it's prediction was found to be within 1% of what the eventually tally showed. New **technology** is often unsettling to people, and it is hard sometimes to trust what computers show. Be patient and specific as you explain how a new data mining model works, what the results mean, and how they can be used.

While the UNIVAC example illustrates the power and utility of predictive computer modeling (despite inherent mistrust), it should not construed as a reason for blind trust either. In the days of UNIVAC, the biggest problem was the newness of the technology. It was doing something no one really expected or could explain, and because few people understood how the computer worked, it was hard to trust it. Today we face a different but equally troubling problem: computers have become ubiquitous, and too often, we don't question enough whether or not the results are accurate and meaningful. In order for data mining models to be effectively deployed, balance must be struck. By clearly communicating a model's function and utility to stake holders, thoroughly testing and proving the model, then planning for and monitoring its implementation, data mining models can be effectively introduced into the organizational flow. Failure to carefully and effectively manage deployment however can sink even the best and most effective models.

DATA MINING AND YOU

Because data mining can be applied to such a wide array of professional fields, this book has been written with the intent of explaining data mining in plain English, using software tools that are accessible and intuitive to everyone. You may not have studied algorithms, data structures, or programming, but you may have questions that can be answered through data mining. It is our hope that by writing in an informal tone and by illustrating data mining concepts with accessible, logical examples, data mining can become a useful tool for you regardless of your previous level of data analysis or computing expertise. Let's start digging!

CHAPTER TWO:
ORGANIZATIONAL UNDERSTANDING AND DATA UNDERSTANDING

CONTEXT AND PERSPECTIVE

Consider some of the activities you've been involved with in the past three or four days. Have you purchased groceries or gasoline? Attended a concert, movie or other public event? Perhaps you went out to eat at a restaurant, stopped by your local post office to mail a package, made a purchase online, or placed a phone call to a utility company. Every day, our lives are filled with interactions – encounters with companies, other individuals, the government, and various other organizations.

In today's technology-driven society, many of those encounters involve the transfer of information electronically. That information is recorded and passed across networks in order to complete financial transactions, reassign ownership or responsibility, and enable delivery of goods and services. Think about the amount of data collected each time even one of these activities occurs.

Take the grocery store for example. If you take items off the shelf, those items will have to be replenished for future shoppers – perhaps even for yourself – after all you'll need to make similar purchases again when that case of cereal runs out in a few weeks. The grocery store must constantly replenish its supply of inventory, keeping the items people want in stock while maintaining freshness in the products they sell. It makes sense that large databases are running behind the scenes, recording data about what you bought and how much of it, as you check out and pay your grocery bill. All of that data must be recorded and then reported to someone whose job it is to reorder items for the store's inventory.

However, in the world of data mining, simply keeping inventory up-to-date is only the beginning. Does your grocery store require you to carry a frequent shopper card or similar device which, when scanned at checkout time, gives you the best price on each item you're buying? If so, they can now begin not only keep track of store-wide purchasing trends, but individual purchasing trends as well. The store can target market to you by sending mailers with coupons for products you tend to purchase most frequently.

Now let's take it one step further. Remember, if you can, what types of information you provided when you filled out the form to receive your frequent shopper card. You probably indicated your address, date of birth (or at least birth year), whether you're male or female, and perhaps the size of your family, annual household income range, or other such information. Think about the range of possibilities now open to your grocery store as they analyze that vast amount of data they collect at the cash register each day:

- Using ZIP codes, the store can locate the areas of greatest customer density, perhaps aiding their decision about the construction location for their next store.
- Using information regarding customer gender, the store may be able to tailor marketing displays or promotions to the preferences of male or female customers.
- With age information, the store can avoid mailing coupons for baby food to elderly customers, or promotions for feminine hygiene products to households with a single male occupant.

These are only a few the many examples of potential uses for data mining. Perhaps as you read through this introduction, some other potential uses for data mining came to your mind. You may have also wondered how ethical some of these applications might be. This text has been designed to help you understand not only the possibilities brought about through data mining, but also the techniques involved in making those possibilities a reality while accepting the responsibility that accompanies the collection and use of such vast amounts of personal information.

LEARNING OBJECTIVES

After completing the reading and exercises in this chapter, you should be able to:
- Define the discipline of Data Mining
- List and define various types of data
- List and define various sources of data
- Explain the fundamental differences between databases, data warehouses and data sets

- Explain some of the ethical dilemmas associated with data mining and outline possible solutions

PURPOSES, INTENTS AND LIMITATIONS OF DATA MINING

Data mining, as explained in Chapter 1 of this text, applies statistical and logical methods to large data sets. These methods can be used to *categorize* the data, or they can be used to create *predictive models*. Categorizations of large sets may include grouping people into similar types of classifications, or in identifying similar characteristics across a large number of observations.

Predictive models however, transform these descriptions into expectations upon which we can base decisions. For example, the owner of a book-selling Web site could project how frequently she may need to restock her supply of a given title, or the owner of a ski resort may attempt to predict the earliest possible opening date based on projected snow arrivals and accumulations.

It is important to recognize that data mining cannot provide answers to every question, nor can we expect that predictive models will always yield results which will in fact turn out to be the reality. Data mining is limited to the data that has been collected. And those limitations may be many. We must remember that the data may not be completely representative of the group of individuals to which we would like to apply our results. The data may have been collected incorrectly, or it may be out-of-date. There is an expression which can adequately be applied to data mining, among many other things: *GIGO,* or *Garbage In, Garbage Out.* The quality of our data mining results will directly depend upon the quality of our data collection and organization. Even after doing our very best to collect high quality data, we must still remember to base decisions not only on data mining results, but also on available resources, acceptable amounts of risk, and plain old common sense.

DATABASE, DATA WAREHOUSE, DATA MART, DATA SET...?

In order to understand data mining, it is important to understand the nature of databases, data collection and data organization. This is fundamental to the discipline of Data Mining, and will directly impact the quality and reliability of all data mining activities. In this section, we will examine the differences between **databases, data warehouses**, and **data sets**. We will also examine some of the variations in terminology used to describe data attributes.

Although we will be examining the differences between databases, data warehouses and data sets, we will begin by discussing what they have in common. In Figure 2-1, we see some data organized into **rows** (shown here as A, B, etc.) and **columns** (shown here as 1, 2, etc.). In varying data environments, these may be referred to by differing names. In a database, rows would be referred to as **tuples** or **records**, while the columns would be referred to as **fields**.

TYPO

	A	B	C	D
1	3989.408	3989.408	140.4029	2654.278
2	140.4029	4125.044	4125.044	1335.467
3	2654.278	1335.467	2789.76	2789.76
4	5777.168	1788.068	5912.553	3123.153
5	2050.529	6039.689	1915.155	4704.363
6	1435.265	2554.287	1571.295	1219.56
7	4006.104	7994.156	3872.258	6659.535
8	671.2763	3318.277	807.9208	1983.314
9	2622.699	1367.091	2758.56	43.64889
10	8364.031	12353.06	8229.223	11018.06

Figure 2-1: Data arranged in columns and rows.

In data warehouses and data sets, rows are sometimes referred to as **observations, examples** or **cases**, and columns are sometimes called **variables** or **attributes**. For purposes of consistency in this book, we will use the terminology of **observations** for rows and **attributes** for columns. It is important to note that RapidMiner will use the term *examples* for rows of data, so keep this in mind throughout the rest of the text.

A **database** is an organized grouping of information within a specific structure. Database containers, such as the one pictured in Figure 2-2, are called **tables** in a database environment. Most databases in use today are **relational databases**—they are designed using many tables which relate to one another in a logical fashion. Relational databases generally contain dozens or even hundreds of tables, depending upon the size of the organization.

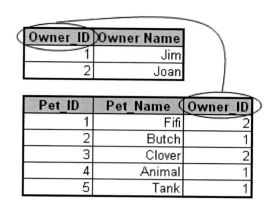

Figure 2-2: A simple database with a relation between two tables.

Figure 2-2 depicts a relational database environment with two tables. The first table contains information about pet owners; the second, information about pets. The tables are related by the single column they have in common: Owner_ID. By relating tables to one another, we can reduce redundancy of data and improve database performance. The process of breaking tables apart and thereby reducing data redundancy is called **normalization.**

Most relational databases which are designed to handle a high number of reads and writes (updates and retrievals of information) are referred to as **OLTP (online transaction processing)** systems. OLTP systems are very efficient for high volume activities such as cashiering, where many items are being recorded via bar code scanners in a very short period of time. However, using OLTP databases for analysis is generally not very efficient, because in order to retrieve data from multiple tables at the same time, a query containing joins must be written. A **query** is simple a method of retrieving data from database tables for viewing. Queries are usually written in a language called **SQL (Structured Query Language; pronounced 'sequel').** Because it is not very useful to only query pet names or owner names, for example, we must **join** two or more tables together in order to retrieve both pets and owners at the same time. Joining requires that the computer match the Owner_ID column in the Owners table to the Owner_ID column in the Pets table. When tables contain thousands or even millions of rows of data, this matching process can be very intensive and time consuming on even the most robust computers.

For much more on database design and management, check out geekgirls.com: (http://www.geekgirls.com/ menu_databases.htm).

In order to keep our transactional databases running quickly and smoothly, we may wish to create a data warehouse. A **data warehouse** is a type of large database that has been denormalized and archived. **Denormalization** is the process of intentionally combining some tables into a single table in spite of the fact that this may introduce duplicate data in some columns (or in other words, attributes).

Pet_ID	Pet_Name	Owner_Name
1	Fifi	Joan
2	Butch	Jim
3	Clover	Joan
4	Animal	Jim
5	Tank	Jim

Figure 2-3: A combination of the tables into a single data set.

Figure 2-3 depicts what our simple example data might look like if it were in a data warehouse. When we design databases in this way, we reduce the number of joins necessary to query related data, thereby speeding up the process of analyzing our data. Databases designed in this manner are called **OLAP (online analytical processing)** systems.

Transactional systems and analytical systems have conflicting purposes when it comes to database speed and performance. For this reason, it is difficult to design a single system which will serve both purposes. This is why data warehouses generally contain archived data. **Archived data** are data that have been copied out of a transactional database. Denormalization typically takes place at the time data are copied out of the transactional system. It is important to keep in mind that if a *copy* of the data is made in the data warehouse, the data may become out-of-synch. This happens when a copy is made in the data warehouse and then later, a change to the original record (observation) is made in the source database. Data mining activities performed on out-of-synch observations may be useless, or worse, misleading. An alternative archiving method would be to *move* the data out of the transactional system. This ensures that data won't get out-of-synch, however, it also makes the data unavailable should a user of the transactional system need to view or update it.

A **data set** is a subset of a database or a data warehouse. It is usually denormalized so that only one table is used. The creation of a data set may contain several steps, including appending or combining tables from source database tables, or simplifying some data expressions. One example of this may be changing a date/time format from '10-DEC-2002 12:21:56' to '12/10/02'. If this latter date format is adequate for the type of data mining being performed, it would make sense to simplify the attribute containing dates and times when we create our data set. Data sets may be made up of a representative sample of a larger set of data, or they may contain all observations relevant to a specific group. We will discuss sampling methods and practices in Chapter 3.

TYPES OF DATA

Thus far in this text, you've read about some fundamental aspects of data which are critical to the discipline of data mining. But we haven't spent much time discussing where that data are going to come from. In essence, there are really two types of data that can be mined: **operational** and **organizational**.

The most elemental type of data, operational data, comes from transactional systems which record everyday activities. Simple encounters like buying gasoline, making an online purchase, or checking in for a flight at the airport all result in the creation of **operational data**. The times, prices and descriptions of the goods or services we have purchased are all recorded. This information can be combined in a data warehouse or may be extracted directly into a data set from the OLTP system.

Often times, transactional data is too detailed to be of much use, or the detail may compromise individuals' privacy. In many instances, government, academic or not-for-profit organizations may create data sets and then make them available to the public. For example, if we wanted to identify regions of the United States which are historically at high risk for influenza, it would be difficult to obtain permission and to collect doctor visit records nationwide and compile this information into a meaningful data set. However, the U.S. Centers for Disease Control and Prevention (CDCP), do exactly that every year. Government agencies do not always make this information immediately available to the general public, but it often can be requested. Other organizations create such summary data as well. The grocery store mentioned at the beginning of this chapter wouldn't necessarily want to analyze records of individual cans of greens beans sold, but they may want to watch trends for daily, weekly or perhaps monthly totals. **Organizational data** sets can help to protect peoples' **privacy**, while still proving useful to data miners watching for trends in a given population.

Another type of data often overlooked within organizations is something called a data mart. A **data mart** is an organizational data store, similar to a data warehouse, but often created in conjunction with business units' needs in mind, such as Marketing or Customer Service, for reporting and management purposes. Data marts are usually intentionally created by an organization to be a type of one-stop shop for employees throughout the organization to find data they might be looking for. Data marts may contain wonderful data, prime for data mining activities, but they must be known, current, and accurate to be useful. They should also be well-managed in terms of privacy and security.

All of these types of organizational data carry with them some concern. Because they are secondary, meaning they have been derived from other more detailed primary data sources, they may lack adequate documentation, and the rigor with which they were created can be highly variable. Such data sources may also not be intended for general distribution, and it is always wise to ensure proper permission is obtained before engaging in data mining activities on any data set. Remember, simply because a data set may have been acquired from the Internet does not mean it is in the public domain; and simply because a data set may exist within your organization does not mean it can be freely mined. Checking with relevant managers, authors and stakeholders is critical before beginning data mining activities.

A NOTE ABOUT PRIVACY AND SECURITY

In 2003, JetBlue Airlines supplied more than one million passenger records to a U.S. government contractor, Torch Concepts. Torch then subsequently augmented the passenger data with additional information such as family sizes and social security numbers—information purchased from a data broker called Acxiom. The data were intended for a data mining project in order to develop potential terrorist profiles. All of this was done without notification or consent of passengers. When news of the activities got out however, dozens of privacy lawsuits were filed against JetBlue, Torch and Acxiom, and several U.S. senators called for an investigation into the incident.

This incident serves several valuable purposes for this book. First, we should be aware that as we gather, organize and analyze data, there are real people behind the figures. These people have certain rights to privacy and protection against crimes such as identity theft. We as data miners have an ethical obligation to protect these individuals' rights. This requires the utmost care in terms of information security. Simply because a government representative or contractor asks for data does not mean it should be given.

Beyond technological security however, we must also consider our moral obligation to those individuals behind the numbers. Recall the grocery store shopping card example given at the beginning of this chapter. In order to encourage use of frequent shopper cards, grocery stores frequently list two prices for items, one with use of the card and one without. For each individual, the answer to this question may vary, however, answer it for yourself: At what price mark-up has the grocery store crossed an ethical line between encouraging consumers to participate in frequent shopper programs, and forcing them to participate in order to afford to buy groceries? Again, your answer will be unique from others', however it is important to keep such moral obligations in mind when gathering, storing and mining data.

The objectives hoped for through data mining activities should never justify unethical means of achievement. Data mining can be a powerful tool for customer relationship management, marketing, operations management, and production, however in all cases the human element must be kept sharply in focus. When working long hours at a data mining task, interacting primarily with hardware, software, and numbers, it can be easy to forget about the people, and therefore it is so emphasized here.

CHAPTER SUMMARY

This chapter has introduced you to the discipline of data mining. Data mining brings statistical and logical methods of analysis to large data sets for the purposes of describing them and using them to create predictive models. Databases, data warehouses and data sets are all unique kinds of digital record keeping systems, however, they do share many similarities. Data mining is generally most effectively executed on data data sets, extracted from OLAP, rather than OLTP systems. Both operational data and organizational data provide good starting points for data mining activities, however both come with their own issues that may inhibit quality data mining activities. These should be mitigated before beginning to mine the data. Finally, when mining data, it is critical to remember the human factor behind manipulation of numbers and figures. Data miners have an ethical responsibility to the individuals whose lives may be affected by the decisions that are made as a result of data mining activities.

REVIEW QUESTIONS

1) What is data mining in general terms?

2) What is the difference between a database, a data warehouse and a data set?

3) What are some of the limitations of data mining? How can we address those limitations?

4) What is the difference between operational and organizational data? What are the pros and cons of each?

5) What are some of the ethical issues we face in data mining? How can they be addressed?

6) What is meant by out-of-synch data? How can this situation be remedied?

7) What is normalization? What are some reasons why it is a good thing in OLTP systems, but not so good in OLAP systems?

EXERCISES

1) Design a relational database with at least three tables. Be sure to create the columns necessary within each table to relate the tables to one another.

2) Design a data warehouse table with some columns which would usually be normalized. Explain why it makes sense to denormalize in a data warehouse.

3) Perform an Internet search to find information about data security and privacy. List three web sites that you found that provided information that could be applied to data mining. Explain how it might be applied.

4) Find a newspaper, magazine or Internet news article related to information privacy or security. Summarize the article and explain how it might be related to data mining.

5) Using the Internet, locate a data set which is available for download. Describe the data set (contents, purpose, size, age, etc.). Classify the data set as operational or organizational. Summarize any requirements placed on individuals who may wish to use the data set.

6) Obtain a copy of an application for a grocery store shopping card. Summarize the type of data requested when filling out the application. Give an example of how that data may aid in a data mining activity. What privacy concerns arise regarding the data being collected?

CHAPTER THREE: DATA PREPARATION

CONTEXT AND PERSPECTIVE

Jerry is the marketing manager for a small Internet design and advertising firm. Jerry's boss asks him to develop a data set containing information about Internet users. The company will use this data to determine what kinds of people are using the Internet and how the firm may be able to market their services to this group of users.

To accomplish his assignment, Jerry creates an online survey and places links to the survey on several popular Web sites. Within two weeks, Jerry has collected enough data to begin analysis, but he finds that his data needs to be denormalized. He also notes that some observations in the set are missing values or they appear to contain invalid values. Jerry realizes that some additional work on the data needs to take place before analysis begins.

LEARNING OBJECTIVES

After completing the reading and exercises in this chapter, you should be able to:

- Explain the concept and purpose of data scrubbing
- List possible solutions for handling missing data
- Explain the role and perform basic methods for data reduction
- Define and handle inconsistent data
- Discuss the important and process of attribute reduction

APPLYING THE CRISP DATA MINING MODEL

Recall from Chapter 1 that the CRISP Data Mining methodology requires three phases *before* any actual data mining models are constructed. In the Context and Perspective paragraphs above, Jerry has a number of tasks before him, each of which fall into one of the first three phases of CRISP. First, Jerry must ensure that he has developed a clear **Organizational Understanding**. What is the purpose of this project for his employer? Why is he surveying Internet users? Which data points are important to collect, which would be nice to have, and which would be irrelevant or even distracting to the project? Once the data are collected, who will have access to the data set and through what mechanisms? How will the business ensure privacy is protected? All of these questions, and perhaps others, should be answered before Jerry even creates the survey mentioned in the second paragraph above.

Once answered, Jerry can then begin to craft his survey. This is where **Data Understanding** enters the process. What database system will he use? What survey software? Will he use a publicly available tool like SurveyMonkey™, a commercial product, or something homegrown? If he uses publicly available tool, how will he access and extract data for mining? Can he trust this third-party to secure his data and if so, why? How will the underlying database be designed? What mechanisms will be put in place to ensure consistency and integrity in the data? These are all questions of data understanding. An easy example of ensuring consistency might be if a person's home city were to be collected as part of the data. If the online survey just provides an open text box for entry, respondents could put just about anything as their home city. They might put New York, NY, N.Y., Nwe York, or any number of other possible combinations, including typos. This could be avoided by forcing users to select their home city from a dropdown menu, but considering the number cities there are in most countries, that list could be unacceptably long! So the choice of how to handle this potential data consistency problem isn't necessarily an obvious or easy one, and this is just one of many data points to be collected. While 'home state' or 'country' may be reasonable to constrain to a dropdown, 'city' may have to be entered freehand into a textbox, with some sort of data correction process to be applied later.

The 'later' would come once the survey has been developed and deployed, and data have been collected. With the data in place, the third CRISP-DM phase, **Data Preparation**, can begin. If you haven't installed OpenOffice and RapidMiner yet, and you want to work along with the examples given in the rest of the book, now would be a good time to go ahead and install these applications. Remember that both are freely available for download and installation via the Internet, and the links to both applications are given in Chapter 1. We'll begin by doing some data preparation in OpenOffice Base (the database application), OpenOffice Calc (the spreadsheet application), and then move on to other data preparation tools in RapidMiner. You should understand that the examples of data preparation in this book are only a subset of possible data preparation approaches.

COLLATION

Suppose that the database underlying Jerry's Internet survey is designed as depicted in the screenshot from OpenOffice Base in Figure 3-1.

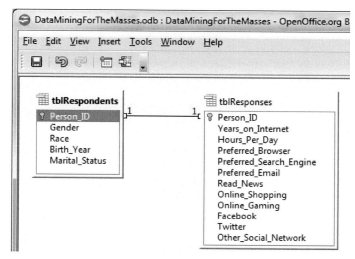

Figure 3-1: A simple relational (one-to-one) database for Internet survey data.

This design would enable Jerry to collect data about people in one table, and data about their Internet behaviors in another. RapidMiner would be able to connect to either of these tables in order to mine the responses, but what if Jerry were interested in mining data from both tables at once?

One simple way to collate data in multiple tables into a single location for data mining is to create a database view. A **view** is a type of pseudo-table, created by writing a SQL statement which is named and stored in the database. Figure 3-2 shows the creation of a view in OpenOffice Base, while Figure 3-3 shows the view in datasheet view.

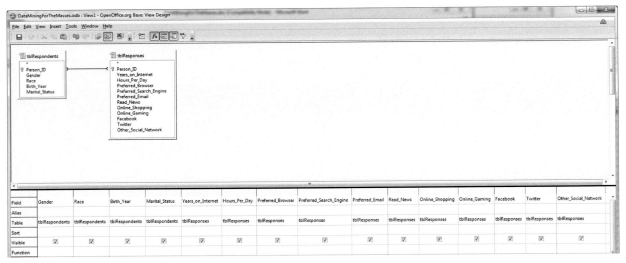

Figure 3-2: Creation of a view in OpenOffice Base.

Gender	Race	Birth_Year	Marital_Status	Years_on_Internet	Hours_Per_Day	Preferred_Browser	Preferred_Search_Engine	Preferred_Email	Read_News	Online_Shopping	Online_Gaming	Facebook	Twitter	Other_Social_Network
M	White	1972	M	8	1	Firefox	Google	Yahoo	Y	N	N	Y	N	
M	Hispanic	1981	S	14	2	Chrome	Google	Hotmail	Y	N	N	Y	N	
F	African American	1977	S	6	2	Firefox	Yahoo	Yahoo		Y		Y	N	
F	White	1961	D	8	6	Firefox	Google	Hotmail	N	Y	N	N	Y	
M	White	1954	M	2	3	Internet Explorer	Bing	Hotmail	Y	Y	Y	N	N	
M	African American	1982	D	15	4	Internet Explorer	Google	Yahoo	Y	N	Y	N	N	
M	African American	1981	D	11	2	Firefox	Google	Yahoo		Y		Y	Y	LinkedIn
M	White	1977	S	3	3	Internet Explorer	Yahoo	Yahoo	Y			Y	99	LinkedIn
F	African American	1969	M	6	2	Firefox	Google	Gmail	N	Y	N	N	N	
M	White	1987	S	12	1	Safari	Yahoo	Yahoo	Y		Y	Y	N	MySpace
F	Hispanic	1959	D	12	5	Chrome	Google	Gmail	Y	N	N	Y	N	Google+

Figure 3-3: Results of the view from Figure 3-2 in datasheet view.

The creation of views is one way that data from a relational database can be collated and organized in preparation for data mining activities. In this example, although the personal information in the 'Respondents' table is only stored once in the database, it is displayed for each record in the 'Responses' table, creating a data set that is more easily mined because it is both richer in information and consistent in its formatting.

DATA SCRUBBING

In spite of our very best efforts to maintain quality and integrity during data collection, it is inevitable that some anomalies will be introduced into our data at some point. The process of data scrubbing allows us to handle these anomalies in ways that make sense for us. In the remainder of this chapter, we will examine data scrubbing in four different ways: handling missing data, reducing data (observations), handling inconsistent data, and reducing attributes.

HANDS ON EXERCISE

Starting now, and throughout the next chapters of this book, there will be opportunities for you to put your hands on your computer and follow along. In order to do this, you will need to be sure to install OpenOffice and RapidMiner, as was discussed in the section *A Note about Tools* in Chapter 1. You will also need to have an Internet connection to access this book's companion web site, where copies of all data sets used in the chapter exercises are available. The companion web site is located at:

https://sites.google.com/site/dataminingforthemasses/

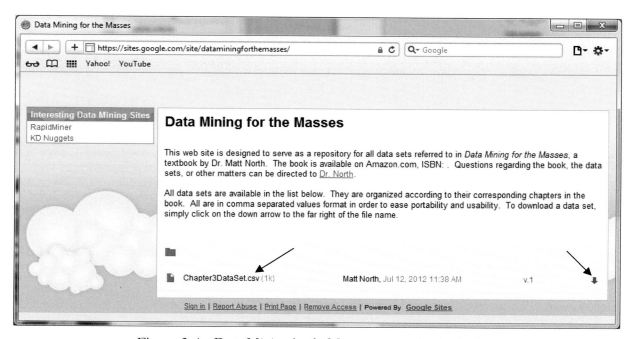

Figure 3-4. *Data Mining for the Masses* companion web site.

You can download the Chapter 3 data set, which is an export of the view created in OpenOffice Base, from the web site by locating it in the list of files and then clicking the down arrow to the far right of the file name, as indicated by the black arrows in Figure 3-4 You may want to consider creating a folder labeled 'data mining' or something similar where you can keep copies of your data—more files will be required and created as we continue through the rest of the book, especially when we get into building data mining models in RapidMiner. Having a central place to keep everything together will simplify things, and upon your first launch of the RapidMiner software, you'll be prompted to create a repository, so it's a good idea to have a space ready. Once you've downloaded the Chapter 3 data set, you're ready to begin learning how to handle and prepare data for mining in RapidMiner.

PREPARING RAPIDMINER, IMPORTING DATA, AND HANDLING MISSING DATA

Our first task in data preparation is to handle missing data, however, because this will be our first time using RapidMiner, the first few steps will involve getting RapidMiner set up. We'll then move straight into handling missing data. **Missing data** are data that do not exist in a data set. As you can see in Figure 3-5, missing data is not the same as zero or some other value. It is blank, and the value is unknown. Missing data are also sometimes known in the database world as **null**. Depending on your objective in data mining, you may choose to leave missing data as they are, or you may wish to replace missing data with some other value.

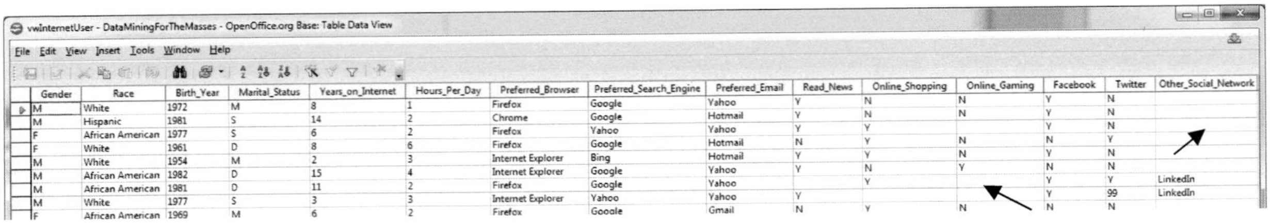

Gender	Race	Birth_Year	Marital_Status	Years_on_Internet	Hours_Per_Day	Preferred_Browser	Preferred_Search_Engine	Preferred_Email	Read_News	Online_Shopping	Online_Gaming	Facebook	Twitter	Other_Social_Network
M	White	1972	M	8	1	Firefox	Google	Yahoo	Y	N	N	Y	N	
M	Hispanic	1981	S	14	2	Chrome	Google	Hotmail	Y	N	N	Y	N	
F	African American	1977	S	6	2	Firefox	Yahoo	Yahoo	Y	Y		Y	N	
F	White	1961	D	8	6	Firefox	Google	Hotmail	N	Y	N	N	Y	
M	White	1954	M	2	3	Internet Explorer	Bing	Hotmail	Y	Y	N	Y	N	
M	African American	1982	D	15	4	Internet Explorer	Google	Yahoo	Y	N	Y	N	N	
M	African American	1981	D	11	2	Firefox	Google	Yahoo		Y		Y	Y	LinkedIn
M	White	1977	S	3	3	Internet Explorer	Yahoo	Yahoo	Y			Y	99	LinkedIn
F	African American	1969	M	6	2	Firefox	Google	Gmail	N	Y	N	N	N	

Figure 3-5: Some missing data within the survey data set.

The creation of views is one way that data from a relational database can be collated and organized in preparation for data mining activities. In this example, our database view has missing data in a number of its attributes. Black arrows indicate a couple of these attributes in Figure 3-5 above. In some instances, missing data are not a problem, they are expected. For example, in the Other Social Network attribute, it is entirely possible that the survey respondent did not indicate that they use social networking sites other than the ones proscribed in the survey. Thus, missing data are probably accurate and acceptable. On the other hand, in the Online Gaming attribute, there are answers of either 'Y' or 'N', indicating that the respondent either does, or does not participate in online gaming. But what do the missing, or null values in this attribute indicate? It is unknown to us. For the purposes of data mining, there are a number of options available for handling missing data.

To learn about handling missing data in RapidMiner, follow the steps below to connect to your data set and begin modifying it:

1) Launch the RapidMiner application. This can be done by double clicking your desktop icon or by finding it in your application menu. The first time RapidMiner is launched, you will get the message depicted in Figure 3-6. Click OK to set up a repository.

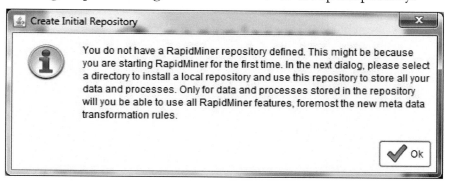

Figure 3-6. The prompt to create an initial data repository for RapidMiner to use.

2) For most purposes (and for all examples in this book), a local repository will be sufficient. Click OK to accept the default option as depicted in Figure 3-7.

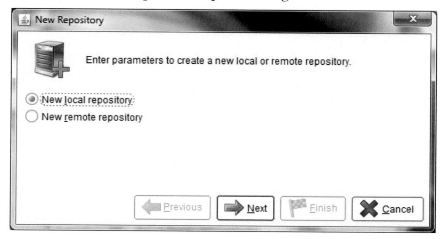

Figure 3-7. Setting up a local data repository.

3) In the example given in Figure 3-8, we have named our repository 'RapidMinerBook, and pointed it to our data folder, RapidMiner Data, which is found on our E: drive. Use the folder icon to browse and find the folder or directory you created for storing your RapidMiner data sets. Then click Finish.

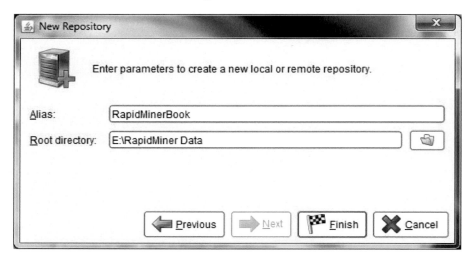

Figure 3-8. Setting the repository name and directory.

4) You may get a notice that updates are available. If this is the case, go ahead and accept the option to update, where you will be presented with a window similar to Figure 3-9. Take advantage of the opportunity to add in the Text Mining module (indicated by the black arrow), since Chapter 12 will deal with Text Mining. Double click the check box to add a green check mark indicating that you wish to install or update the module, then click Install.

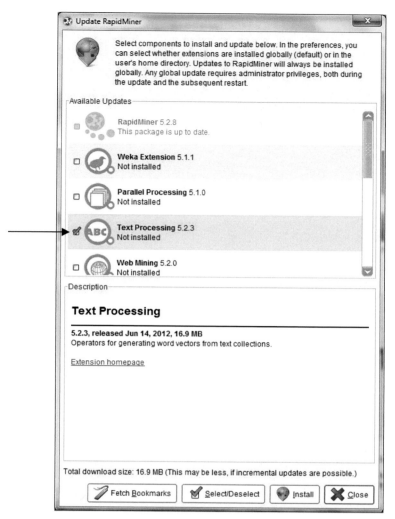

Figure 3-9. Installing updates and adding the Text Mining module.

5) Once the updates and installations are complete, RapidMiner will open and your window should look like Figure 3-10:

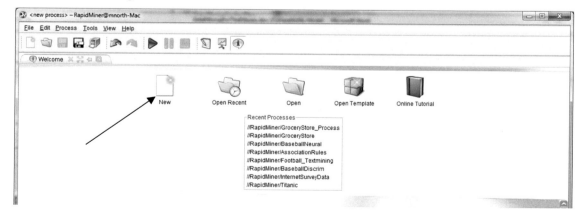

Figure 3-10. The RapidMiner start screen.

6) Next we will need to start a new data mining project in RapidMiner. To do this we click on the 'New' icon as indicated by the black arrow in Figure 3-10. The resulting window should look like Figure 3-11.

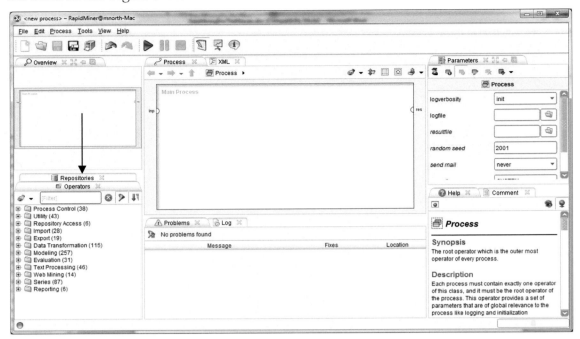

Figure 3-11. Getting started with a new project in RapidMiner.

7) Within RapidMiner there are two main areas that hold useful tools: **Repositories** and **Operators**. These are accessed by the tabs indicated by the black arrow in Figure 3-11. The Repositories area is the place where you will connect to each data set you wish to mine. The Operators area is where all data mining tools are located. These are used to build models and otherwise manipulate data sets. Click on Repositories. You will find that the initial repository we created upon our first launch of the RapidMiner software is present in the list.

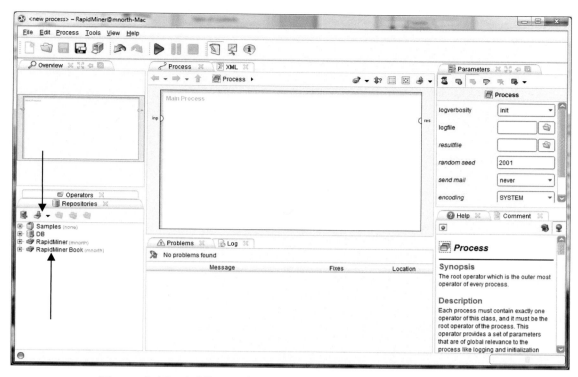

Figure 3-12. Adding a data set to a repository in RapidMiner.

8) Because the focus of this book is to introduce data mining to the broadest possible audience, we will not use all of the tools available in RapidMiner. At this point, we could do a number of complicated and technical things, such as connecting to a remote enterprise database. This however would likely be overwhelming and inaccessible to many readers. For the purposes of this text, we will therefore only be connecting to **comma separate values (CSV)** files. You should know that most data mining projects incorporate extremely large data sets encompassing dozens of attributes and thousands or even millions of observations. We will use smaller data sets in this text, but the foundational concepts illustrated are the same for large or small data. The Chapter 3 data set downloaded from the companion web site is very small, comprised of only 15 attributes and 11 observations. Our next step is to connect to this data set. Click on the Import icon, which is the second icon from the left in the Repositories area, as indicated by the black arrow in Figure 3-12.

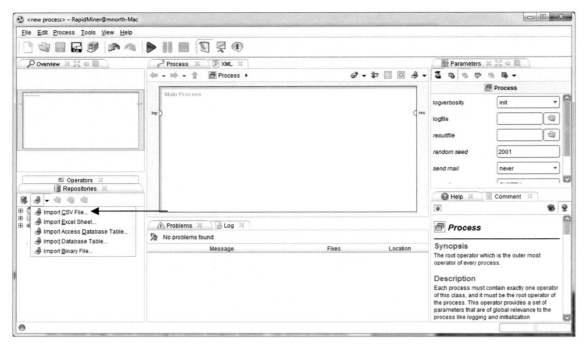

Figure 3-13. Importing a CSV file.

9) You will see by the black arrow in Figure 3-13 that you can import from a number of different data sources. Note that by importing, you are bringing your data into a RapidMiner file, rather than working with data that are already stored elsewhere. If your data set is extremely large, it may take some time to import the data, and you should be mindful of disk space that is available to you. As data sets grow, you may be better off using the first (leftmost) icon to set up a remote repository in order to work with data already stored in other areas. As previously explained, all examples in this text will be conducted by importing CSV files that are small enough to work with quickly and easily. Click on the Import CSV File option.

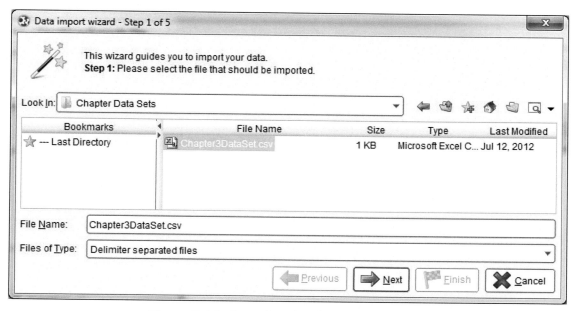

Figure 3-14. Locating the data set to import.

10) When the data import wizard opens, navigate to the folder where your data set is stored and select the file. In this example, only one file is visible: the Chapter 3 data set downloaded from the companion web site. Click Next.

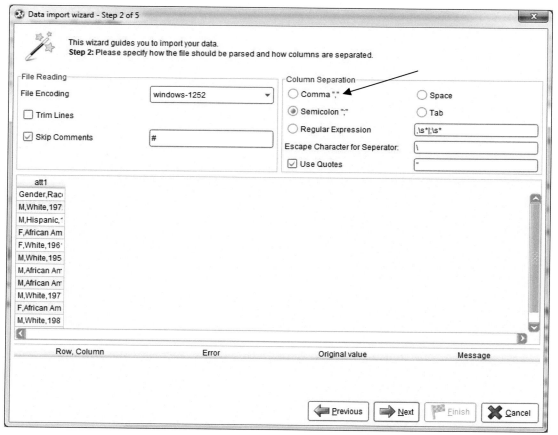

Figure 3-15. Configuring attribute separation.

11) By default, RapidMiner looks for semicolons as attribute separators in our data. We must change the column separation delimiter to be Comma, in order to be able to see each attribute separated correctly. **Note:** If your data naturally contain commas, then you should be careful as you are collecting or collating your data to use a delimiter that does not naturally occur in the data. A semicolon or a pipe (|) symbol can often help you avoid unintended column separation.

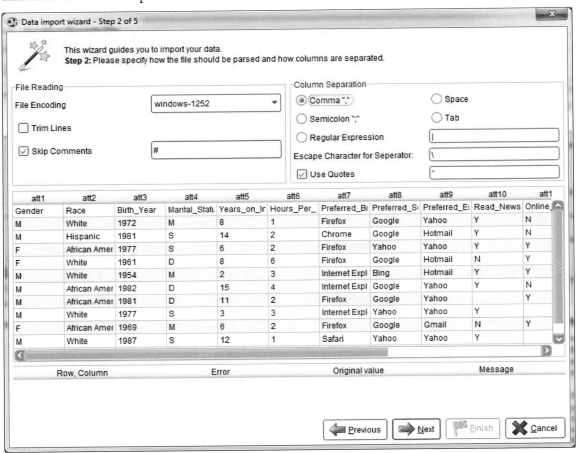

Figure 3-16. A preview of attributes separated into columns
with the Comma option selected.

12) Once the preview shows columns for each attribute, click Next. Note that RapidMiner has treated our attribute names as if they are our first row of data, or in other words, our first observation. To fix this, click the Annotation dropdown box next to this row and set it to **Name**, as indicated in Figure 3-17. With the attribute names designated correctly, click Next.

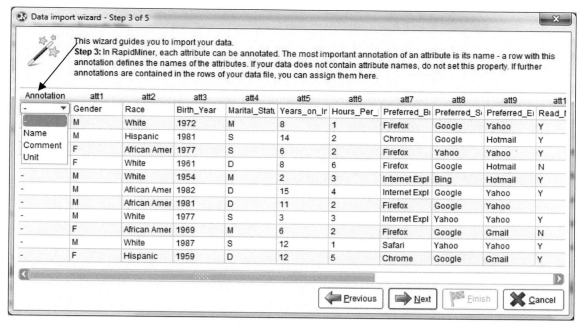

Figure 3-17. Setting the attribute names.

13) In step 4 of the data import wizard, RapidMiner will take its best guess at a **data type** for each attribute. The data type is the kind of data an attribute holds, such as numeric, text or date. These can be changed in this screen, but for our purposes in Chapter 3, we will accept the defaults. Just below each attribute's data type, RapidMiner also indicates a **Role** for each attribute to play. By default, all columns are imported simply with the role of 'attribute', however we can change these here if we know that one attribute is going to play a specific role in a data mining model that we will create. Since roles can be set within RapidMiner's main process window when building data mining models, we will accept the default of 'attribute' whenever we import data sets in exercises in this text. Also, you may note that the check boxes above each attribute in this window allow you to *not* import some of the attributes if you don't want to. This is accomplished by simply clearing the checkbox. Again, attributes can be excluded from models later, so for the purposes of this text, we will always include all attributes when importing data. All of these functions are indicated by the black arrows in Figure 3-18. Go ahead and accept these defaults as they stand and click Next.

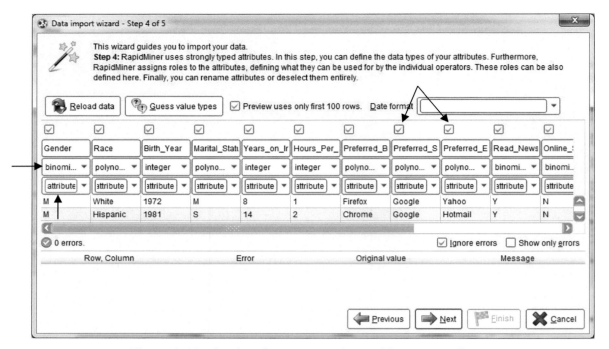

Figure 3-18. Setting data types, roles and import attributes.

14) The final step is to choose a repository to store the data set in, and to give the data set a name within RapidMiner. In Figure 3-19, we have chosen to store the data set in the RapidMiner Book repository, and given it the name Chapter3. Once we click Finish, this data set will become available to us for any type of data mining process we would like to build upon it.

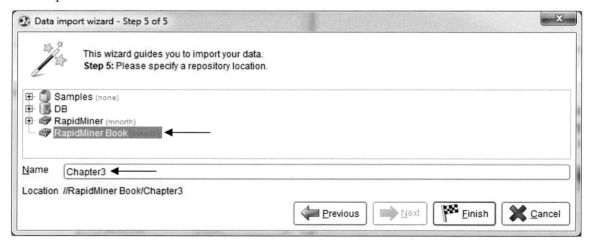

Figure 3-19. Selecting the repository and setting a data set name
for our imported CSV file.

15) We can now see that the data set is available for use in RapidMiner. To begin using it in a RapidMiner data mining process, simply drag the data set and drop it in the Main Process window, as has been done in Figure 3-20.

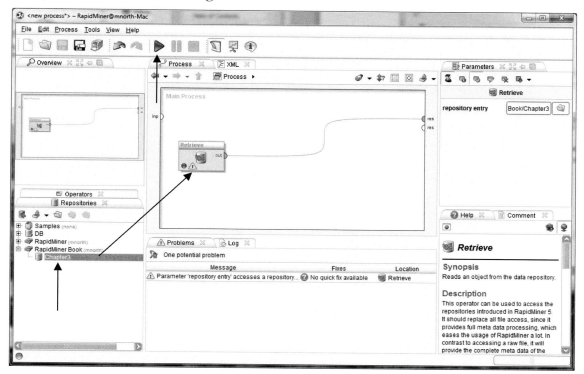

Figure 3-20. Adding a data set to a process in RapidMiner.

16) Each rectangle in a process in RapidMiner is an **operator**. The Retrieve operator simply gets a data set and makes it available for use. The small half-circles on the sides of the operator, and of the Main Process window, are called **ports**. In Figure 3-20, an output (*out*) port from our data set's Retrieve operator is connected to a result set (*res*) port via a **spline**. The splines, combined with the operators connected by them, constitute a data mining **stream**. To run a data mining stream and see the results, click the blue, triangular Play button in the toolbar at the top of the RapidMiner window. This will change your view from **Design Perspective**, which is the view pictured in Figure 3-20 where you can change your data mining stream, to **Results Perspective**, which shows your stream's results, as pictured in Figure 3-21. When you hit the Play button, you may be prompted to save your process, and you are encouraged to do so. RapidMiner may also ask you if you wish to overwrite a saved process each time it is run, and you can select your preference on this prompt as well.

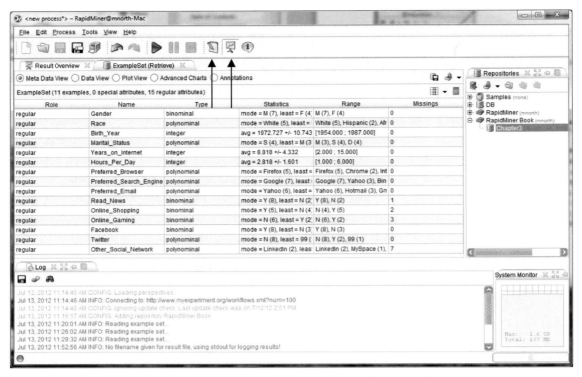

Figure 3-21. Results perspective for the Chapter3 data set.

17) You can toggle between design and results perspectives using the two icons indicated by the black arrows in Figure 3-21. As you can see, there is a rich set of information in results perspective. In the **meta data** view, basic descriptive statistics are given. It is here that we can also get a sense for the number of observations that have missing values in each attribute of the data set. The columns in meta data view can be stretched to make their contents more readable. This is accomplished by hovering your mouse over the faint vertical gray bars between each column, then clicking and dragging to make them wider. The information presented here can be very helpful in deciding where missing data are located, and what to do about it. Take for example the Online_Gaming attribute. The results perspective shows us that we have six 'N' responses in that attribute, two 'Y' responses, and three missing. We could use the **mode**, or most common response to replace the missing values. This of course assumes that the most common response is accurate for all observations, and this may not be accurate. As data miners, we must be responsible for thinking about each change we make in our data, and whether or not we threaten the integrity of our data by making that change. In some instances the consequences could be drastic. Consider, for instance, if the mode for an attribute of Felony_Conviction were 'Y'. Would we really want to convert all missing values in this attribute to 'Y' simply because that is the mode in our data set? Probably not; the

implications about the persons represented in each observation of our data set would be unfair and misrepresentative. Thus, we will change the missing values in the current example to illustrate how to handle missing values in RapidMiner, recognizing that what we are about to do won't always be the right way to handle missing data. In order to have RapidMiner handle the change from missing to 'N' for the three observations in our Online_Gaming variable, click the design perspective icon.

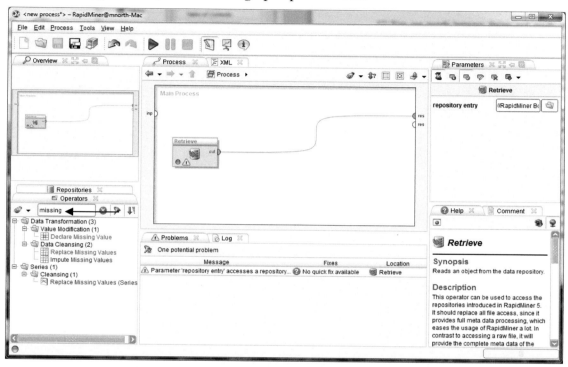

Figure 3-22. Finding an operator to handle missing values.

18) In order to find a tool in the Operators area, you can navigate through the folder tree in the lower left hand corner. RapidMiner offers many tools, and sometimes, finding the one you want can be tricky. There is a handy search box, indicated by the black arrow in Figure 3-22, that allows you to type in key words to find tools that might do what you need. Type the word 'missing' into this box, and you will see that RapidMiner automatically searches for tools with this word in their name. We want to replace missing values, and we can see that within the Data Transformation tool area, inside a sub-area called Value Modification, there is an operator called Replace Missing Values. Let's add this operator to our stream. Click and hold on the operator name, and drag it up to your spline. When you point your mouse cursor on the spline, the spline will turn slightly bold, indicating that when you let go of your mouse button, the operator will be connected into the stream. If you let go and the Replace Missing Values operator fails to connect into your stream, you can reconfigure

your splines manually. Simply click on the *out* port in your Retrieve operator, and then click on the *exa* port on the Replace Missing Values operator. *Exa* stands for example set, and remember that 'examples' is the word RapidMiner uses for observations in a data set. Be sure the *exa* port from the Replace Missing Values operator is connected to your result set (*res*) port so that when you run your process, you will have output. Your model should now look similar to Figure 3-23.

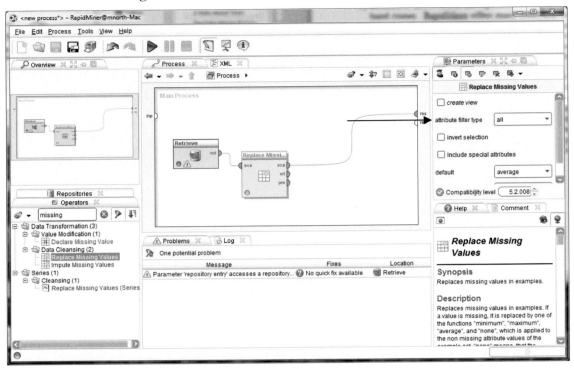

Figure 3-23. Adding a missing value operator to the stream.

19) When an operator is selected in RapidMiner, it has an orange rectangle around it. This will also enable you to modify that operator's **parameters**, or properties. The Parameters pane is located on the right side of the RapidMiner window, as indicated by the black arrow in Figure 3-23. For this exercise, we have decided to change all missing values in the Online_Gaming attribute to be 'N', since this is the most common response in that attribute. To do this, change the 'attribute filter type' to 'single', and you will see that a dropdown box appears, allowing you to choose the Online_Gaming attribute as the target for modification. Next, expand the 'default' dropdown box, and select 'value', which will cause a 'replenishment value' box to appear. Type the replacement value 'N' in this box. Note that you may need to expand your RapidMiner window, or use the vertical scroll bar on the left of the Parameters pane in order to see all options, as the options change based on what you have selected. When you are finished, your parameters should look like the

ones in Figure 3-24. Parameter settings that were changed are highlighted with black arrows.

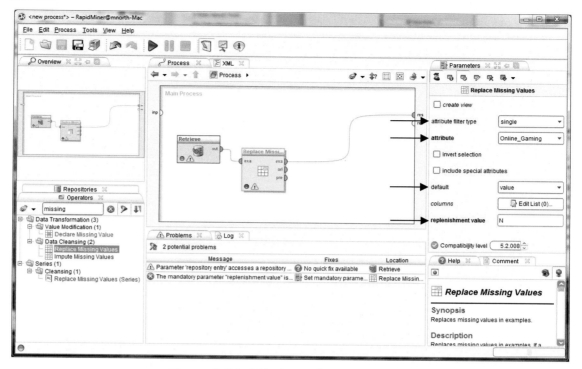

Figure 3-24. Missing value parameters.

20) You should understand that there are many other options available to you in the parameters pane. We will not explore all of them here, but feel free to experiment with them. For example, instead of changing a single attribute at a time, you could change a subset of the attributes in your data set. You will learn much about the flexibility and power of RapidMiner by trying out different tools and features. When you have your parameter set, click the play button. This will run your process and switch you to results perspective once again. Your results should look like Figure 3-25.

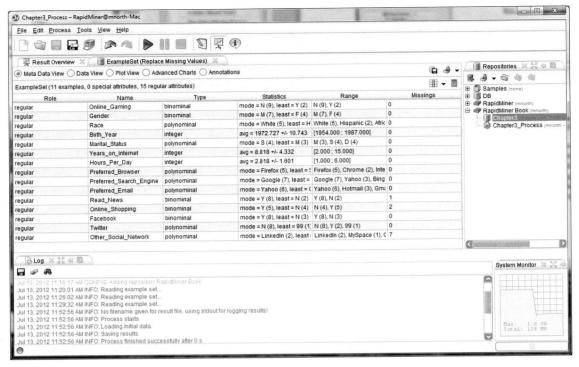

Figure 3-25. Results of changing missing data.

21) You can see now that the Online_Gaming attribute has been moved to the top of our list, and that there are zero missing values. Click on the Data View radio button, above and to the left hand side of the attribute list to see your data in a spreadsheet-type view. You will see that the Online_Gaming variable is now populated with only 'Y' and 'N' values. We have successfully replaced all missing values in that attribute. While in Data View, take note of how missing values are annotated in other variables, Online_Shopping for example. A question mark (?) denotes a missing value in an observation. Suppose that for this variable, we do not wish to replace the null values with the mode, but rather, that we wish to remove those observations from our data set prior to mining it. This is accomplished through data reduction.

DATA REDUCTION

Go ahead and switch back to design perspective. The next set of steps will teach you to reduce the number of observations in your data set through the process of filtering.

1) In the search box within the Operators tab, type in the word 'filter'. This will help you locate the 'Filter Examples' operator, which is what we will use in this example. Drag the

Filter Examples operator over and connect it into your stream, right after the Replace Missing Values operator. Your window will look like Figure 3-26.

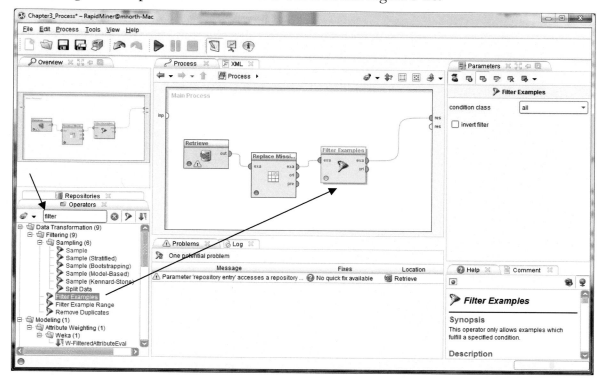

Figure 3-26. Adding a filter to the stream.

2) In the condition class, choose 'attribute_value_filter', and for the parameter_string, type the following: **Online_Shopping=.** <u>Be sure to include the period.</u> This parameter string refers to our attribute, Online_Shopping, and it tells RapidMiner to filter out all observations where the value in that attribute is missing. This is a bit confusing, because in Data View in results perspective, missings are denoted by a question mark (?), but when entering the parameter string, missings are denoted by a period (.). Once you've typed these parameter values in, your screen will look like Figure 3-27.

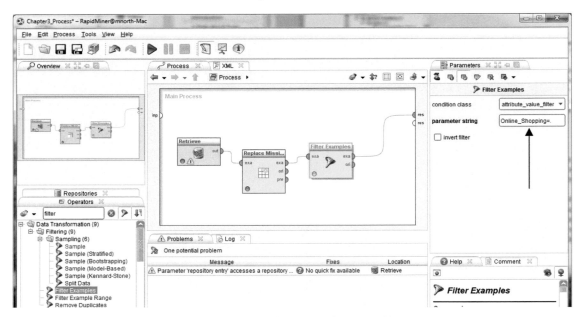

Figure 3-27. Adding observation filter parameters.

Go ahead and run your model by clicking the play button. In results perspective, you will now see that your data set has been reduced from eleven observations (or examples) to nine. This is because the two observations where the Online_Shopping attribute had a missing value have been removed. You'll be able to see that they're gone by selecting the Data View radio button. They have not been deleted from the original source data, they are simply removed from the data set at the point in the stream where the filter operator is located and will no longer be considered in any downstream data mining operations. In instances where the missing value cannot be safely assumed or computed, removal of the entire observation is often the best course of action. When attributes are numeric in nature, such as with ages or number of visits to a certain place, an arithmetic measure of central tendency, such as **mean, median** or **mode** might be an acceptable replacement for missing values, but in more subjective attributes, such as whether one is an online shopper or not, you may be better off simply filtering out observations where the datum is missing. (One cool trick you can try in RapidMiner is to use the Invert Filter option in design perspective. In this example, if you check that check box in the parameters pane of the Filter Examples operator, you will *keep* the missing observations, and filter out the rest.)

Data mining can be confusing and overwhelming, especially when data sets get large. It doesn't have to be though, if we manage our data well. The previous example has shown how to filter out observations containing undesired data (or missing data) in an attribute, but we can also reduce data to test out a data mining model on a smaller subset of our data. This can greatly reduce processing time while testing a model to see if it will work to answer our questions. Follow the steps below to take a **sample** of our data set in RapidMiner.

1) Using the search techniques previously demonstrated, use the Operators search feature to find an operator called 'Sample' and add this to your stream. In the parameters pane, set the sample to be to be a 'relative' sample, and then indicate you want to retain 50% of your observations in the resulting data set by typing **.5** into the sample ratio field. Your window should look like Figure 3-28.

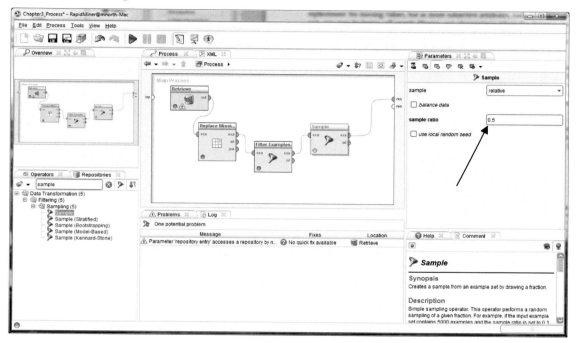

Figure 3-28. Taking a 50% random sample of the data set.

2) When you run your model now, you will find that your results only contain four or five observations, randomly selected from the nine that were remaining after our filter operator removed records that had missing Online_Shopping values.

Thus you can see that there are many ways, and various reasons to reduce data by decreasing the number of observations in your data set. We'll now move on to handling inconsistent data, but before doing so, <u>it is going to be important to reset our data back to its original form</u>. While filtering, we removed an observation that we will need in order to illustrate what inconsistent data is, and to demonstrate how to handle it in RapidMiner. This is a good time to learn how to remove operators from your stream. Switch back to design perspective and click on your Sampling operator. Next, right click and choose Delete, or simply press the Delete key on your keyboard. Delete the Filter Examples operator at this time as well. Note that your spline that was connected to the *res* port is also deleted. This is not a problem, you can reconnect the *exa* port from the Replace Missing Values operator to the *res* port, or you will find that the spline will reappear when you complete the steps under Handling Inconsistent Data.

HANDLING INCONSISTENT DATA

Inconsistent data is different from missing data. Inconsistent data occurs when a value <u>does exist</u>, however that value is not valid or meaningful. Refer back to Figure 3-25, a close up version of that image is shown here as Figure 3-29.

regular	Online_Shopping	binominal	mode = Y (5), least = N (4)	N (4), Y (5)
regular	Facebook	binominal	mode = Y (8), least = N (3)	Y (8), N (3)
regular	Twitter	polynominal	mode = N (8), least = 99 (1)	N (8), Y (2), 99 (1)
regular	Other_Social_Network	polynominal	mode = LinkedIn (2), least :	LinkedIn (2), MySpace (1), (

Figure 3-29. Inconsisten data in the Twitter attribute.

What is that 99 doing there? It seems that the only two valid values for the Twitter attribute should be 'Y' and 'N'. This is a value that is inconsistent and is therefore meaningless. As data miners, we can decide if we want to filter this observation out, as we did with the missing Online_Shopping records, or, we could use an operator designed to allow us to replace certain values with others.

1) Return to design perspective if you are not already there. Ensure that you have deleted your sampling and filter operators from your stream, so that your window looks like Figure 3-30.

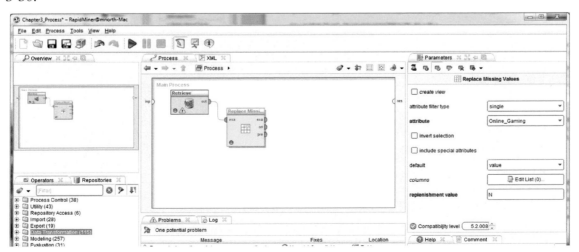

Figure 3-30. Returning to a full data set in RapidMiner.

2) Note that we don't need to remove the Replace Missing Values operator, because it is not removing any observations in our data set. It only changes the values in the Online_Gaming attribute, which won't affect our next operator. Use the search feature in the Operators tab to find an operator called Replace. Drag this operator into your stream. If your splines had been disconnected during the deletion of the sampling and filtering operators, as is the case in Figure 3-30, you will see that your splines are automatically reconnected when you add the Replace operator to the stream.

3) In the parameters pane, change the attribute filter type to single, then indicate Twitter as the attribute to be modified. In truth, in this data set there is only one instance of the value 99 across all attributes and observations, so this change to a single attribute is not actually necessary in this example, but it is good to be thoughtful and intentional with every step in a data mining process. Most data sets will be far larger and more complex that the Chapter 3 data set we are currently working with. In the 'replace what' field, type the value 99, since this is the value we're looking to replace. Finally, in the 'replace by' field, we must decide what we want to have in the place of the 99. If we leave this field blank, then the observation will have a missing (?) when we run the model and switch to Data View in results perspective. We could also choose the mode of 'N', and given that 80% of the survey respondents indicated that they did not use Twitter, this would seem a safe course of action. You may choose the value you would like to use. For the book's example, we will enter 'N' and then run our model. You can see in Figure 3-31 that we now have nine values of 'N', and two of 'Y' for our Twitter attribute.

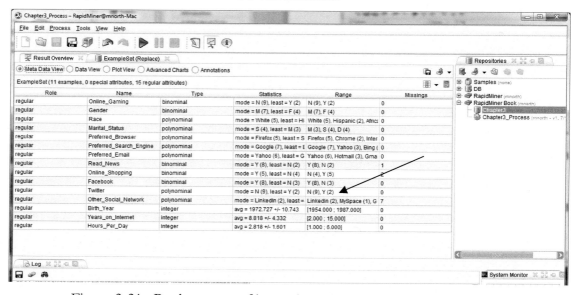

Figure 3-31. Replacement of inconsistent value with a consistent one.

Keep in mind that not all inconsistent data is going to be as easy to handle as replacing a single value. It would be entirely possible that in addition to the inconsistent value of 99, values of 87, 96, 101, or others could be present in a data set. If this were the case, it might take multiple replacements and/or missing data operators to prepare the data set for mining. In numeric data we might also come across data which are accurate, but which are also statistical outliers. These might also be considered to be inconsistent data, so an example in a later chapter will illustrate the handling of statistical outliers. Sometimes data scrubbing can become tedious, but it will ultimately affect the usefulness of data mining results, so these types of activities are important, and attention to detail is critical.

ATTRIBUTE REDUCTION

In many data sets, you will find that some attributes are simply irrelevant to answering a given question. In Chapter 4 we will discuss methods for evaluating correlation, or the strength of relationships between given attributes. In some instances, you will not know the extent to which a certain attribute will be useful without statistically assessing that attribute's correlation to the other data you will be evaluating. In our process stream in RapidMiner, we can remove attributes that are not very interesting in terms of answering a given question without completely deleting them from the data set. Remember, simply because certain variables in a data set aren't interesting for answering a certain question doesn't mean those variables won't ever be interesting. This is why we recommended bringing in all attributes when importing the Chapter 3 data set earlier in this chapter—uninteresting or irrelevant attributes are easy to exclude within your stream by following these steps:

1) Return to design perspective. In the operator search field, type Select Attribute. The Select Attributes operator will appear. Drag it onto the end of your stream so that it fits between the Replace operator and the result set port. Your window should look like Figure 3-32.

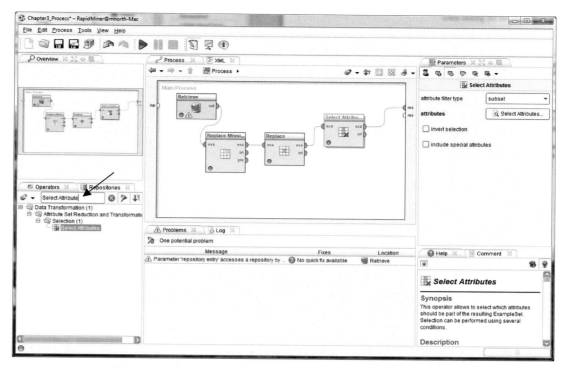

Figure 3-32. Selecting a subset of a data set's attributes.

2) In the Parameters pane, set the attribute filter type to 'subset', then click the Select Attributes button; a window similar to Figure 3-33 will appear.

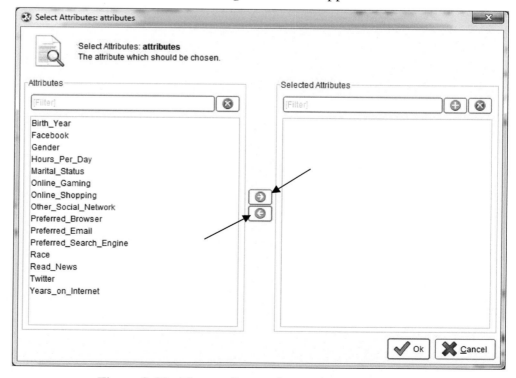

Figure 3-33. The attribute subset selection window.

3) Using the green right and left arrows, you can select which attributes you would like to keep. Suppose we were going to study the demographics of Internet users. In this instance, we might select Birth_Year, Gender, Marital_Status, Race, and perhaps Years_on_Internet, and move them to the right under Selected Attributes using the right green arrow. You can select more than one attribute at a time by holding down your control or shift keys (on a Windows computer) while clicking on the attributes you want to select or deselect. We could then click OK, and these would be the only attributes we would see in results perspective when we run our model. All subsequent downstream data mining operations added to our model will act only upon this subset of our attributes.

CHAPTER SUMMARY

This chapter has introduced you to a number of concepts related to data preparation. Recall that Data Preparation is the third step in the CRISP-DM process. Once you have established Organizational Understanding as it relates to your data mining plans, and developed Data Understanding in terms of what data you need, what data you have, where it is located, and so forth; you can begin to prepare your data for mining. This has been the focus of this chapter.

The chapter used a small and very simple data set to help you learn to set up the RapidMiner data mining environment. You have learned about viewing data sets in OpenOffice Base, and learned some ways that data sets in relational databases can be collated. You have also learned about comma separated values (CSV) files.

We have then stepped through adding CSV files to a RapidMiner data repository in order to handle missing data, reduce data through observation filtering, handle inconsistencies in data, and reduce the number of attributes in a model. All of these methods will be used in future chapters to prepare data for modeling.

Data mining is most successful when conducted upon a foundation of well-prepared data. Recall the quotation from Chapter 1 from *Alice's Adventures in Wonderland*—which way you go does not matter very much if you don't know, or don't care, where you are going. Likewise, the value of where you arrive when you complete a data mining exercise will largely depend upon how well you prepared to get there. Sometimes we hear the phrase "It's better than nothing". Well, in data mining, results gleaned from poorly prepared data might be "Worse than nothing", because they may be misleading. Decisions based upon them could lead an organization down a detrimental and costly path. Learn to value the process of data preparation, and you will learn to be a better data miner.

REVIEW QUESTIONS

1) What are the four main processes of data preparation discussed in this chapter? What do they accomplish and why are they important?

2) What are some ways to collate data from a relational database?

3) For what kinds of problems might a data set need to be scrubbed?

4) Why is it often better to perform reductions using operators rather than excluding attributes or observations as data are imported?

5) What is a data repository in RapidMiner and how is one created?

6) How might inconsistent data cause later trouble in data mining activities?

EXERCISE

1) Locate a data set of any number of attributes and observations. You may have access to data sets through personal data collection or through your employment, although if you use an employer's data, make sure to do so only by permission! You can also search the Internet for data set libraries. A simple search on the term 'data sets' in your favorite search engine will yield a number of web sites that offer libraries of data sets that you can use for academic and learning purposes. Download a data set that looks interesting to you and complete the following:

2) Format the data set into a CSV file. It may come in this format, or you may need to open the data in OpenOffice Calc or some similar software, and then use the File > Save As feature to save your data as a CSV file.

3) Import your data into your RapidMiner repository. Save it in the repository as Chapter3_Exercise.

4) Create a new, blank process stream in RapidMiner and drag your data set into the process window.

5) Run your process and examine your data set in both meta data view and Data View. Note if any attributes have missing or inconsistent data.

6) If you found any missing or inconsistent data, use operators to handle these. Perhaps try browsing through the folder tree in the Operators tab and experiment with some operators that were not covered in this chapter.

7) Try filtering out some observations based on some attibute's value, and filter out some attributes.

8) Document where you found your data set, how you prepared it for import into RapidMiner, and what data preparation activities you applied to it.

SECTION TWO: DATA MINING MODELS AND METHODS

CHAPTER FOUR:
CORRELATION

CONTEXT AND PERSPECTIVE

Sarah is a regional sales manager for a nationwide supplier of fossil fuels for home heating. Recent volatility in market prices for heating oil specifically, coupled with wide variability in the size of each order for home heating oil, has Sarah concerned. She feels a need to understand the types of behaviors and other factors that may influence the demand for heating oil in the domestic market. What factors are related to heating oil usage, and how might she use a knowledge of such factors to better manage her inventory, and anticipate demand? Sarah believes that data mining can help her begin to formulate an understanding of these factors and interactions.

LEARNING OBJECTIVES

After completing the reading and exercises in this chapter, you should be able to:

- Explain what correlation is, and what it isn't.
- Recognize the necessary format for data in order to perform correlation analysis.
- Develop a correlation model in RapidMiner.
- Interpret the coefficients in a correlation matrix and explain their significance, if any.

ORGANIZATIONAL UNDERSTANDING

Sarah's goal is to better understand how her company can succeed in the home heating oil market. She recognizes that there are many factors that influence heating oil consumption, and believes that by investigating the relationship between a number of those factors, she will be able to better monitor and respond to heating oil demand. She has selected correlation as a way to model the relationship between the factors she wishes to investigate. **Correlation** is a statistical measure of how strong the relationships are between attributes in a data set.

DATA UNDERSTANDING

In order to investigate her question, Sarah has enlisted our help in creating a correlation matrix of six attributes. Working together, using Sarah's employer's data resources which are primarily drawn from the company's billing database, we create a data set comprised of the following attributes:

- **Insulation**: This is a density rating, ranging from one to ten, indicating the thickness of each home's insulation. A home with a density rating of one is poorly insulated, while a home with a density of ten has excellent insulation.

- **Temperature**: This is the average outdoor ambient temperature at each home for the most recent year, measure in degree Fahrenheit.

- **Heating_Oil**: This is the total number of units of heating oil purchased by the owner of each home in the most recent year.

- **Num_Occupants**: This is the total number of occupants living in each home.

- **Avg_Age**: This is the average age of those occupants.

- **Home_Size**: This is a rating, on a scale of one to eight, of the home's overall size. The higher the number, the larger the home.

DATA PREPARATION

A CSV data set for this chapter's example is available for download at the book's companion web site (https://sites.google.com/site/dataminingforthemasses/). If you wish to follow along with the example, go ahead and download the Chapter04DataSet.csv file now and save it into your RapidMiner data folder. Then, complete the following steps to prepare the data set for correlation mining:

1) Import the Chapter 4 CSV data set into your RapidMiner data repository. Save it with the name Chapter4. If you need a refresher on how to bring this data set into your RapidMiner repository, refer to steps 7 through 14 of the Hands On Exercise in Chapter 3. The steps will be the same, with the exception of which file you select to import. Import all attributes, and accept the default data types. When you are finished, your repository should look similar to Figure 4-1.

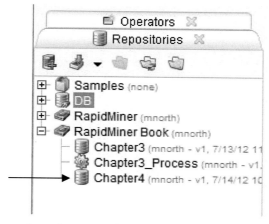

Figure 4-1. The chapter four data set added to the author's RapidMiner Book repository.

2) If your RapidMiner application is not open to a new, blank process window, click the new process icon, or click File > New to create a new process. Drag your Chapter4 data set into your main process window. Go ahead and click the run (play) button to examine the data set's meta data. If you are prompted, you may choose to save your new model. For this book's example, we'll save the model as Chapter4_Process.

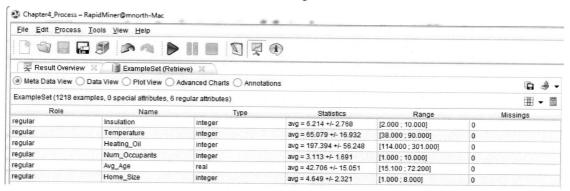

Figure 4-2. Meta Data view of the chapter four data set.

We can see in Figure 4-2 that our six attributes are shown. There are a total of 1,218 homes represented in the data set. Our data set appears to be very clean, with no missing values in any of the six attributes, and no inconsistent data apparent in our ranges or other descriptive statistics. If you wish, you can take a minute to switch to Data View to familiarize yourself with the data. It feels like these data are in good shape, and are in no further need of data preparation operators, so we are ready to move on to...

MODELING

3) Switch back to design perspective. On the Operators tab in the lower left hand corner, use the search box and begin typing in the word *correlation*. The tool we are looking for is called Correlation Matrix. You may be able to find it before you even finish typing the full search term. Once you've located it, drag it over into your process window and drop it into your stream. By default, the *exa* port will connect to the *res* port, but in this chapter's example we are interested in creating a matrix of correlation coefficients that we can analyze. Thus, is it important for you to connect the *mat* (matrix) port to a *res* port, as illustrated in Figure 4-3.

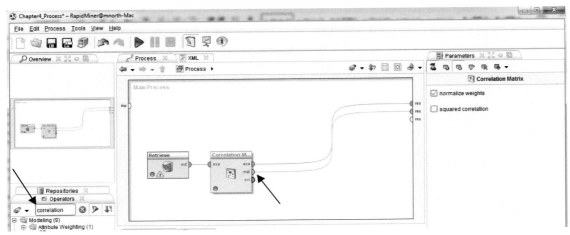

Figure 4-3. The addition of a Correlation Matrix to our stream, with the *mat* (matrix) port connected to a result set (*res*) port.

4) Correlation is a relatively simple statistical analysis tool, so there are few parameters to modify. We will accept the defaults, and run the model. The results will be similar to Figure 4-4.

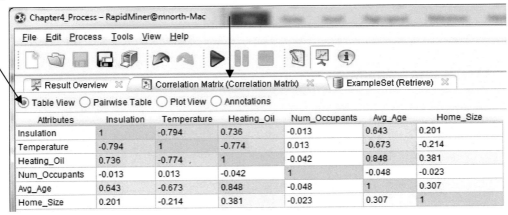

Attributes	Insulation	Temperature	Heating_Oil	Num_Occupants	Avg_Age	Home_Size
Insulation	1	-0.794	0.736	-0.013	0.643	0.201
Temperature	-0.794	1	-0.774	0.013	-0.673	-0.214
Heating_Oil	0.736	-0.774	1	-0.042	0.848	0.381
Num_Occupants	-0.013	0.013	-0.042	1	-0.048	-0.023
Avg_Age	0.643	-0.673	0.848	-0.048	1	0.307
Home_Size	0.201	-0.214	0.381	-0.023	0.307	1

Figure 4-4. Results of a Correlation Matrix.

5) In Figure 4-4, we have our **correlation coefficients** in a matrix. Correlation coefficients are relatively easy to decipher. They are simply a measure of the strength of the relationship between each possible set of attributes in the data set. Because we have six attributes in this data set, our matrix is six columns wide by six rows tall. In the location where an attribute intersects with itself, the correlation coefficient is '1', because everything compared to itself has a perfectly matched relationship. All other pairs of attributes will have a correlation coefficient of less than one. To complicate matters a bit, correlation coefficients can actually be negative as well, so all correlation coefficients will fall somewhere between -1 and 1. We can see that this is the case in Figure 4-4, and so we can now move on to the CRISP-DM step of...

EVALUATION

All correlation coefficients between 0 and 1 represent **positive correlations**, while all coefficients between 0 and -1 are **negative correlations**. While this may seem straightforward, there is an important distinction to be made when interpreting the matrix's values. This distinction has to do with the direction of movement between the two attributes being analyzed. Let's consider the relationship between the Heating_Oil consumption attribute, and the Insulation rating level attribute. The coefficient there, as seen in our matrix in Figure 4-4, is 0.736. This is a positive number, and therefore, a positive correlation. But what does that mean? Correlations that are positive mean that as one attribute's value rises, the other attribute's value also rises. *But*, a positive correlation also means that as one attribute's value falls, the other's also falls. Data analysts sometimes make the mistake in thinking that a negative correlation exists if an attribute's values are decreasing, but if its corresponding attribute's values are also decreasing, the correlation is still a positive one. This is illustrated in Figure 4-5.

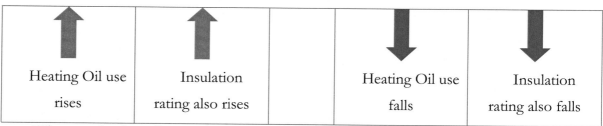

Whenever both attribute values move in the same direction, the correlation is <u>positive</u>.

Figure 4-5. Illustration of positive correlations.

Next, consider the relationship between the Temperature attribute and the Insulation rating attribute. In our Figure 4-4 matrix, we see that the coefficient there is -0.794. In this example, the correlation is negative, as illustrated in Figure 4-6.

Temperature rises — Insulation rating falls — Temperature falls — Insulation rating rises

Whenever attribute values move in opposite directions, the correlation is <u>negative</u>.

Figure 4-6. Illustration of negative correlations.

So correlation coefficients tell us something about the relationship between attributes, and this is helpful, but they also tell us something about the *strength* of the correlation. As previously mentioned, all correlations will fall between 0 and 1 or 0 and -1. The closer a correlation coefficient is to 1 or to -1, the stronger it is. Figure 4-7 illustrates the correlation strength along the continuum from -1 to 1.

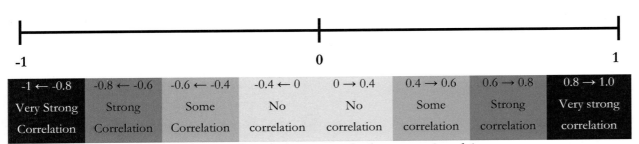

| -1 ← -0.8 Very Strong Correlation | -0.8 ← -0.6 Strong Correlation | -0.6 ← -0.4 Some Correlation | -0.4 ← 0 No correlation | 0 → 0.4 No correlation | 0.4 → 0.6 Some correlation | 0.6 → 0.8 Strong correlation | 0.8 → 1.0 Very strong correlation |

Figure 4-7. Correlation strengths between -1 and 1.

RapidMiner attempts to help us recognize correlation strengths through color coding. In the Figure 4-4 matrix, we can see that some of the cells are tinted with shades of purple in graduated colors, in order to more strongly highlight those with stronger correlations. It is important to recognize that these are only general guidelines and not hard-and-fast rules. A correlation coefficient around .2 does show some interaction between attributes, even if it is not statistically significant. This should be kept in mind as we proceed to…

DEPLOYMENT

The concept of deployment in data mining means doing something with what you've learned from your model; taking some action based upon what your model tells you. In this chapter's example, we conducted some basic, exploratory analysis for our fictional figure, Sarah. There are several possible outcomes from this investigation.

We learned through our investigation, that the two most strongly correlated attributes in our data set are Heating_Oil and Avg_Age, with a coefficient of 0.848. Thus, we know that in this data set, as the average age of the occupants in a home increases, so too does the heating oil usage in that home. What we *do not know* is why that occurs. Data analysts often make the mistake of interpreting correlation as causation. <u>The assumption that correlation proves causation is dangerous and often false</u>.

Consider for a moment the correlation coefficient between Avg_Age and Temperature: -0.673. Referring back to Figure 4-7, we see that this is considered to be a relatively strong negative correlation. As the age of a home's residents increases, the average temperature outside decreases; and as the temperature rises, the age of the folks inside goes down. But could the average age of a home's occupants have any effect on that home's average yearly outdoor temperature? Certainly not. If it did, we could control the temperature by simply moving people of different ages in and out of homes. This of course is silly. While statistically, there is a correlation between these two attributes in our data set, there is no logical reason that movement in one *causes* movement in the other. The relationship is probably coincidental, but if not, there must be some other explanation that our model cannot offer. Such limitations must be recognized and accepted in all data mining deployment decisions.

Another false interpretation about correlations is that the coefficients are percentages, as if to say that a correlation coefficient of 0.776 between two attributes is an indication that there is 77.6% shared variability between those two attributes. This is not correct. While the coefficients do tell a story about the shared variability between attributes, the underlying mathematical formula used to calculate correlation coefficients solely measures strength, as indicated by proximity to 1 or -1, of the interaction between attributes. No percentage is calculated or intended.

With these interpretation parameters explained, there may be several things that Sarah *can do* in order to take action based upon our model. A few options might include:

- Dropping the Num_Occupants attribute. While the number of people living in a home might logically seem like a variable that would influence energy usage, in our model it did not correlate in any significant way with anything else. Sometimes there are attributes that don't turn out to be very interesting.

- Investigating the role of home insulation. The Insulation rating attribute was fairly strongly correlated with a number of other attributes. There may be some opportunity there to partner with a company (or start one...?) that specializes in adding insulation to existing homes. If she is interested in contributing to conservation, working on a marketing promotion to show the benefits of adding insulation to a home might be a good course of action, however if she wishes to continue to sell as much heating oil as she can, she may feel conflicted about participating in such a campaign.

- Adding greater granularity in the data set. This data set has yielded some interesting results, but frankly, it's pretty general. We have used average yearly temperatures and total annual number of heating oil units in this model. But we also know that temperatures fluctuate throughout the year in most areas of the world, and thus monthly, or even weekly measures would not only be likely to show more detailed results of demand and usage over time, but the correlations between attributes would probably be more interesting. From our model, Sarah now knows how certain attributes interact with one another, but in the day-to-day business of doing her job, she'll probably want to know about usage over time periods shorter than one year.

- Adding additional attributes to the data set. It turned out that the number of occupants in the home didn't correlate much with other attributes, but that doesn't mean that other attributes would be equally uninteresting. For example, what if Sarah had access to the number of furnaces and/or boilers in each home? Home_size was slightly correlated with Heating_Oil usage, so perhaps the number of instruments that consume heating oil in each home would tell an interesting story, or at least add to her insight.

Sarah would also be wise to remember that the CRISP-DM approach is cyclical in nature. Each month as new orders come in and new bills go out, as new customers sign up for a heating oil account, there are additional data available to add into the model. As she learns more about how each attribute in her data set interacts with others, she can increase our correlation model by adding not only new attributes, but also, new observations.

CHAPTER SUMMARY

This chapter has introduced the concept of correlation as a data mining model. It has been chosen as the first model for this book because it is relatively simple to construct, run and interpret, thus serving as an easy starting point upon which to build. Future models will become more complex, but continuing to develop your skills in RapidMiner and getting comfortable with the tools will make the more complex models easier for you to achieve as we move forward.

Recall from Chapter 1 (Figure 1-2) that data mining has two somewhat interconnected sides: Classification, and Prediction. Correlation has been shown to be primarily on the side of Classification. We do not infer causation using correlation metrics, nor do we use correlation coefficients to predict one attribute's value based on another's. We can however quickly find general trends in data sets using correlations, and we can anticipate how strongly an observed movement in one attribute will occur in conjunction with movement in another.

Correlation can be a quick and easy way to see how elements of a given problem may be interacting with one another. Whenever you find yourself asking how certain factors in a problem you're trying to solve interact with one another, consider building a correlation matrix to find out. For example, does customer satisfaction change based on time of year? Does the amount of rainfall change the price of a crop? Does household income influence which restaurants a person patronizes? The answer to each of these questions is probably 'yes', but correlation can not only help us know if that's true, it can also help us learn how strongly the interactions are when, and if, they occur.

1) What are some of the limitations of correlation models?

2) What is a correlation coefficient? How is it interpreted?

3) What is the difference between a positive and a negative correlation? If two attributes have values that decrease at essentially the same rate, is that a negative correlation? Why or why not?

4) How is correlation strength measured? What are the ranges for strengths of correlation?

5) The number of heating oil consuming devices was suggested as a possibly interesting attribute that could be added to the example data set for this chapter. Can you think of others? Why might they be interesting? To what other attributes in the data set do you think your suggested attributes might be correlated? What would be the value in knowing if they are?

EXERCISE

It is now your turn to develop a correlation model, generate a coefficient matrix, and analyze the results. To complete this chapter's exercise, follow the steps below.

1) Select a professional sporting organization that you enjoy, or of which you are aware. Locate that organization's web site and search it for statistics, facts and figures about the athletes in that organization.

2) Open OpenOffice Calc, and starting in Cell A across Row 1 of the spreadsheet, define some attributes (at least three or four) to hold data about each athlete. Some possible attributes you may wish to consider could be annual_salary, points_per_game, years_as_pro, height, weight, age, etc. The list is potentially unlimited, will vary based on the type of sport you choose, and will depend on the data available to you on the web site you've selected. Measurements of the athletes' salaries and performance in competition are

likely to be the most interesting. You may include the athletes' names, however keep in mind that correlations can only be conducted on numeric data, so the name attribute would need to be reduced out of your data set before creating your correlation matrix. (Remember the Select Attributes operator!)

3) Look up the statistics for each of your selected attributes and enter them as observations into your spreadsheet. Try to find as many as you can—at least thirty is a good rule of thumb in order to achieve at least a basic level of statistical validity. More is better.

4) Once you've created your data set, use the menu to save it as a CSV file. Click File, then Save As. Enter a file name, and change 'Save as type:' to be Text CSV (.csv). Be sure to save the file in your data mining data folder.

5) Open RapidMiner and import your data set into your RapidMiner repository. Name it Chapter4Exercise, or something descriptive so that you will remember what data are contained in the data set when you look in your repository.

6) Add the data set to a new process in RapidMiner. Ensure that the *out* port is connected to a *res* port and run your model. Save your process with a descriptive name if you wish. Examine your data in results perspective and ensure there are no missing, inconsistent, or other potentially problematic data that might need to be handled as part of your Data Preparation phase. Return to design perspective and handle any data preparation tasks that may be necessary.

7) Add a Correlation Matrix operator to your stream and ensure that the *mat* port is connected to a *res* port. Run your model again. Interpret your correlation coefficients as displayed on the matrix tab.

8) Document your findings. What correlations exist? How strong are they? Are they surprising to you and if so, why? What other attributes would you like to add? Are there any you'd eliminate now that you've mined your data?

Challenge step!

9) While still in results perspective, click on the ExampleSet tab (which exists assuming you left the *exa* port connected to a *res* port when you were in design perspective). Click on the Plot View radio button. Examine correlations that you found in your model visually by creating a scatter plot of your data. Choose one attribute for your x-Axis and a correlated one for your y-Axis. Experiment with the **Jitter** slide bar. What is it doing? (Hint: Try an Internet search on the term 'jittering statistics'.) For an additional visual experience, try a Scatter 3D or Scatter 3D Color plot. Consider Figures 4-8 and 4-9 as examples. Note that with 3D plots in RapidMiner, you can click and hold to rotate your plot in order to better see the interactions between the data.

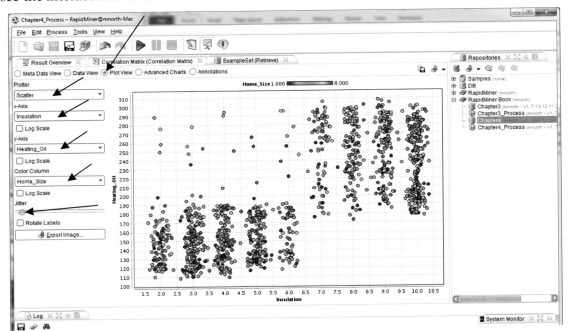

Figure 4-8. A two-dimensional scatterplot with a
colored third dimension and a slight jitter.

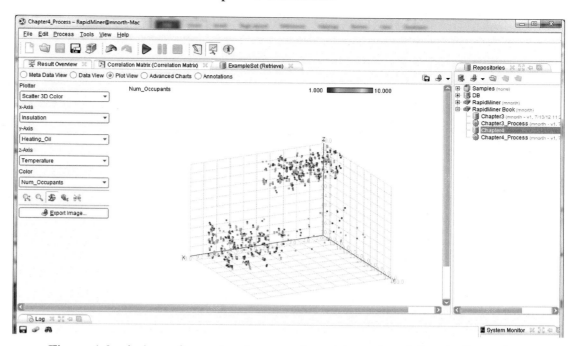

Figure 4-9. A three-dimensional scatterplot with a colored fourth dimension.

CHAPTER FIVE:
ASSOCIATION RULES

CONTEXT AND PERSPECTIVE

Roger is a city manager for a medium-sized, but steadily growing, city. The city has limited resources, and like most municipalities, there are more needs than there are resources. He feels like the citizens in the community are fairly active in various community organizations, and believes that he may be able to get a number of groups to work together to meet some of the needs in the community. He knows there are churches, social clubs, hobby enthusiasts and other types of groups in the community. What he doesn't know is if there are connections between the groups that might enable natural collaborations between two or more groups that could work together on projects around town. He decides that before he can begin asking community organizations to begin working together and to accept responsibility for projects, he needs to find out if there are any existing associations between the different types of groups in the area.

LEARNING OBJECTIVES

After completing the reading and exercises in this chapter, you should be able to:

- Explain what association rules are, how they are found and the benefits of using them.
- Recognize the necessary format for data in order to create association rules.
- Develop an association rule model in RapidMiner.
- Interpret the rules generated by an association rule model and explain their significance, if any.

ORGANIZATIONAL UNDERSTANDING

Roger's goal is to identify and then try to take advantage of existing connections in his local community to get some work done that will benefit the entire community. He knows of many of the organizations in town, has contact information for them and is even involved in some of them himself. His family is involved in an even broader group of organizations, so he understands on a personal level the diversity of groups and their interests. Because people he and his family knows are involved in other groups around town, he is aware in a more general sense of many different types of organizations, their interests, objectives and potential contributions. He knows that to start, his main concern is finding types of organizations that seem to be connected with one another. Identifying individuals to work with at each church, social club or political organization will be overwhelming without first categorizing the organizations into groups and looking for associations between the groups. Only once he's checked for existing connections will he feel ready to begin contacting people and asking them to use their cross-organizational contacts and take on project ownership. His first need is to find where such associations exist.

DATA UNDERSTANDING

In order to answer his question, Roger has enlisted our help in creating an **association rules** data mining model. Association rules are a data mining methodology that seeks to find frequent connections between attributes in a data set. Association rules are very common when doing shopping basket analysis. Marketers and vendors in many sectors use this data mining approach to try to find which products are most frequently purchased together. If you have ever purchased items on an e-Commerce retail site like Amazon.com, you have probably seen the fruits of association rule data mining. These are most commonly found in the recommendations sections of such web sites. You might notice that when you search for a smartphone, recommendations for screen protectors, protective cases, and other accessories such as charging cords or data cables are often recommended to you. The items being recommended are identified by mining for items that previous customers bought in conjunction with the item you search for. In other words, those items are found to be *associated* with the item you are looking for, and that association is so frequent in the web site's data set, that the *association* might be considered a *rule*. Thus is born the name of this data mining approach: "association rules". While association rules are most common in shopping basket analysis, this modeling technique can be applied to a broad range of questions. We will help Roger by creating an association rule model to try to find linkages across types of community organizations.

Working together, we using Roger's knowledge of the local community to create a short survey which we will administer online via a web site. In order to ensure a measure of data integrity and to try to protect against possible abuse, our web survey is password protected. Each organization invited to participate in the survey is given a unique password. The leader of that organization is asked to share the password with his or her membership and to encourage participation in the survey. Community members are given a month to respond, and each time an individual logs on complete the survey, the password used is recorded so that we can determine how many people from each organization responded. After the month ends, we have a data set comprised of the following attributes:

- **Elapsed_Time**: This is the amount of time each respondent spent completing our survey. It is expressed in decimal minutes (e.g. 4.5 in this attribute would be four minutes, thirty seconds).

- **Time_in_Community**: This question on the survey asked the person if they have lived in the area for 0-2 years, 3-9 years, or 10+ years; and is recorded in the data set as Short, Medium, or Long respectively.

- **Gender**: The survey respondent's gender.

- **Working**: A yes/no column indicating whether or not the respondent currently has a paid job.

- **Age**: The survey respondent's age in years.

- **Family**: A yes/no column indicating whether or not the respondent is currently a member of a family-oriented community organization, such as Big Brothers/Big Sisters, childrens' recreation or sports leagues, genealogy groups, etc.

- **Hobbies**: A yes/no column indicating whether or not the respondent is currently a member of a hobby-oriented community organization, such as amateur radio, outdoor recreation, motorcycle or bicycle riding, etc.

- **Social_Club**: A yes/no column indicating whether or not the respondent is currently a member of a community social organization, such as Rotary International, Lion's Club, etc.

- **Political**: A yes/no column indicating whether or not the respondent is currently a member of a political organization with regular meetings in the community, such as a political party, a grass-roots action group, a lobbying effort, etc.

- **Professional:** A yes/no column indicating whether or not the respondent is currently a member of a professional organization with local chapter meetings, such as a chapter of a law or medical society, a small business owner's group, etc.

- **Religious:** A yes/no column indicating whether or not the respondent is currently a member of a church in the community.

- **Support_Group:** A yes/no column indicating whether or not the respondent is currently a member of a support-oriented community organization, such as Alcoholics Anonymous, an anger management group, etc.

In order to preserve a level of personal privacy, individual respondents' names were not collected through the survey, and no respondent was asked to give personally identifiable information when responding.

DATA PREPARATION

A CSV data set for this chapter's exercise is available for download at the book's companion web site (https://sites.google.com/site/dataminingforthemasses/). If you wish to follow along with the exercise, go ahead and download the Chapter05DataSet.csv file now and save it into your RapidMiner data folder. Then, complete the following steps to prepare the data set for association rule mining:

1) Import the Chapter 5 CSV data set into your RapidMiner data repository. Save it with the name Chapter5. If you need a refresher on how to bring this data set into your RapidMiner repository, refer to steps 7 through 14 of the Hands On Exercise in Chapter 3. The steps will be the same, with the exception of which file you select to import. Import all attributes, and accept the default data types. This is the same process as was done in Chapter 4, so hopefully by now, you are getting comfortable with the steps to import data into RapidMiner.

2) Drag your Chapter5 data set into a new process window in RapidMiner, and run the model in order to inspect the data. When running the model, if prompted, save the process as Chapter5_Process, as shown in Figure 5-1.

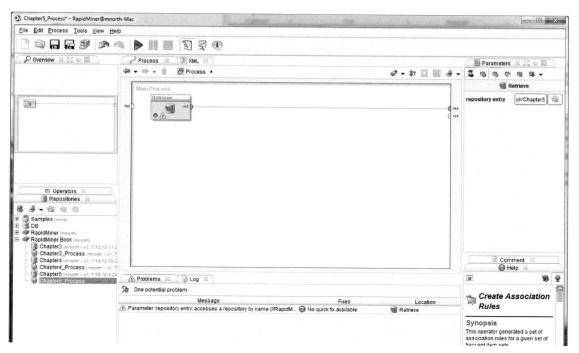

Figure 5-1. Adding the data for the Chapter 5 example model.

3) In results perspective, look first at Meta Data view (Figure 5-2). Note that we do not have any missing values among any of the 12 attributes across 3,483 observations. In examining the statistics, we do not see any inconsistent data. For numeric data types, RapidMiner has given us the **average** (avg), or **mean**, for each attribute, as well the **standard deviation** for each attribute. Standard deviations are measurements of how dispersed or varied the values in an attribute are, and so can be used to watch for inconsistent data. A good rule of thumb is that any value that is smaller than two standard deviations below the mean (or arithmetic average), or two standard deviations above the mean, is a statistical outlier. For example, in the Age attribute in Figure 5-2, the average age is 36.731, while the standard deviation is 10.647. Two standard deviations above the mean would be 58.025 (36.731+(2*10.647)), and two standard deviations below the mean would be 15.437 (36.731-(2*10.647)). If we look at the Range column in Figure 5-2, we can see that the Age attribute has a range of 17 to 57, so all of our observations fall within two standard deviations of the mean. We find no inconsistent data in this attribute. This won't always be the case, so a data miner should always be watchful for such indications of inconsistent data. It's important to realize also that while two standard deviations is a guideline, it's not a hard-and-fast rule. Data miners should be thoughtful about why some observations may be legitimate and yet far from the mean, or why some values that fall within two standard deviations of the mean should still be scrutinized. One other item should be noted as we

examine Figure 5-2: the yes/no attributes about whether or not a person was a member of various types of community organizations was recorded as a 0 or 1 and those attributes were imported as 'integer' data types. The association rule operators we'll be using in RapidMiner require attributes to be of 'binominal' data type, so we still have some data preparation yet to do.

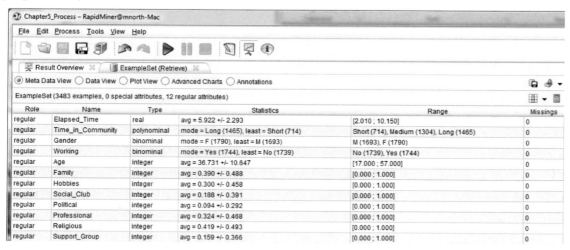

Figure 5-2. Meta data of our community group involvement survey.

4) Switch back to design perspective. We have a fairly good understanding of our objectives and our data, but we know that some additional preparation is needed. First off, we need to reduce the number of attributes in our data set. The elapsed time each person took to complete the survey isn't necessarily interesting in the context of our current question, which is whether or not there are existing connections between types of organizations in our community, and if so, where those linkages exist. In order to reduce our data set to only those attributes related to our question, add a Select Attributes operator to your stream (as was demonstrated in Chapter 3), and select the following attributes for inclusion, as illustrated in Figure 5-3: Family, Hobbies, Social_Club, Political, Professional, Religious, Support_Group. Once you have these attributes selected, click OK to return to your main process.

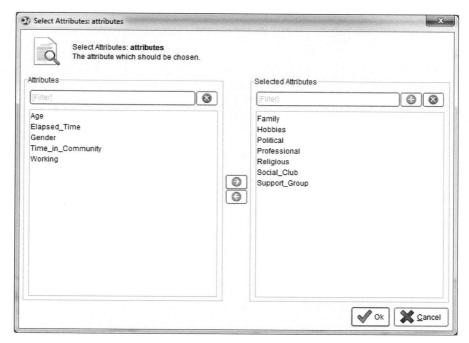

Figure 5-3. Selection of attributes to include

in the association rules model.

5) One other step is needed in our data preparation. This is to change the data types of our selected attributes from integer to binominal. As previously mentioned, the association rules operators need this data type in order to function properly. In the search box on the Operators tab in design view, type 'Numerical to' (without the single quotes) to locate the operators that will change attributes with a numeric data type to some other data type. The one we will use is Numerical to Binominal. Drag this operator into your stream.

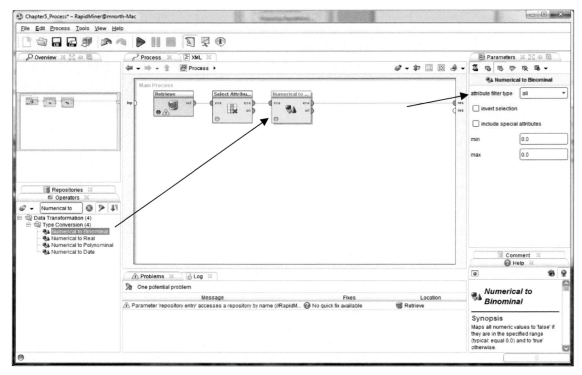

Figure 5-4. Adding a data type converstion operator to a data mining model.

6) For our purposes, all attributes which remain after application of the Select Attributes operator need to be converted from numeric to binominal, so as the black arrow indicates in Figure 5-4, we will convert 'all' from the former data type to the latter. We could convert a subset or a single attribute, by selecting one of those options in the attribute filter type dropdown menu. We have done this in the past, but in this example, we can accept the default and covert all attributes at once. You should also observe that within RapidMiner, the data type **binominal** is used instead of **binomial**, a term many data analysts are more used to. There is an important distinction. *Binomial* means one of two numbers (usually 0 and 1), so the basic underlying data type is still numeric. *Binominal* on the other hand, means one of two values which may be numeric *or* character based. Click the play button to run your model and see how this conversion has taken place in our data set. In results perspective, you should see the transformation, as depicted in Figure 5-5.

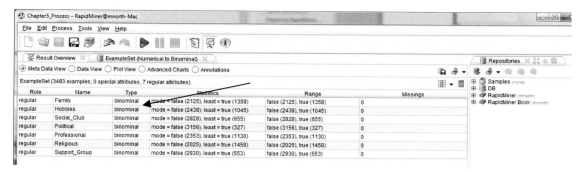

Figure 5-5. The results of a data type transformation.

7) For each attribute in our data set, the values of 1 or 0 that existed in our source data set now are reflected as either 'true' or 'false'. Our data preparation phase is now complete and we are ready for...

MODELING

8) Switch back to design perspective. We will use two specific operators in order to generate our association rule data mining model. Understand that there are many other operators offered in RapidMiner that can be used in association rule models. At the outset, we established that this book is not a RapidMiner training manual and thus, will not cover every possible operator that could be used in a given model. Thus, please do not assume that this chapter's example is demonstrating the one and only way to mine for association rules. This is one of several possible approaches, and you are encouraged to explore other operators and their functionality.

To proceed with the example, use the search field in the operators tab to look for an operator called FP-Growth. Note that you might find one called W-FPGrowth. This is simply a slightly different implementation of the FP-Growth algorithm that will look for associations in our data, so do not be confused by the two very similar names. For this chapter's example, select the operator that is just called FP-Growth. Go ahead and drag it into your stream. The FP in FP-Growth stands for **Frequency Pattern**. Frequency pattern analysis is handy for many kinds of data mining, and is a necessary component of association rule mining. Without having frequencies of attribute combinations, we cannot determine whether any of the patterns in the data occur often enough to be considered rules. Your stream should now look like Figure 5-6.

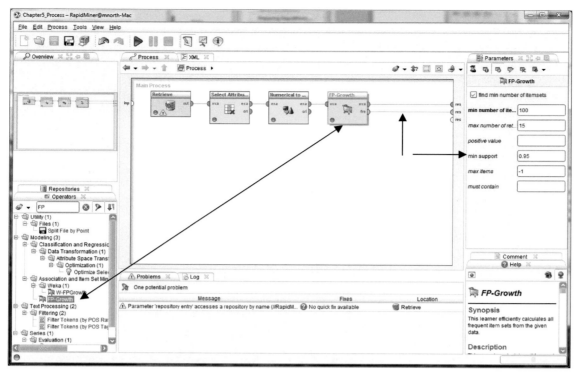

Figure 5-6. Addition of an FP-Growth operator to an association rule model.

9) Take note of the *min support* parameter on the right hand side. We will come back to this parameter during the evaluation portion of this chapter's example. Also, be sure that both your *exa* port and your *fre* port are connected to *res* ports. The *exa* port will generate a tab of your examples (your data set's observations and meta data), while the *fre* port will generate a matrix of any frequent patterns the operator might find in your data set. Run your model to switch to results perspective.

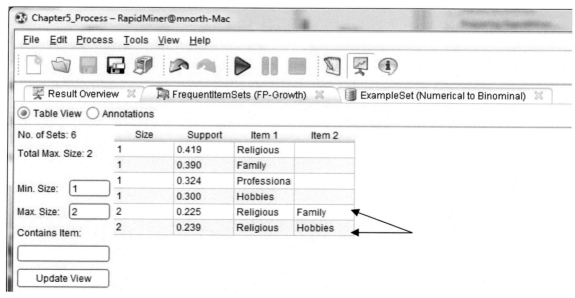

Figure 5-7. Results of an FP-Growth operator.

10) In results perspective, we see that some of our attributes appear to have some frequent patterns in them, and in fact, we begin to see that three attributes look like they might have some association with one another. The black arrows point to areas where it seems that Religious organizations might have some natural connections with Family and Hobby organizations. We can investigate this possible connection further by adding one final operator to our model. Return to design perspective, and in the operators search box, look for 'Create Association' (again, without the single quotes). Drag the Create Association Rules operator over and drop it into the spline that connects the *fre* port to the *res* port. This operator takes in frequent pattern matrix data and seeks out any patterns that occur so frequently that they could be considered rules. Your model should now look like Figure 5-8.

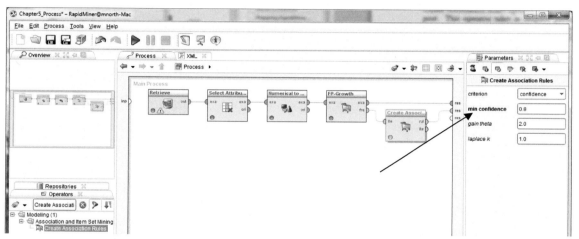

Figure 5-8. Addition of Create Association Rules operator.

11) The Create Association Rules operator can generate both a set of rules (through the *rul* port) and a set of associated items (through the *ite* port). We will simply generate rules, and for now, accept the default parameters for the Create Association Rules, though note the *min confidence* parameter, which we will address in the evaluation phase of our mining. Run your model.

Figure 5-9. The results of our association rule model.

12) Bummer. No rules found. Did we do all that work for nothing? It seemed like we had some hope for some associations back in step 9, what happened? Remember from Chapter 1 that the CRISP-DM process is cyclical in nature, and sometimes, you have to go back and forth between steps before you will create a model that yields results. Such is the case here. We have nothing to consider here, so perhaps we need to tweak some of our model's parameters. This may be a process of trial and error, which will take us back and forth between our current CRISP-DM step of Modeling and…

EVALUATION

13) So we've evaluated our model's first run. No rules found. Not much to evaluate there, right? So let's switch back to design perspective, and take a look at those parameters we highlighted briefly in the previous steps. There are two main factors that dictate whether or not frequency patterns get translated into association rules: **Confidence percent** and **Support percent**. Confidence percent is a measure of how confident we are that when one attribute is flagged as true, the associated attribute will also be flagged as true. In the classic shopping basket analysis example, we could look at two items often associated with one another: cookies and milk. If we examined ten shopping baskets and found that cookies were purchased in four of them, and milk was purchased in seven, and that further, in three of the four instances where cookies were purchased, milk was also in those baskets, we would have a 75% confidence in the association rule: cookies → milk. This is calculated by dividing the three instances where cookies and milk coincided by the four instances where they *could have* coincided (3/4 = .75, or 75%). The rule cookies → milk had a chance to occur four times, but it only occurred three, so our confidence in this rule is not absolute.

Now consider the reciprocal of the rule: milk → cookies. Milk was found in seven of our ten hypothetical baskets, while cookies were found in four. We know that the coincidence, or frequency of connection between these two products is three. So our confidence in milk → cookies falls to only 43% (3/7 = .429, or 43%). Milk had a chance to be found with cookies seven times, but it was only found with them three times, so our confidence in milk → cookies is a good bit lower than our confidence in cookies → milk. If a person comes to the store with the intention of buying cookies, we are more confident that they will also buy milk than if their intentions were reversed. This concept is referred to in association rule mining as **Premise → Conclusion**. Premises are sometimes also referred to as **antecedents**, while conclusions are sometimes referred to as **consequents**. For each pairing, the confidence percentages will differ based on which attribute is the premise and which the conclusion. When associations between three or more attributes are found, for example, cookies, crackers → milk, the confidence percentages are calculated based on the two attributes being found with the third. This can become complicated to do manually, so it is nice to have RapidMiner to find these combinations and run the calculations for us!

The support percent is an easier measure to calculate. This is simply the number of times that the rule *did* occur, divided by the number of observations in the data set. The number of items in the data set is the absolute number of times the association *could have* occurred, since every customer could have purchased cookies and milk together in their shopping basket. The fact is, they didn't, and such a phenomenon would be highly unlikely in any analysis. Possible, but unlikely. We know that in our hypothetical example, cookies and milk were found together in three out of ten shopping baskets, so our support percentage for this association is 30% (3/10 = .3, or 30%). There is no reciprocal for support percentages since this metric is simply the number of times the association did occur over the number of times it could have occurred in the data set.

So now that we understand these two pivotal parameters in association rule mining, let's make a parameter modification and see if we find any association rules in our data. You should be in design perspective again, but if not, switch back now. Click on your Create Association Rules operator and change the *min confidence* parameter to .5 (see Figure 5-10). This indicates to RapidMiner that any association with at least 50% confidence should be displayed as a rule. With this as the confidence percent threshold, if we were using the hypothetical shopping baskets discussed in the previous paragraphs to explain confidence and support, cookies → milk would return as a rule because its confidence percent was 75%, while milk → cookies would not, due to that association's 43% confidence percent. Let's run our model again with the .5 confidence value and see what we get.

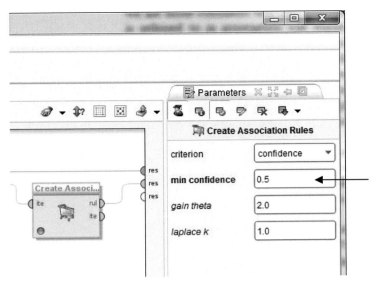

Figure 5-10. Chaning the confidence percent threshold.

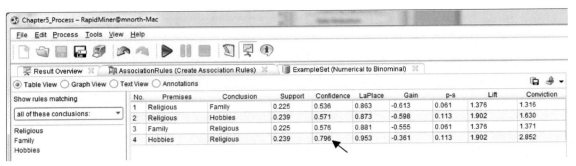

Figure 5-11. Four rules found with the 50% confidence threshold.

14) Eureka! We have found rules, and our hunch that Religious, Family and Hobby organizations are related was correct (remember Figure 5-7). Look at rule number four. It just barely missed being considered a rule with an 80% confidence threshold at 79.6%. Our other associations have lower confidence percentages, but are still quite good. We can see that for each of these four rules, more than 20% of the observations in our data set support them. Remember that since support is not reciprocal, the support percents for rules 1 and 3 are the same, as they are for rules 2 and 4. As the premises and conclusions were reversed, their confidence percentages did vary however. Had we set our confidence percent threshold at .55 (or 55% percent), rule 1 would drop out of our results, so Family → Religious would be a rule but Religious → Family would not. The other calculations to the right (LaPlace...Conviction) are additional arithmetic indicators of the strength of the rules' relationships. As you compare these values to support and confidence percents, you will see that they track fairly consistently with one another.

If you would like, you may return to design perspective and experiment. If you click on the FP-Growth operator, you can modify the *min support* value. Note that while support percent is the metric calculated and displayed by the Create Association Rules operator, the *min support* parameter in the FP-Growth actually calls for a confidence level. The default of .95 is very common in much data analysis, but you may want to lower it a bit and re-run your model to see what happens. Lowering *min support* to .5 does yield additional rules, including some with more than two attributes in the association rules. As you experiment you can see that a data miner might need to go back and forth a number of times between modeling and evaluating before moving on to…

DEPLOYMENT

We have been able to help Roger with his question. Do existing linkages between types of community groups exist? Yes, they do. We have found that the community's churches, family, and hobby organizations have some common members. It may be a bit surprising that the political and professional groups do not appear to be interconnected, but these groups may also be more specialized (e.g. a local chapter of the bar association) and thus may not have tremendous cross-organizational appeal or need. It seems that Roger will have the most luck finding groups that will collaborate on projects around town by engaging churches, hobbyists and family-related organizations. Using his contacts among local pastors and other clergy, he might ask for volunteers from their congregations to spearhead projects to clean up city parks used for youth sports (family organization association rule) or to improve a local biking trail (hobby organization association rule).

CHAPTER SUMMARY

This chapter's fictional scenario with Roger's desire to use community groups to improve his city has shown how association rule data mining can identify linkages in data that can have a practical application. In addition to learning about the process of creating association rule models in RapidMiner, we introduced a new operator that enabled us to change attributes' data types. We also used CRISP-DM's cyclical nature to understand that sometimes data mining involves some back and forth 'digging' before moving on to the next step. You learned how support and confidence percentages are calculated and about the importance of these two metrics in identifying rules and determining their strength in a data set.

REVIEW QUESTIONS

1) What are association rules? What are they good for?

2) What are the two main metrics that are calculated in association rules and how are they calculated?

3) What data type must a data set's attributes be in order to use Frequent Pattern operators in RapidMiner?

4) How are rule results interpreted? In this chapter's example, what was our strongest rule? How do we know?

EXERCISE

In explaining support and confidence percentages in this chapter, the classic example of shopping basket analysis was used. For this exercise, you will do a shopping basket association rule analysis. Complete the following steps:

1) Using the Internet, locate a sample shopping basket data set. Search terms such as 'association rule data set' or 'shopping basket data set' will yield a number of downloadable examples. With a little effort, you will be able to find a suitable example.

2) If necessary, convert your data set to CSV format and import it into your RapidMiner repository. Give it a descriptive name and drag it into a new process window.

3) As necessary, conduct your Data Understanding and Data Preparation activities on your data set. Ensure that all of your variables have consistent data and that their data types are appropriate for the FP-Growth operator.

4) Generate association rules for your data set. Modify your confidence and support values in order to identify their most ideal levels such that you will have some interesting rules with reasonable confidence and support. Look at the other measures of rule strength such as LaPlace or Conviction.

5) Document your findings. What rules did you find? What attributes are most strongly associated with one another. Are there products that are frequently connected that surprise you? Why do you think this might be? How much did you have to test different support and confidence values before you found some association rules? Were any of your association rules good enough that you would base decisions on them? Why or why not?

Challenge Step!

6) Build a new association rule model using your same data set, but this time, use the W-FPGrowth operator. (Hints for using the W-FPGrowth operator: (1) This operator creates its own rules without help from other operators; and (2) This operator's support and confidence parameters are labeled U and C, respectively.

Exploration!

7) The Apriori algorithm is often used in data mining for associations. Search the RapidMiner Operators tree for Apriori operators and add them to your data set in a new process. Use the Help tab in RapidMiner's lower right hand corner to learn about these operators' parameters and functions (be sure you have the operator selected in your main process window in order to see its help content).

CHAPTER SIX:
K-MEANS CLUSTERING

CONTEXT AND PERSPECTIVE

Sonia is a program director for a major health insurance provider. Recently she has been reading in medical journals and other articles, and found a strong emphasis on the influence of weight, gender and cholesterol on the development of coronary heart disease. The research she's read confirms time after time that there is a connection between these three variables, and while there is little that can be done about one's gender, there are certainly life choices that can be made to alter one's cholesterol and weight. She begins brainstorming ideas for her company to offer weight and cholesterol management programs to individuals who receive health insurance through her employer. As she considers where her efforts might be most effective, she finds herself wondering if there are natural groups of individuals who are most at risk for high weight and high cholesterol, and if there are such groups, where the natural dividing lines between the groups occur.

LEARNING OBJECTIVES

After completing the reading and exercises in this chapter, you should be able to:

- Explain what k-means clusters are, how they are found and the benefits of using them.
- Recognize the necessary format for data in order to create k-means clusters.
- Develop a k-means cluster data mining model in RapidMiner.
- Interpret the clusters generated by a k-means model and explain their significance, if any.

ORGANIZATIONAL UNDERSTANDING

Sonia's goal is to identify and then try to reach out to individuals insured by her employer who are at high risk for coronary heart disease because of their weight and/or high cholesterol. She understands that those at low risk, that is, those with low weight and cholesterol, are unlikely to participate in the programs she will offer. She also understands that there are probably policy holders with high weight and low cholesterol, those with high weight *and* high cholesterol, and those with low weight and high cholesterol. She further recognizes there are likely to be a lot of people somewhere in between. In order to accomplish her goal, she needs to search among the thousands of policy holders to find groups of people with similar characteristics and craft programs and communications that will be relevant and appealing to people in these different groups.

DATA UNDERSTANDING

Using the insurance company's claims database, Sonia extracts three attributes for 547 randomly selected individuals. The three attributes are the insured's weight in pounds as recorded on the person's most recent medical examination, their last cholesterol level determined by blood work in their doctor's lab, and their gender. As is typical in many data sets, the gender attribute uses 0 to indicate Female and 1 to indicate Male. We will use this sample data from Sonia's employer's database to build a cluster model to help Sonia understand how her company's clients, the health insurance policy holders, appear to group together on the basis of their weights, genders and cholesterol levels. We should remember as we do this that means are particularly susceptible to undue influence by extreme outliers, so watching for inconsistent data when using the **k-Means clustering** data mining methodology is very important.

DATA PREPARATION

As with previous chapters, a data set has been prepared for this chapter's example, and is available as Chapter06DataSet.csv on the book's companion web site. If you would like to follow along with this example exercise, go ahead and download the data set now, and import it into your RapidMiner data repository. At this point you are probably getting comfortable with importing CSV data sets into a RapidMiner repository, but remember that the steps are outlined in Chapter 3 if you need to review them. Be sure to designate the attribute names correctly and to check your data types as you import. Once you have imported the data set, drag it into a new, blank process window so that you can begin to set up your k-means clustering data mining model. Your process should look like Figure 6-1.

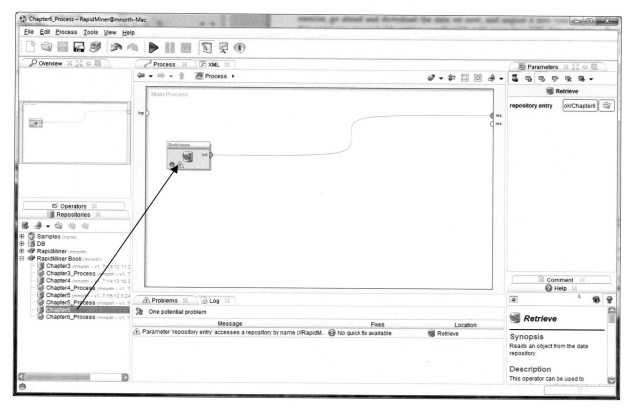

Figure 6-1. Cholesterol, Weight and Gender data set added to a new process.

Go ahead and click the play button to run your model and examine the data set. In Figure 6-2 we can see that we have 547 observations across our three previously defined attributes. We can see the averages for each of the three attributes, along with their accompanying standard deviations and ranges. None of these values appear to be inconsistent (remember the earlier comments about using standard deviations to find statistical outliers). We have no missing values to handle, so our data appear to be very clean and ready to be mined.

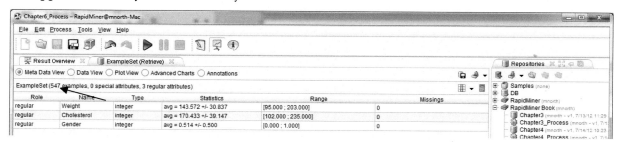

Figure 6-2. A view of our data set's meta data.

MODELING

The '*k*' in k-means clustering stands for some number of groups, or clusters. The aim of this data mining methodology is to look at each observation's individual attribute values and compare them to the means, or in other words averages, of potential groups of other observations in order to find natural groups that are similar to one another. The k-means algorithm accomplishes this by sampling some set of observations in the data set, calculating the averages, or means, for each attribute for the observations in that sample, and then comparing the other attributes in the data set to that sample's means. The system does this repetitively in order to 'circle-in' on the best matches and then to formulate groups of observations which become the clusters. As the means calculated become more and more similar, clusters are formed, and each observation whose attributes values are most like the means of a cluster become members of that cluster. Using this process, k-means clustering models can sometimes take a long time to run, especially if you indicate a large number of "max runs" through the data, or if you seek for a large number of clusters (*k*). To build your k-means cluster model, complete the following steps:

1) Return to design view in RapidMiner if you have not done so already. In the operators search box, type k-means (be sure to include the hyphen). There are three operators that conduct k-means clustering work in RapidMiner. For this exercise, we will choose the first, which is simply named "k-Means". Drag this operator into your stream, and shown in Figure 6-3.

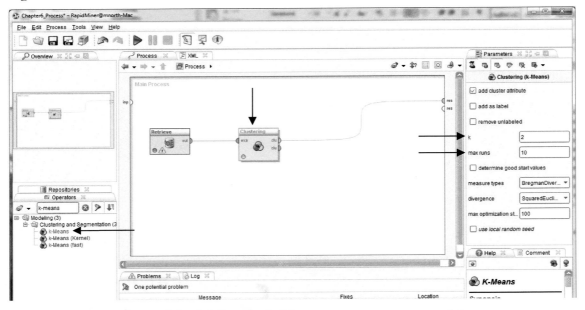

Figure 6-3. Adding the k-Means operator to our model.

2) Because we did not need to add any other operators in order to prepare our data for mining, our model in this exercise is very simple. We could, at this point, run our model and begin to interpret the results. This would not be very interesting however. This is because the default for our *k,* or our number of clusters, is 2, as indicated by the black arrow on the right hand side of Figure 6-3. This means we are asking RapidMiner to find only two clusters in our data. If we only wanted to find those with high and low levels of risk for coronary heart disease, two clusters would work. But as discussed in the Organizational Understanding section earlier in the chapter, Sonia has already recognized that there are likely a number of different types of groups to be considered. Simply splitting the data set into two clusters is probably not going to give Sonia the level of detail she seeks. Because Sonia felt that there were probably at least 4 potentially different groups, let's change the *k* value to four, as depicted in Figure 6-4. We could also increase of number of 'max runs', but for now, let's accept the default and run the model.

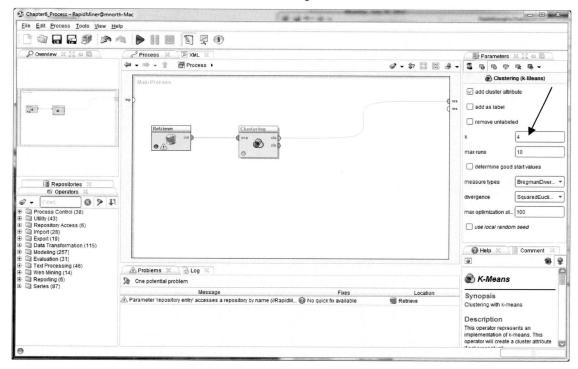

Figure 6-4. Setting the desired number of clusters for our model.

3) When the model is run, we find an initial report of the number of items that fell into each of our four clusters. (Note that the clustered are numbered starting from 0, a result of RapidMiner being written in the Java programming language.) In this particular model, our

clusters are fairly well balanced. While Cluster 1, with only 118 observations (Figure 6-5), is smaller than the other clusters, it is not unreasonably so.

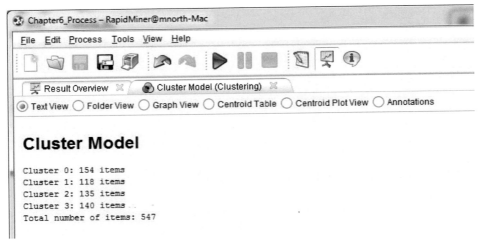

Figure 6-5. The distribution of observations across our four clusters.

We could go back at this point and adjust our number of clusters, our number of 'max runs', or even experiment with the other parameters offered by the k-Means operator. There are other options for measurement type or divergence algorithms. Feel free to try out some of these options if you wish. As was the case with Association Rules, there may be some back and forth trial-and-error as you test different parameters to generate model output. When you are satisfied with your model parameters, you can proceed to...

EVALUATION

Recall that Sonia's major objective in the hypothetical scenario posed at the beginning of the chapter was to try to find natural breaks between different types of heart disease risk groups. Using the k-Means operator in RapidMiner, we have identified four clusters for Sonia, and we can now evaluate their usefulness in addressing Sonia's question. Refer back to Figure 6-5. There are a number of radio buttons which allow us to select options for analyzing our clusters. We will start by looking at our Centroid Table. This view of our results, shown in Figure 6-6, give the means for each attribute in each of the four clusters we created.

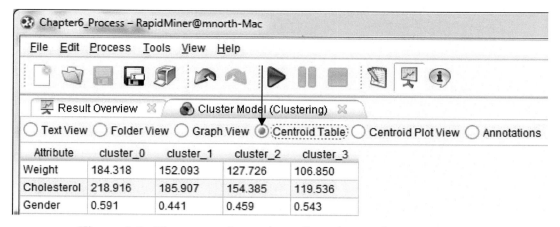

Figure 6-6. The means for each attribute in our four (*k*) clusters.

We see in this view that cluster 0 has the highest average weight and cholesterol. With 0 representing Female and 1 representing Male, a mean of 0.591 indicates that we have more men than women represented in this cluster. Knowing that high cholesterol and weight are two key indicators of heart disease risk that policy holders can do something about, Sonia would likely want to start with the members of cluster 0 when promoting her new programs. She could then extend her programming to include the people in clusters 1 and 2, which have the next incrementally lower means for these two key risk factor attributes. You should note that in this chapter's example, the clusters' numeric order (0, 1, 2, 3) corresponds to decreasing means for each cluster. This is coincidental. Sometimes, depending on your data set, cluster 0 might have the highest means, but cluster 2 might have then next highest, so it's important to pay close attention to your centroid values whenever you generate clusters.

So we know that cluster 0 is where Sonia will likely focus her early efforts, but how does she know who to try to contact? Who are the members of this highest risk cluster? We can find this information by selecting the Folder View radio button. Folder View is depicted in Figure 6-7.

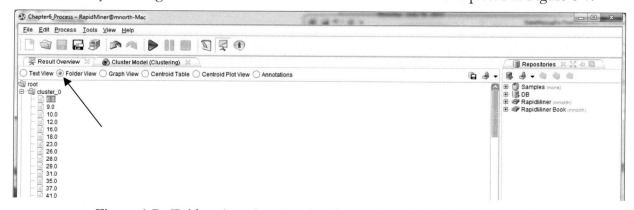

Figure 6-7. Folder view showing the observations included in Cluster 0.

By clicking the small + sign next to cluster 0 in Folder View, we can see all of the observations that have means which are similar to the mean for this cluster. Remember that these means are calculated for each attribute. You can see the details for any observation in the cluster by clicking on it. Figure 6-8 shows the results of clicking on observation 6 (6.0):

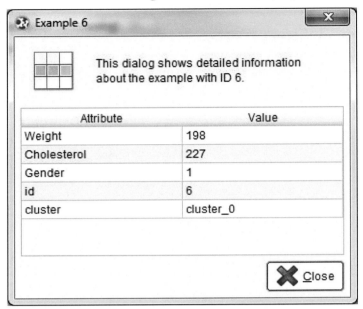

Figure 6-8. The details of an observation within cluster 0.

The means for cluster 0 were just over 184 pounds for weight and just under 219 for cholesterol. The person represented in observation 6 is heavier and has higher cholesterol than the average for this highest risk group. Thus, this is a person Sonia is really hoping to help with her outreach program. But we know from the Centroid Table that there are 154 individuals in the data set who fall into this cluster. Clicking on each one of them in Folder View probably isn't the most efficient use of Sonia's time. Furthermore, we know from our Data Understanding paragraph earlier in this chapter that this model is built on only a sample data set of policy holders. Sonia might want to extract these attributes for all policy holders from the company's database and run the model again on that data set. Or, if she is satisfied that the sample has given her what she wants in terms of finding the breaks between the groups, she can move forward with…

DEPLOYMENT

We can help Sonia extract the observations from cluster 0 fairly quickly and easily. Return to design perspective in RapidMiner. Recall from Chapter 3 that we can filter out observations in our data set. In that chapter, we discussed filtering out observations as a Data Preparation step, but we can use the same operator in our Deployment as well. Using the search field in the Operators tab, locate the Filter Examples operator and connect it to your k-Means Clustering operator, as is depicted in Figure 6-9. Note that we have not disconnected the *clu* (cluster) port from the 'res' (result set) port, but rather, we have connected a second *clu* port to our *exa* port on the Filter Examples operator, and connected the *exa* port from Filter Examples to its own *res* port.

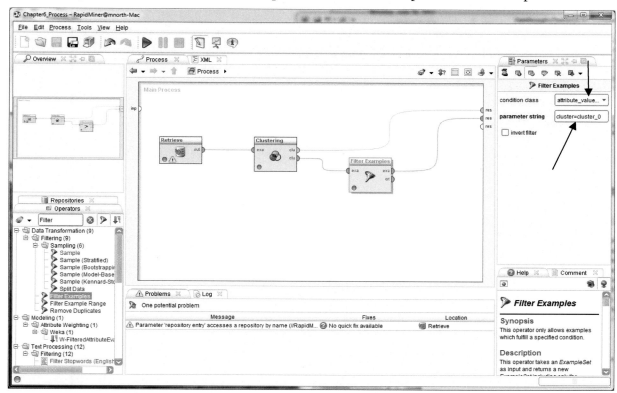

Figure 6-9. Filtering our cluster model's output for only observations in cluster 0.

As indicated by the black arrows in Figure 6-9, we are filtering out our observations based on an attribute filter, using the parameter string cluster=cluster_0. This means that only those observations in the data set that are classified in the cluster_0 group will be retained. Go ahead and click the play button to run the model again.

You will see that we have not lost our Cluster Model tab. It is still available to us, but now we have added an ExampleSet tab, which contains only those 154 observations which fell into cluster 0. As with the result of previous models we've created, we have descriptive statistics for the various attributes in the data set.

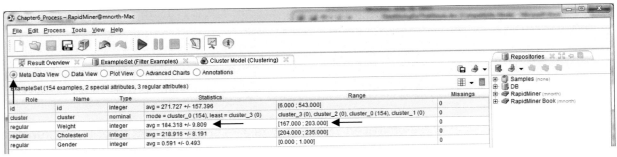

Figure 6-10. Filtered results for only cluster 0 observations.

Sonia could use these figures to begin contacting potential participants in her programs. With the high risk group having weights between 167 and 203 pounds, and cholesterol levels between 204 and 235 (these are taken from the Range statistics in Figure 6-10), she could return to her company's database and issue a SQL query like this one:

SELECT First_Name, Last_Name, Policy_Num, Address, Phone_Num

FROM PolicyHolders_view

WHERE Weight >= 167

AND Cholesterol >= 204;

This would give her the contact list for every person, male or female, insured by her employer who would fall into the higher risk group (cluster 0) in our data mining model. She could change the parameter criteria in our Filter Examples operator to be cluster=cluster_1 and re-run the model to get the descriptive statistics for those in the next highest risk group, and modify her SQL statement to get the contact list for that group from her organizational database; something akin to this query:

SELECT First_Name, Last_Name, Policy_Num, Address, Phone_Num

FROM PolicyHolders_view

WHERE (Weight >= 140 AND Weight <= 169)

AND (Cholesterol >= 168 AND Cholesterol <= 204);

If she wishes to also separate her groups by gender, she could add that criteria as well, such as "AND Gender = 1" in the WHERE clause of the SQL statement. As she continues to develop her health improvement programs, Sonia would have the lists of individuals that she most wants to target in the hopes of raising awareness, educating policy holders, and modifying behaviors that will lead to lower incidence of heart disease among her employer's clients.

CHAPTER SUMMARY

k-Means clustering is a data mining model that falls primarily on the side of Classification when referring to the Venn diagram from Chapter 1 (Figure 1-2). For this chapter's example, it does not necessarily predict which insurance policy holders *will* or *will not* develop heart disease. It simply takes known indicators from the attributes in a data set, and groups them together based on those attributes' similarity to group averages. Because any attributes that can be quantified can also have means calculated, k-means clustering provides an effective way of grouping observations together based on what is typical or normal for that group. It also helps us understand where one group begins and the other ends, or in other words, where the natural breaks occur between groups in a data set.

k-Means clustering is very flexible in its ability to group observations together. The k-Means operator in RapidMiner allows data miners to set the number of clusters they wish to generate, to dictate the number of sample means used to determine the clusters, and to use a number of different algorithms to evaluate means. While fairly simple in its set-up and definition, k-Means clustering is a powerful method for finding natural groups of observations in a data set.

REVIEW QUESTIONS

1) What does the *k* in k-Means clustering stand for?

2) How are clusters identified? What process does RapidMiner use to define clusters and place observations in a given cluster?

3) What does the Centroid Table tell the data miner? How do you interpret the values in a Centroid Table?

4) How do descriptive statistics aid in the process of evaluating and deploying a k-Means clustering model?

5) How might the presence of outliers in the attributes of a data set influence the usefulness of a k-Means clustering model? What could be done to address the problem?

EXERCISE

Think of an example of a problem that could be at least partially addressed by being able to group observations in a data set into clusters. Some examples might be grouping kids who might be at risk for delinquency, grouping product sale volumes, grouping workers by productivity and effectiveness, etc. Search the Internet or other resources available to you for a data set that would allow you to investigate your question using a k-means model. As with all exercises in this text, please ensure that you have permission to use any data set that might belong to your employer or another entity. When you have secured your data set, complete the following steps:

1) Ensure that your data set is saved as a CSV file. Import your data set into your RapidMiner repository and save it with a meaningful name. Drag it into a new process window in RapidMiner.

2) Conduct any data preparation that you need for your data set. This may include handling inconsistent data, dealing with missing values, or changing data types. Remember that in order to calculate means, each attribute in your data set will need to be numeric. If, for example, one of your attributes contains the values 'yes' and 'no', you may need to change these to be 1 and 0 respectively, in order for the k-Means operator to work.

3) Connect a k-Means operator to your data set, configure your parameters (especially set your k to something meaningful for your question) and then run your model.

4) Investigate your Centroid Table, Folder View, and the other evaluation tools.

5) Report your findings for your clusters. Discuss what is interesting about them and describe what iterations of modeling you went through, such as experimentation with different parameter values, to generate the clusters. Explain how your findings are relevant to your original question.

Challenge Step!

6) Experiment with the other k-Means operators in RapidMiner, such as Kernel or Fast. How are they different from your original model. Did the use of these operators change your clusters, and if so, how?

CHAPTER SEVEN:
DISCRIMINANT ANALYSIS

CONTEXT AND PERSPECTIVE

Gill runs a sports academy designed to help high school aged athletes achieve their maximum athletic potential. On the boys side of his academy, he focuses on four major sports: Football, Basketball, Baseball and Hockey. He has found that while many high school athletes enjoy participating in a number of sports in high school, as they begin to consider playing a sport at the college level, they would prefer to specialize in one sport. As he's worked with athletes over the years, Gill has developed an extensive data set, and he now is wondering if he can use past performance from some of his previous clients to predict prime sports for up-and-coming high school athletes. Ultimately, he hopes he can make a recommendation to each athlete as to the sport in which they should most likely choose to specialize. By evaluating each athlete's performance across a battery of test, Gill hopes we can help him figure out for which sport each athlete has the highest aptitude.

LEARNING OBJECTIVES

After completing the reading and exercises in this chapter, you should be able to:

- Explain what discriminant analysis is, how it is used and the benefits of using it.

- Recognize the necessary format for data in order to perform discriminant analysis.

- Explain the differences and similarities between k-Means clustering and discriminant analysis.

- Develop a discriminant analysis data mining model in RapidMiner using a training data set.

- Interpret the model output and apply it to a scoring data set in order to deploy the model.

ORGANIZATIONAL UNDERSTANDING

Gill's objective is to examine young athletes and, based upon their performance across a number of metrics, help them decide which sport is the most prime for their specialized success. Gill recognizes that all of his clients possess some measure of athleticism, and that they enjoy participating in a number of sports. Being young, athletic, and adaptive, most of his clients are quite good at a number of sports, and he has seen over the years that some people are so naturally gifted that they would excel in any sport they choose for specialization. Thus, he recognizes, as a limitation of this data mining exercise, that he may not be able to use data to determine an athlete's "best" sport. Still, he has seen metrics and evaluations work in the past, and has seen that some of his previous athletes really were pre-disposed to a certain sport, and that they were successful as they went on to specialize in that sport. Based on his industry experience, he has decided to go ahead with an experiment in mining data for athletic aptitude, and has enlisted our help.

DATA UNDERSTANDING

In order to begin to formulate a plan, we sit down with Gill to review his data assets. Every athlete that has enrolled at Gill's academy over the past several years has taken a battery test, which tested for a number of athletic and personal traits. The battery has been administered to both boys and girls participating in a number of different sports, but for this preliminary study we have decided with Gill that we will look at data only for boys. Because the academy has been operating for some time, Gill has the benefit of knowing which of his former pupils have gone on to specialize in a single sport, and which sport it was for each of them. Working with Gill, we gather the results of the batteries for all former clients who have gone on to specialize, Gill adds the sport each person specialized in, and we have a data set comprised of 493 observations containing the following attributes:

- **Age**: This is the age in years (one decimal precision for the part of the year since the client's last birthday) at the time that the athletic and personality trait battery test was administered. Participants ranged in age from 13-19 years old at the time they took the battery.

- **Strength**: This is the participant's strength measured through a series of weight lifting exercises and recorded on a scale of 0-10, with 0 being limited strength and 10 being sufficient strength to perform all lifts without any difficulty. No participant scored 8, 9 or 10, but some participants did score 0.

- **Quickness**: This is the participant's performance on a series of responsiveness tests. Participants were timed on how quickly they were able to press buttons when they were illuminated or to jump when a buzzer sounded. Their response times were tabulated on a scale of 0-6, with 6 being extremely quick response and 0 being very slow. Participants scored all along the spectrum for this attribute.

- **Injury**: This is a simple yes (1) / no (0) column indicating whether or not the young athlete had already suffered an athletic-related injury that was severe enough to require surgery or other major medical intervention. Common injuries treated with ice, rest, stretching, etc. were entered as 0. Injuries that took more than three week to heal, that required physical therapy or surgery were flagged as 1.

- **Vision**: Athletes were not only tested on the usual 20/20 vision scale using an eye chart, but were also tested using eye-tracking technology to see how well they were able to pick up objects visually. This test challenged participants to identify items that moved quickly across their field of vision, and to estimate speed and direction of moving objects. Their scores were recorded on a 0 to 4 scale with 4 being perfect vision and identification of moving objects. No participant scored a perfect 4, but the scores did range from 0 to 3.

- **Endurance**: Participants were subjected to an array of physical fitness tests including running, calisthenics, aerobic and cardiovascular exercise, and distance swimming. Their performance was rated on a scale of 0-10, with 10 representing the ability to perform all tasks without fatigue of any kind. Scores ranged from 0 to 6 on this attribute. Gill has acknowledged to us that even finely tuned professional athletes would not be able to score a 10 on this portion of the battery, as it is specifically designed to test the limits of human endurance.

- **Agility**: This is the participant's score on a series of tests of their ability to move, twist, turn, jump, change direction, etc. The test checked the athlete's ability to move nimbly, precisely, and powerfully in a full range of directions. This metric is comprehensive in nature, and is influenced by some of the other metrics, as agility is often dictated by one's strength, quickness, etc. Participants were scored between 0 and 100 on this attribute, and in our data set from Gill, we have found performance between 13 and 80.

- **Decision_Making**: This portion of the battery tests the athlete's process of deciding what to do in athletic situations. Athlete's participated in simulations that tested their choices of whether or not to swing a bat, pass a ball, move to a potentially advantageous location of a playing surface, etc. Their scores were to have been recorded on a scale of 0 to 100, though Gill has indicated that no one who completed the test should have been able to score lower than a 3, as three points are awarded simply for successfully entering and exiting the decision making part of the battery. Gill knows that all 493 of his former athletes represented in this data set successfully entered and exited this portion, but there are a few scores lower than 3, and also a few over 100 in the data set, so we know we have some data preparation in our future.

- **Prime_Sport**: This attribute is the sport each of the 453 athletes went on to specialize in after they left Gill's academy. This is the attribute Gill is hoping to be able to predict for his current clients. For the boys in this study, this attribute will be one of four sports: football (American, not soccer; sorry soccer fans), Basketball, Baseball, or Hockey.

As we analyze and familiarize ourselves with these data, we realize that all of the attributes with the exception of Prime_Sport are numeric, and as such, we could exclude Prime_Sport and conduct a k-means clustering data mining exercise on the data set. Doing this, we might be able group individuals into one sport cluster or another based on the means for each of the attributes in the data set. However, having the Prime_Sport attribute gives us the ability to use a different type of data mining model: **Discriminant Analysis**. Discriminant analysis is a lot like k-means clustering, in that it groups observations together into like-types of values, but it also gives us something more, and that is the ability to *predict*. Discriminant analysis then helps us cross that intersection seen in the Venn diagram in Chapter 1 (Figure 1-2). It is still a data mining methodology for classifying observations, but it classifies them *in a predictive way*. When we have a data set that contains an attribute that we know is useful in predicting the same value for other observations that do not yet have that attribute, then we can use **training data** and **scoring data** to mine predictively. Training data are simply data sets that have that known prediction attribute. For the observations in the training data set, the outcome of the prediction attribute is already known. The prediction attribute is also sometimes referred to as the **dependent attribute (or variable)** or the **target attribute**. It is the thing you are trying to predict. RapidMiner will ask us to set this attribute to be the **label** when we build our model. Scoring data are the observations which have all of the same attributes as the training data set, with the exception of the prediction attribute. We can use the training data set to allow RapidMiner to evaluate the values of all our attributes in the context of the resulting prediction variable (in this case, Prime_Sport), and then compare those values to the scoring data set and predict the Prime_Sport for each observation in the scoring data set. That may seem a little confusing, but our chapter example should help clarify it, so let's move on to the next CRISP-DM step.

DATA PREPARATION

This chapter's example will be a slight divergence from other chapters. Instead of there being a single example data set in CSV format for you to download, there are two this time. You can access the Chapter 7 data sets on the book's companion web site (https://sites.google.com/site/dataminingforthemasses/).

They are labeled Chapter07DataSet_Scoring.csv and Chapter07DataSet_Training.csv. Go ahead and download those now, and import both of them into your RapidMiner repository as you have in past chapters. Be sure to designate the attribute names in the first row of the data sets as you import them. Be sure you give each of the two data sets descriptive names, so that you can tell they are for Chapter 7, and also so that you can tell the difference between the training data set and the scoring data set. After importing them, **drag only the training data set into a new process window**, and then follow the steps below to prepare for and create a discriminant analysis data mining model.

1) Thus far, when we have added data to a new process, we have allowed the operator to simply be labeled 'Retrieve', which is done by RapidMiner by default. For the first time, we will have more than one Retrieve operator in our model, because we have a training data set and a scoring data set. In order to easily differentiate between the two, let's start by renaming the Retrieve operator for the training data set that you've dragged and dropped into your main process window. Right click on this operator and select Rename. You will then be able to type in a new name for this operator. For this example, we will name the operator 'Training', as is depicted in Figure 7-1.

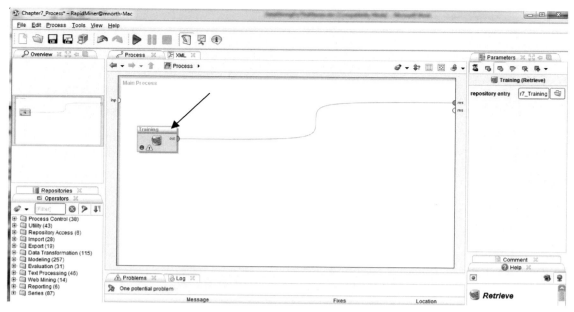

Figure 7-1. Our Retrieve operator renamed as 'Training'.

2) We know from our Data Preparation phase that we have some data that need to be fixed before we can mine this data set. Specifically, Gill noticed some inconsistencies in the Decision_Making attribute. Run your model and let's examine the meta data, as seen in Figure 7-2.

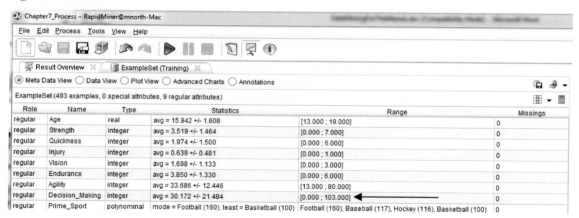

Figure 7-2. Identifying inconsistent data in the Decision_Making attribute.

3) While still in results perspective, switch to the Data View radio button. Click on the column heading for the Decision_Making attribute. This will sort the attribute from smallest to largest (note the small triangle indicating that the data are sorted in ascending order using this attribute). In this view (Figure 7-3) we see that we have three observations with scores smaller than three. We will need to handle these observations.

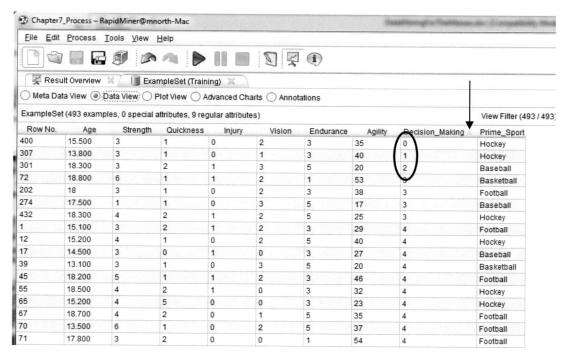

Figure 7-3. The data set sorted in ascending order by the Decision_Making attribute.

4) Click on the Decision_Making attribute again. This will re-sort the attribute in descending order. Again, we have some values that need to be addressed (Figure 7-4).

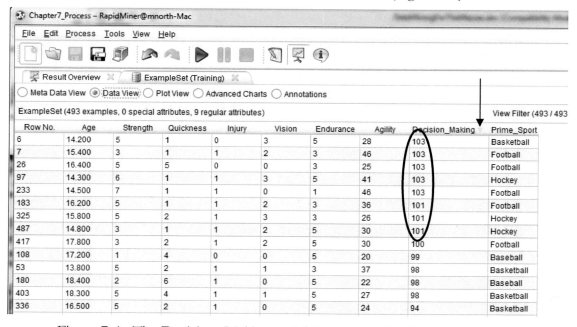

Figure 7-4. The Decision_Making variable, re-sorted in descending order.

5) Switch back to design perspective. Let's address these inconsistent data by removing them from our training data set. We could set these inconsistent values to missing then set missing values to another value, such as the mean, but in this instance we don't really know

what *should have* been in this variable, so changing these to the mean seems a bit arbitrary. Removing this inconsistencies means only removing 11 of our 493 observations, so rather than risk using bad data, we will simply remove them. To do this, add two Filter Examples operators in a row to your stream. For each of these, set the condition class to attribute_value_filter, and for the parameter strings, enter 'Decision_Making>=3' (without single quotes) for the first one, and 'Decision_Making<=100' for the second one. This will reduce our training data set down to 482 observations. The set-up described in this step is shown in Figure 7-5.

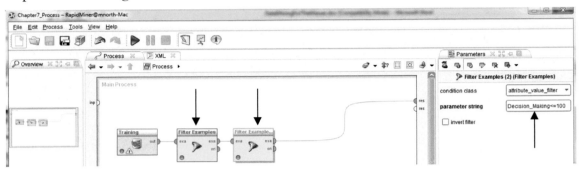

Figure 7-5. Filtering out observations with inconsistent data.

6) If you would like, you can run the model to confirm that your number of observations (examples) has been reduced to 482. Then, in design perspective, use the search field in the Operators tab to look for 'Discriminant' and locate the operator for Linear Discriminant Analysis. Add this operator to your stream, as shown in Figure 7-6.

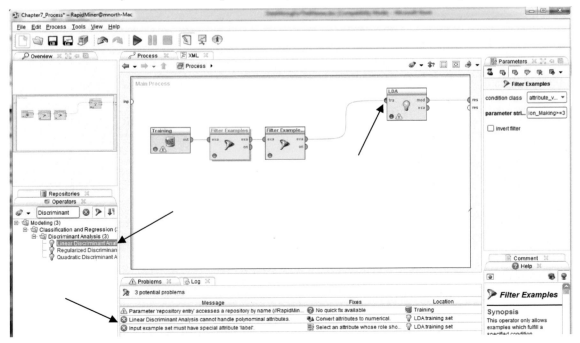

Figure 7-6. Addition of the Linear Discriminant Analysis operator to the model.

7) The *tra* port on the LDA (or Linear Discriminant Analysis) operator indicates that this tool does expect to receive input from a training data set like the one we've provided, but despite this, we still have received two errors, as indicated by the black arrow at the bottom of the Figure 7-6 image. The first error is because of our Prime_Sport attribute. It is data typed as polynominal, and LDA likes attributes that are numeric. This is OK, because the predictor attribute can have a polynominal data type, and the Prime_Sport attribute is the one we want to predict, so this error will be resolved shortly. This is because it is related to the second error, which tells us that the LDA operator wants one of our attributes to be designated as a 'label'. In RapidMiner, the label is the attribute that you want to predict. At the time that we imported our data set, we could have designated the Prime_Sport attribute as a label, rather than as a normal attribute, but it is very simple to change an attribute's role right in your stream. Using the search field in the Operators tab, search for an operator called Set Role. Add this to your stream and then in the parameters area on the right side of the window, select Prime_Sport in the name field, and in target role, select label. We still have a warning (which does not prevent us from continuing), but you will see the errors have now disappeared at the bottom of the RapidMiner window (Figure 7-7).

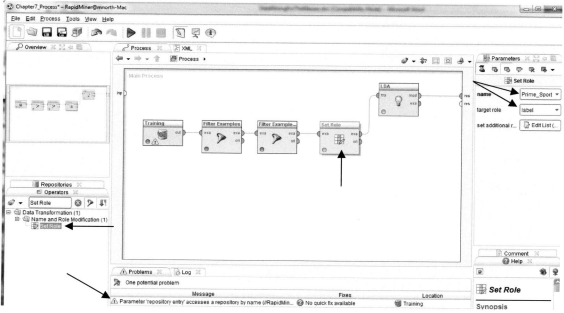

Figure 7-7. Setting an attribute's role in RapidMiner.

With our inconsistent data removed and our errors resolved, we are now prepared to move on to...

MODELING

8) We now have a functional stream. Go ahead and run the model as it is now. With the *mod* port connected to the *res* port, RapidMiner will generate Discriminant Analysis output for us.

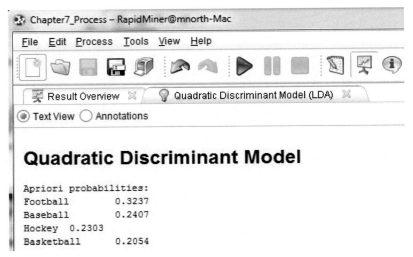

Figure 7-8. The results of discriminant analysis on our training data set.

9) The probabilities given in the results will total to 1. This is because at this stage of our Discriminant Analysis model, all that has been calculated is the likelihood of an observation landing in one of the four categories in our target attribute of Prime_Sport. Because this is our training data set, RapidMiner can calculate theses probabilities easily—every observation is already classified. Football has a probability of 0.3237. If you refer back to Figure 7-2, you will see that Football as Prime_Sport comprised 160 of our 493 observations. Thus, the probability of an observation having Football is 160/493, or 0.3245. But in steps 3 and 4 (Figures 7-3 and 7-4), we removed 11 observations that had inconsistent data in their Decision_Making attribute. Four of these were Football observations (Figure 7-4), so our Football count dropped to 156 and our total count dropped to 482: 156/482 = 0.3237. Since we have no observations where the value for Prime_Sport is missing, each possible value in Prime_Sport will have some portion of the total count, and the sum of these portions will equal 1, as is the case in Figure 7-8. These probabilities, coupled with the values for each attribute, will be used to predict the Prime_Sport classification for each of Gill's current clients represented in our scoring data set. Return now to design perspective and in the Repositories tab, drag the Chapter 7 scoring data set over and drop it in the main process window. Do not connect it to your

existing stream, but rather, allow it to connect directly to a *res* port. Right click the operator and rename it to 'Scoring'. These steps are illustrated in Figure7-9.

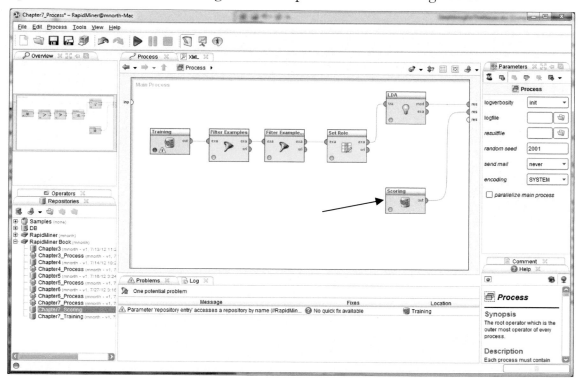

Figure 7-9. Adding the scoring data set to our model.

10) Run the model again. RapidMiner will give you an additional tab in results perspective this time which will show the meta data for the scoring data set (Figure 7-10).

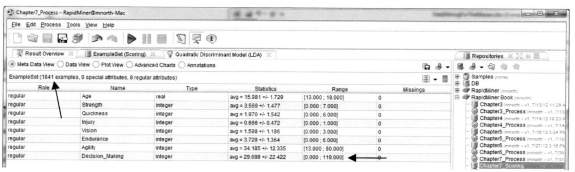

Figure 7-10. Results perspective meta data for our scoring data set.

11) The scoring data set contains 1,841, however, as indicated by the black arrow in the Range column of Figure 7-10, the Decision_Making attribute has some inconsistent data again. Repeating the process previously outlined in steps 3 and 4, return to design perspective and use two consecutive Filter Examples operators to remove any observations that have values below 3 or above 100 in the Decision_Making attribute (Figure 7-11). This will

leave us with 1,767 observations, and you can check this by running the model again (Figure 7-12).

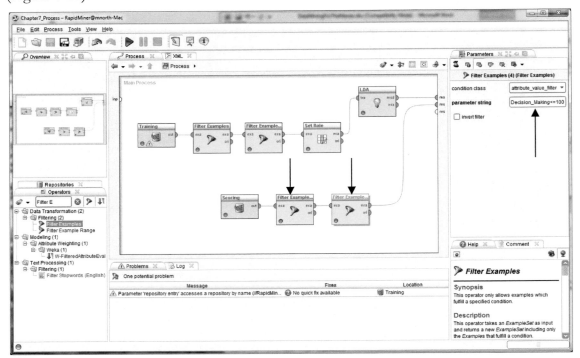

Figure 7-11. Filtering out observations containing inconsistent Decision_Making values.

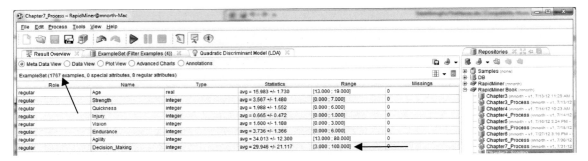

Figure 7-12. Verification that observations with inconsistent values have been removed.

12) We now have just one step remaining to complete our model and predict the Prime_Sport for the 1,767 boys represented in our scoring data set. Return to design perspective, and use the search field in the Operators tab to locate an operator called Apply Model. Drag this operator over and place it in the Scoring data set's stream, as is shown in Figure 7-13.

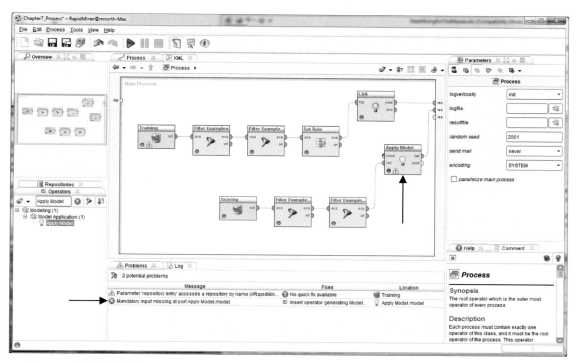

Figure 7-13. Adding the Apply Model operator to our Discriminant Analysis model.

13) As you can see in Figure 7-13, the Apply Model operator has given us an error. This is because the Apply Model operator expects the output of a model generation operator as its input. This is an easy fix, because our LDA operator (which generated a model for us) has a *mod* port for its output. We simply need to disconnect the LDA's *mod* port from the *res* port it's currently connected to, and connect it instead to the Apply Model operator's *mod* input port. To do this, click on the *mod* port for the LDA operator, and then click on the *mod* port for the Apply Model operator. When you do this, the following warning will pop up:

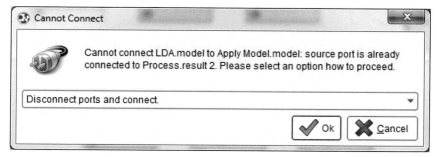

Figure 7-14. The port reconnection warning in RapidMiner.

14) Click OK to indicate to RapidMiner that you do in fact wish to reconfigure the spline to connect *mod* port to *mod* port. The error message will disappear and your scoring model will be ready for prediction (Figure 7-15).

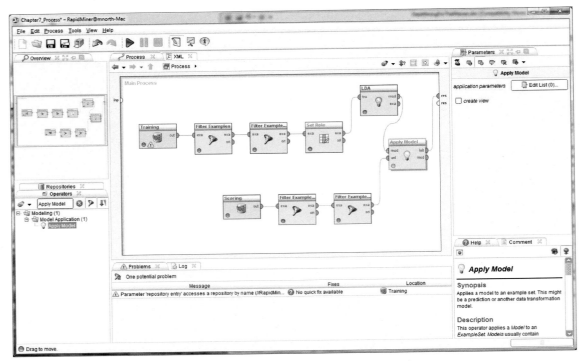

Figure 7-15. Discriminant analysis model with training and scoring data streams.

15) Run the model by clicking the play button. RapidMiner will generate five new attributes and add them to our results perspective (Figure 7-16), preparing us for...

EVALUATION

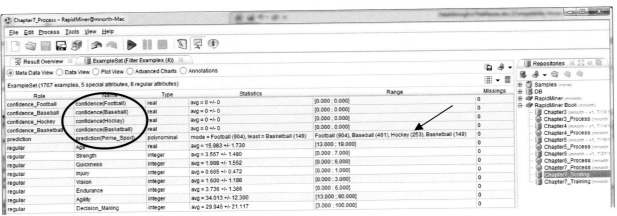

Figure 7-16. Prediction attributes generated by RapidMiner.

The first four attributes created by RapidMiner are confidence percentages, which indicate the relative strength of RapidMiner's prediction when compared to the other values the software might have predicted for each observation. In this example data set, RapidMiner has not generated confidence percentages for each of our four target sports. If RapidMiner had found some significant possibility that an observation might have more than one possible Prime_Sport, it would have calculated the percent probability that the person represented by an observation would succeed in one sport and in the others. For example, if an observation yielded a statistical possibility that the Prime_Sport for a person could have been any of the four, but Baseball was the strongest statistically, the confidence attributes on that observation might be: confidence(Football): 8%; confidence(Baseball): 69%; confidence(Hockey): 12%; confidence(Basketball): 11%. In some predictive data mining models (including some later in this text), your data *will* yield partial confidence percentages such as this. This phenomenon did not occur however in the data sets we used for this chapter's example. This is most likely explained by the fact discussed earlier in the chapter: all athletes will display some measure of aptitude in many sports, and so their battery test scores will likely be varied across the specializations. In statistical language, this is often referred to as **heterogeneity**.

Not finding confidence percentages does not mean that our experiment has been a failure however. The fifth new attribute, generated by RapidMiner when we applied our LDA model to our scoring data, is the prediction of Prime_Sport for each of our 1,767 boys. Click on the Data View radio button, and you will see that RapidMiner has applied our discriminant analysis model to our scoring data, resulting in a predicted Prime_Sport for each boy based on the specialization sport of previous academy attendees (Figure 7-17).

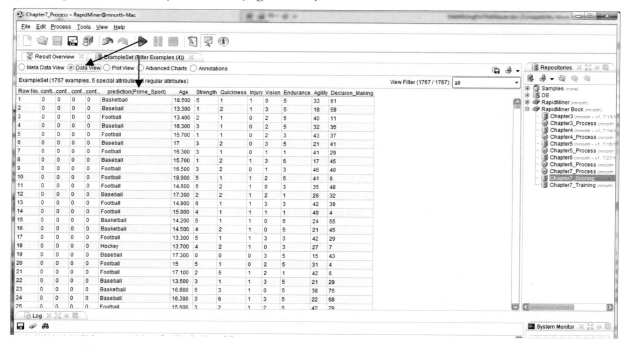

Figure 7-17. Prime_Sport predictions for each boy in the scoring data set.

DEPLOYMENT

Gill now has a data set with a prediction for each boy that has been tested using the athletic battery at his academy. What to do with these predictions will be a matter of some thought and discussion. Gill can extract these data from RapidMiner and relate them back to each boy individually. For relatively small data sets, such as this one, we could move the results into a spreadsheet by simply copying and pasting them. Just as a quick exercise in moving results to other formats, try this:

1) Open a blank OpenOffice Calc spreadsheet.

2) In RapidMiner, click on the 1 under Row No. in Data View of results perspective (the cell will turn gray).

3) Press Ctrl+A (the keyboard command for 'select all' in Windows; you can use equivalent keyboard command for Mac or Linux as well). All cells in Data View will turn gray.

4) Press Ctrl+C (or the equivalent keyboard command for 'copy' if not using Windows).

5) In your blank OpenOffice Calc spreadsheet, right click in cell A1 and choose Paste Special... from the context menu.

6) In the pop up dialog box, select Unformatted Text, then click OK.

7) A Text Import pop up dialog box will appear with a preview of the RapidMiner data. Accept the defaults by clicking OK. The data will be pasted into the spreadsheet. The attribute names will have to be transcribed and added to the top row of the spreadsheet, but the data are now available outside of RapidMiner. Gill can match each prediction back to each boy in the scoring data set. The data are still in order, but remember that a few were removed because on inconsistent data, so care should be exercised when matching the predictions back to the boys represented by each observation. Bringing a unique identifying number into the training and scoring data sets might aid the matching once

predictions have been generated. This will be demonstrated in an upcoming chapter's example.

Chapter 14 of this book will spend some time talking about ethics in data mining. As previously mentioned, Gill's use of these predictions is going to require some thought and discussion. Is it ethical to push one of his young clients in the direction of one specific sport based on our model's prediction that that activity as a good match for the boy? Simply because previous academy attendees went on to specialize in one sport or another, can we assume that current clients would follow the same path? The final chapter will offer some suggestions for ways to answer such questions, but it is wise for us to at least consider them now in the context of the chapter examples.

It is likely that Gill, being experienced at working with young athletes and recognizing their strengths and weaknesses, will be able to use our predictions in an ethical way. Perhaps he can begin by grouping his clients by their predicted Prime_Sports and administering more 'sport-specific' drills—say, jumping tests for basketball, skating for hockey, throwing and catching for baseball, etc. This may allow him to capture more specific data on each athlete, or even to simply observe whether or not the predictions based on the data are in fact consistent with observable performance on the field, court, or ice. This is an excellent example of why the CRISP-DM approach is *cyclical*: the predictions we've generated for Gill are a starting point for a new round of assessment and evaluation, not the ending or culminating point. Discriminant analysis has given Gill some idea about where his young proteges may have strengths, and this can point him in certain directions when working with each of them, but he will inevitably gather more data and learn whether or not the use of this data mining methodology and approach is helpful in guiding his clients to a sport in which they might choose to specialize as they mature.

CHAPTER SUMMARY

Discriminant analysis helps us to cross the threshold between Classification and Prediction in data mining. Prior to Chapter 7, our data mining models and methodologies focused primarily on categorization of data. With Discriminant Analysis, we can take a process that is very similar in nature to k-means clustering, and with the right target attribute in a training data set, generate predictions for a scoring data set. This can become a powerful addition to k-means models, giving us the ability to apply our clusters to other data sets that haven't yet been classified.

Discriminant analysis can be useful where the classification for some observations is known and is not known for others. Some classic applications of discriminant analysis are in the fields of biology and organizational behavior. In biology, for example, discriminant analysis has been successfully applied to the classification of plant and animal species based on the traits of those living things. In organizational behavior, this type of data modeling has been used to help workers identify potentially successful career paths based on personality traits, preferences and aptitudes. By coupling known past performance with unknown but similarly structured data, we can use discriminant analysis to effectively train a model that can then score the unknown records for us, giving us a picture of what categories the unknown observations would likely be in.

REVIEW QUESTIONS

1) What type of attribute does a data set need in order to conduct discriminant analysis instead of k-means clustering?

2) What is a 'label' role in RapidMiner and why do you need an attribute with this role in order to conduct discriminant analysis?

3) What is the difference between a training data set and a scoring data set?

4) What is the purpose of the Apply Model operator in RapidMiner?

5) What are confidence percent attributes used for in RapidMiner? What was the likely reason that did we not find any in this chapter's example? Are there attributes about young athletes that you can think of that were not included in our data sets that might have helped up find some confidence percents? (Hint: think of things that are fairly specific to only one or two sports.)

6) What would be problematic about including both male and female athletes in this chapter's example data?

EXERCISE

For this chapter's exercise, you will compile your own data set based on people you know and the cars they drive, and then create a linear discriminant analysis of your data in order to predict categories for a scoring data set. Complete the following steps:

1) Open a new blank spreadsheet in OpenOffice Calc. At the bottom of the spreadsheet there will be three default tabs labeled Sheet1, Sheet2, Sheet3. Rename the first one Training and the second one Scoring. You can rename the tabs by double clicking on their labels. You can delete or ignore the third default sheet.

2) On the training sheet, starting in cell A1 and going across, create attribute labels for six attributes: Age, Gender, Marital_Status, Employment, Housing, and Car_Type.

3) Copy each of these attribute names except Car_Type into the Scoring sheet.

4) On the Training sheet, enter values for each of these attributes for several people that you know who have a car. These could be family members, friends and neighbors, coworkers or fellow students, etc. Try to do at least 20 observations; 30 or more would be better. Enter husband and wife couples as two separate observations, so long as each spouse has a different vehicle. Use the following to guide your data entry:

   a. For Age, you could put the person's actual age in years, or you could put them in buckets. For example, you could put 10 for people aged 10-19; 20 for people aged 20-29; etc.

   b. For Gender, enter 0 for female and 1 for male.

   c. For Marital_Status, use 0 for single, 1 for married, 2 for divorced, and 3 for widowed.

   d. For Employment, enter 0 for student, 1 for full-time, 2 for part-time, and 3 for retired.

   e. For Housing, use 0 for lives rent-free with someone else, 1 for rents housing, and 2 for owns housing.

   f. For Car_Type, you can record data in a number of ways. This will be your label, or the attribute you wish to predict. You could record each person's car by make (e.g.

Toyota, Honda, Ford, etc.), or you could record it by body style (e.g. Car, Truck, SUV, etc.). Be consistent in assigning classifications, and note that depending on the size of the data set you create, you won't want to have too many possible classificatons, or your predictions in the scoring data set will be spread out too much. With small data sets containing only 20-30 observations, the number of categories should be limited to three or four. You might even consider using Japanese, American, European as your Car_Types values.

5) Once you've compiled your Training data set, switch to the Scoring sheet in OpenOffice Calc. Repeat the data entry process for at least 20 people (more is better) that you know who *do not* have a car. You will use the training set to try to predict the type of car each of these people would drive if they had one.

6) Use the File > Save As menu option in OpenOffice Calc to save your Training and Scoring sheets as CSV files.

7) Import your two CSV files into your RapidMiner respository. Be sure to give them descriptive names.

8) Drag your two data sets into a new process window. If you have prepared your data well in OpenOffice Calc, you shouldn't have any missing or inconsistent data to contend with, so data preparation should be minimal. Rename the two retrieve operators so you can tell the difference between your training and scoring data sets.

9) One necessary data preparation step is to add a Set Role operator and define the Car_Type attribute as your label.

10) Add a Linear Discriminant Analysis operator to your Training stream.

11) Apply your LDA model to your scoring data and run your model. Evaluate and report your results. Did you get any confidence percentages? Do the predicted Car_Types seem reasonable and consistent with your training data? Why or why not?

Challenge Step!

12) Change your LDA operator to a different type of discriminant analysis (e.g. Quadratic) operator. Re-run your model. Consider doing some research to learn about the difference between linear and quadratic discriminant analysis. Compare your new results to the LDA results and report any interesting findings or differences.

CHAPTER EIGHT:
LINEAR REGRESSION

CONTEXT AND PERSPECTIVE

Sarah, the regional sales manager from the Chapter 4 example, is back for more help. Business is booming, her sales team is signing up thousands of new clients, and she wants to be sure the company will be able to meet this new level of demand. She was so pleased with our assistance in finding correlations in her data, she now is hoping we can help her do some prediction as well. She knows that there is some correlation between the attributes in her data set (things like temperature, insulation, and occupant ages), and she's now wondering if she can use the data set from Chapter 4 to predict heating oil usage for new customers. You see, these new customers haven't begun consuming heating oil yet, there are a lot of them (42,650 to be exact), and she wants to know how much oil she needs to expect to keep in stock in order to meet these new customers' demand. Can she use data mining to examine household attributes and known past consumption quantities to anticipate and meet her new customers' needs?

LEARNING OBJECTIVES

After completing the reading and exercises in this chapter, you should be able to:

- Explain what linear regression is, how it is used and the benefits of using it.
- Recognize the necessary format for data in order to perform predictive linear regression.
- Explain the basic algebraic formula for calculating linear regression.
- Develop a linear regression data mining model in RapidMiner using a training data set.
- Interpret the model's coefficients and apply them to a scoring data set in order to deploy the model.

ORGANIZATIONAL UNDERSTANDING

Sarah's new data mining objective is pretty clear: she wants to anticipate demand for a consumable product. We will use a **linear regression** model to help her with her desired predictions. She has data, 1,218 observations from the Chapter 4 data set that give an attribute profile for each home, along with those homes' annual heating oil consumption. She wants to use this data set as training data to predict the usage that 42,650 new clients will bring to her company. She knows that these new clients' homes are similar in nature to her existing client base, so the existing customers' usage behavior should serve as a solid gauge for predicting future usage by new customers.

DATA UNDERSTANDING

As a review, our data set from Chapter 4 contains the following attributes:

- **Insulation**: This is a density rating, ranging from one to ten, indicating the thickness of each home's insulation. A home with a density rating of one is poorly insulated, while a home with a density of ten has excellent insulation.

- **Temperature**: This is the average outdoor ambient temperature at each home for the most recent year, measure in degree Fahrenheit.

- **Heating_Oil**: This is the total number of units of heating oil purchased by the owner of each home in the most recent year.

- **Num_Occupants**: This is the total number of occupants living in each home.

- **Avg_Age**: This is the average age of those occupants.

- **Home_Size**: This is a rating, on a scale of one to eight, of the home's overall size. The higher the number, the larger the home.

We will use the Chapter 4 data set as our training data set in this chapter. Sarah has assembled a separate Comma Separated Values file containing all of these same attributes, except of course for Heating_Oil, for her 42,650 new clients. She has provided this data set to us to use as the scoring data set in our model.

DATA PREPARATION

You should already have downloaded and imported the Chapter 4 data set, but if not, you can get it from the book's companion web site (https://sites.google.com/site/dataminingforthemasses/). Download and import the Chapter 8 data set from the companion web site as well. Once you have both the Chapter 4 and Chapter 8 data sets imported into your RapidMiner data repository, complete the following steps:

1) Drag and drop both data sets into a new process window in RapidMiner. Rename the Chapter 4 data set to 'Training (CH4), and the Chapter 8 data set to 'Scoring (CH8)'. Connect both *out* ports to *res* ports, as shown in Figure 8-1, and then run your model.

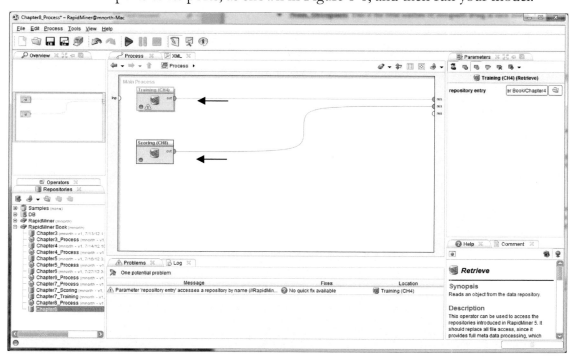

Figure 8-1. Using both Chapter 4 and 8 data sets to set up a linear regression model.

2) Figures 8-2 and 8-3 show side-by-side comparisons of the training and scoring data sets. When using linear regression as a predictive model, it is extremely important to remember that the ranges for all attributes in the scoring data must be within the ranges for the corresponding attributes in the training data. This is because a training data set cannot be relied upon to predict a target attrtibute for observations whose values fall outside the training data set's values.

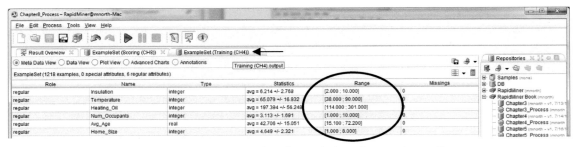

Figure 8-2. Value ranges for the training data set's attributes.

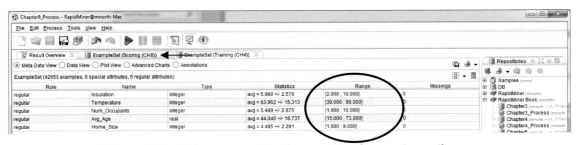

Figure 8-3. Value ranges for the scoring data set's attributes.

3) We can see that in comparing Figures 8-2 and 8-3, the ranges are the same for all attributes except Avg_Age. In the scoring data set, we have some observations where the Avg_Age is slightly below the training data set's lower bound of 15.1, and some observations where the scoring Avg_Age is slightly above the training set's upper bound of 72.2. You might think that these values are so close to the training data set's values that it would not matter if we used our training data set to predict heating oil usage for the homes represented by these observations. While it is likely that such a slight deviation from the range on this attribute would not yield wildly inaccurate results, we cannot use linear regression prediction values as evidence to support such an assumption. Thus, we will need to remove these observations from our data set. Add two Filter Examples operators with the parameters attribute_value_filter and Avg_Age>=15.1 | Avg_Age <=72.2. When you run your model now, you should have 42,042 observations remaining. Check the ranges again to ensure that none of the scoring attributes now have ranges outside those of the training attributes. Then return to design perspective.

4) As was the case with discriminant analysis, linear regression is a predictive model, and thus will need an attribute to be designated as the label—this is the target, the thing we want to predict. Search for the Set Role operator in the Operators tab and drag it into your training

stream. Change the parameters to designate Heating_Oil as the label for this model (Figure 8-4).

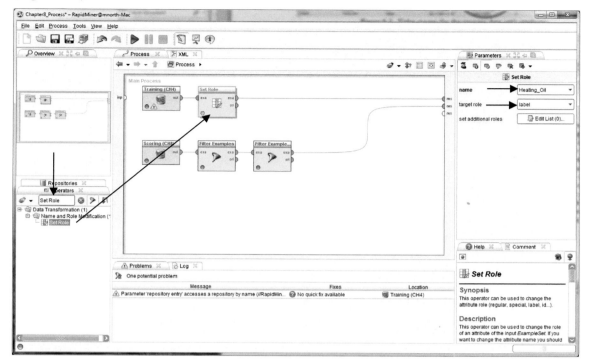

Figure 8-4. Adding an operator to designate Heating_Oil as our label.

With this step complete our data sets are now prepared for…

MODELING

5) Using the search field in the Operators tab again, locate the Linear Regression operator and drag and drop it into your training data set's stream (Figure 8-5).

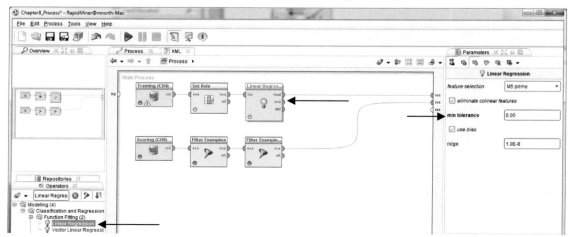

Figure 8-5. Adding the Linear Regression model operator to our stream.

6) Note that the Linear Regression operator uses a default tolerance of .05 (also known in statistical language as the **confidence level** or **alpha level**). This value of .05 is very common in statistical analysis of this type, so we will accept this default. The final step to complete our model is to use an Apply Model operator to connect our training stream to our scoring stream. Be sure to connect both the *lab* and *mod* ports coming from the Apply Model operator to *res* ports. This is illustrated in Figure 8-6.

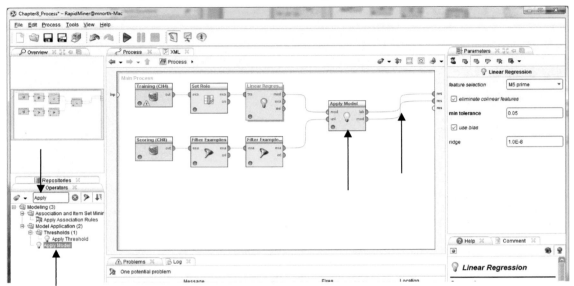

Figure 8-6. Applying the model to the scoring data set.

7) Run the model. Having two splines coming from the Apply Model operator and connecting to *res* ports will result in two tabs in results perspective. Let's examine the LinearRegression tab first, as we begin our...

EVALUATION

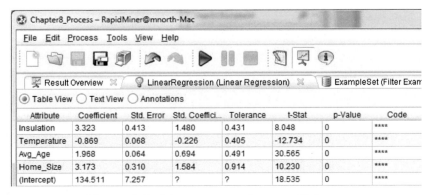

Attribute	Coefficient	Std. Error	Std. Coeffici...	Tolerance	t-Stat	p-Value	Code
Insulation	3.323	0.413	1.480	0.431	8.048	0	****
Temperature	-0.869	0.068	-0.226	0.405	-12.734	0	****
Avg_Age	1.968	0.064	0.694	0.491	30.565	0	****
Home_Size	3.173	0.310	1.584	0.914	10.230	0	****
(Intercept)	134.511	7.257	?	?	18.535	0	****

Figure 8-7. Linear regression coefficients.

Linear regression modeling is all about determing how close a given observation is to an imaginary line representing the average, or center of all points in the data set. That imaginary line gives us the first part of the term "linear regression". The formula for calculating a prediction using linear regression is $y=mx+b$. You may recognize this from a former algebra class as the formula for calculating the slope of a line. In this formula, the variable y, is the target, the label, the thing we want to predict. So in this chapter's example, y is the amount of Heating_Oil we expect each home to consume. But how will we predict y? We need to know what m, x, and b are. The variable m is the value for a given predictor attribute, or what is sometimes referred to as an **independent variable**. Insulation, for example, is a predictor of heating oil usage, so Insulation is a predictor attribute. The variable x is that attribute's coefficient, shown in the second column of Figure 8-7. The coefficient is the amount of weight the attribute is given in the formula. Insulation, with a coefficient of 3.323, is weighted heavier than any of the other predictor attributes in this data set. Each observation will have its Insulation value multipled by the Insulation coefficient to properly weight that attribute when calculating y (heating oil usage). The variable b is a constant that is added to all linear regression calculations. It is represented by the Intercept, shown in figure 8-7 as 134.511. So suppose we had a house with insulation density of 5; our formula using these Insulation values would be $y=(5*3.323)+134.511$.

But wait! We had more than one predictor attribute. We started out using a combination of five attributes to try to predict heating oil usage. The formula described in the previous paragraph only uses one. Furthermore, our LinearRegression result set tab pictured in Figure 8-7 only has four predictor variables. What happened to Num_Occupants?

The answer to the latter question is that Num_Occupants was not a **statistically significant** predictor of heating oil usage in this data set, and therefore, RapidMiner removed it as a predictor. In other words, when RapidMiner evaluated the amount of influence each attribute in the data set had on heating oil usage for each home represented in the training data set, the number of occupants was so non-influential that its weight in the formula was set to zero. An example of why this might occur could be that two older people living in a house may use the same amount of heating oil as a young family of five in the house. The older couple might take longer showers, and prefer to keep their house much warmer in the winter time than would the young family. The variability in the number of occupants in the house doesn't help to explain each home's heating oil usage very well, and so it was removed as a predictor in our model.

But what about the former question, the one about having multiple independent variables in this model? How can we set up our linear formula when we have multiple predictors? This is done by using the formula: $y=mx+mx+mx...+b$. Let's take an example. Suppose we wanted to predict heating oil usage, using our model, for a home with the following attributes:

- Insulation: 6

- Temperature: 67

- Avg_Age: 35.4

- Home_Size: 5

Our formula for this home would be: $y=(6*3.323)+(67*-0.869)+(35.4*1.968)+(5*3.173)+134.511$

Our prediction for this home's annual number of heating oil units ordered (y) is 181.758, or basically 182 units. Let's check our model's predictions as we discuss possibilities for…

DEPLOYMENT

While still in results perspective, switch to the ExampleSet tab, and select the Data View radio button. We can see in this view (Figure 8-8) that RapidMiner has quickly and efficiently predicted the number of units of heating oil each of Sarah's company's new customers will likely use in their first year. This is seen in the prediction(Heating_Oil) attribute.

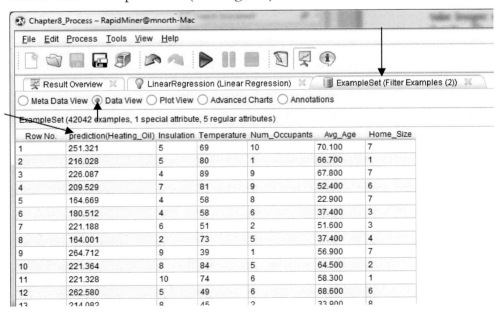

Figure 8-8. Heating oil predictions for 42,042 new clients.

Let's check the first of our 42,042 households by running the linear regression formula for row 1:

$$(5*3.323)+(69*-0.869)+(70.1*1.968)+(7*3.173)+134.511 = 251.321$$

Note that in this formula we skipped the Num_Occupants attribute because it is not predictive. The formula's result does indeed match RapidMiner's prediction for this home. Sarah now has a prediction for each of the new clients' homes, with the exception of those that had Avg_Age values that were out of range. How might Sarah use this data? She could start by summing the prediction attribute. This will tell her the total new units of heating oil her company is going to need to be able to provide in the coming year. This can be accomplished by exporting her data to a spreasheet and summing the column, or it can even be done within RapidMiner using an Aggregate operator. We will demonstrate this briefly.

1) Switch back to design perspective.

2) Search for the Aggreate operator in the Operators tab and add it between the *lab* and *res* ports, as shown in Figure 8-9. It is not depicted in Figure 8-9, but if you wish to generate a tab in results perspective that shows all of your obsevations and their predictions, you can connect the *ori* port on the Aggregate operator to a *res* port.

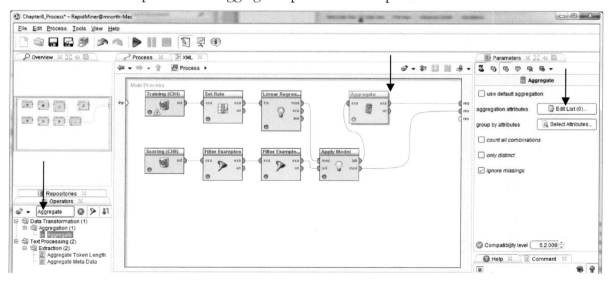

Figure 8-9. Adding an Aggregate operator to our linear regression model.

3) Click on the Edit List button. A window similar to Figure 8-10 will appear. Set the prediction(Heating_Oil) attribute as the aggregation attribute, and the aggregation function to 'sum'. If you would like you can add other aggretations. In the Figure 8-10 example, we have added an average for prediction(Heating_Oil) as well.

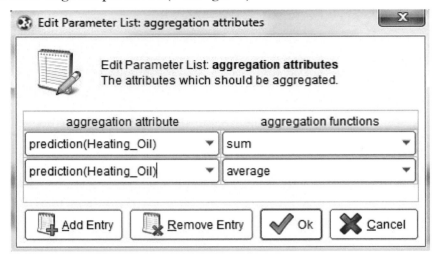

Figure 8-10. Configuring aggregations in RapidMiner.

4) When you are satisfied with your aggregations, click OK to return to your main process window, then run the model. In results perspective, select the ExampleSet(Aggregate) tab, then select the Data View radio button. The sum and average for the prediction attribute will be shown, as depicted in Figure 8-11.

Figure 8-11. Aggregate descriptive statistics for our predicted attribute.

From this image, we can see that Sarah's company is likely to sell some 8,368,088 units of heating oil to these new customers. The company can expect that on average, their new customers will order about 200 units each. These figures are for all 42,042 clients together, but Sarah is probably going to be more interested in regional trends. In order to deploy this model to help her more specifically address her new customers' needs, she should probably extract the predictions, match them back to their source records which might contain the new clients' addresses, enabling her to break the predictions down by city, county, or region of the country. Sarah could then work with her colleagues in Operations and Order Fulfillment to ensure that regional heating oil distribution centers around the country have appropriate amounts of stock on hand to meet anticipated need. If Sarah wanted to get even more granular in her analysis of these data, she could break her training and scoring datas set down into months using a month attribute, and then run the predictions again to reveal fluctuations in usuage throughout the course of the year.

CHAPTER SUMMARY

Linear regression is a predictive model that uses training and scoring data sets to generate numeric predictions in data. It is important to remember that linear regression uses numeric data types for all of its attributes. It uses the algebraic formula for calculating the slope of a line to determine where an observation would fall along an imaginary line through the scoring data. Each attribute in the data set is evaluated statistically for its ability to predict the target attribute. Attributes that are not strong predictors are removed from the model. Those attributes that are good predictors are assigned coefficients which give them weight in the prediction formula. Any observations whose attribute values fall in the range of corresponding training attribute values can be plugged into the formula in order to predict the target.

Once linear regression predictions are calculated, the results can be summarized in order to determine if there are differences in the predictions in subsets of the scoring data. As more data are collected, they can be added into the training data set in order to create a more robust training data set, or to expand the ranges of some attributes to include even more values. It is very important to remember that the ranges for the scoring attributes must fall within the ranges for the training attributes in order to ensure valid predictions.

REVIEW QUESTIONS

1) What data type does linear regression expect for all attributes? What data type will the predicted attribute be when it is calculated?

2) Why are the attribute ranges so important when doing linear regression data mining?

3) What are linear regression coefficients? What does 'weight' mean?

4) What is the linear regression mathematical formula, and how is it arranged?

5) How are linear regression results interpreted?

Extra thought question:

6) If you have an attribute that you want to use in a linear regression model, but it contains text data, such as the make or model of a car, what could you do in order to be able to use that attribute in your model?

EXERCISE

In the Chapter 4 exercise, you compiled your own data set about professional athletes. For this exercise, we will enhance this data set and then build a linear regression model on it. Complete the following steps:

1) Open the data set you compiled for the Chapter 4 exercise. If you did not do that exercise, please turn back to Chapter 4 and complete steps 1 – 4.

2) Split your data set's observations in two: a training portion and a scoring portion. Be sure that you have at least 20 observations in your training data set, and at least 10 in your scoring data set. More would be better, so if you only have 30 observations total, perhaps it would be good to take some time to look up ten or so more athletes to add to your scoring data set. Also, we are going to try to predict each athlete's salary, so if Salary is not one of your attributes, look it up for each athlete in your training data set (don't look it up for the scoring data set athletes, we're going to try to predict these). Also, if there are other attributes that you don't have, but that you think would be great predictors of salary, look these up, and add them to both your training and scoring data sets. These might be things like points per game, defensive statistics, etc. Be sure your attributes are numeric.

3) Import both of your data sets into your RapidMiner repository. Be sure to give them descriptive names. Drag and drop them into a new process, and rename them as Training and Scoring so that you can tell them apart.

4) Use a Set Role operator to designate the Salary attribute as the label for the training data.

5) Add a linear regression operator and apply your model to your scoring data set.

6) Run your model. In results perspective, examine your attribute coefficients and the predictions for the athletes' salaries in your scoring data set.

7) Report your results:

    a. Which attributes have the greatest weight?

    b. Were any attributes dropped from the data set as non-predictors? If so, which ones and why do you think they weren't effective predictors?

    c. Look up a few of the salaries for some of your scoring data athletes and compare their actual salary to the predicted salary. Is it very close? Why or why not, do you think?

    d. What other attributes do you think would help your model better predict professional athletes' salaries?

CHAPTER NINE:
LOGISTIC REGRESSION

CONTEXT AND PERSPECTIVE

Remember Sonia, the health insurance program director from Chapter 6? Well, she's back for more help too! Her k-means clustering project was so helpful in finding groups of folks who could benefit from her programs, that she wants to do more. This time around, she is concerned with helping those who have suffered heart attacks. She wants to help them improve lifestyle choices, including management of weight and stress, in order to improve their chances of *not* suffering a second heart attack. Sonia is wondering if, with the right training data, we can predict the chances of her company's policy holders suffering second heart attacks. She feels like she could really help some of her policy holders who have suffered heart attacks by offering weight, cholesterol and stress management classes or support groups. By lowering these key heart attack risk factors, her employer's clients will live healthier lives, and her employer's risk at having to pay costs associated with treatment of second heart attacks will also go down. Sonia thinks she might even be able to educate the insured individuals about ways to save money in other aspects of their lives, such as their life insurance premiums, by being able to demonstrate that they are now a lower risk policy holder.

LEARNING OBJECTIVES

After completing the reading and exercises in this chapter, you should be able to:

- Explain what logistic regression is, how it is used and the benefits of using it.
- Recognize the necessary format for data in order to perform predictive logistic regression.
- Develop a logistic regression data mining model in RapidMiner using a training data set.
- Interpret the model's outputs and apply them to a scoring data set in order to deploy the model.

ORGANIZATIONAL UNDERSTANDING

Sonia's desire is to expand her data mining activities to determine what kinds of programs she should develop to help victims of heart attacks avoid suffering a recurrence. She knows that several risk factors such as weight, high cholesterol and stress contribute to heart attacks, particularly in those who have already suffered one. She also knows that the cost of providing programs developed to help mitigate these risks is a fraction of the cost of providing medical care for a patient who has suffered multiple heart attacks. Getting her employer on board with funding the programs is the easy part. Figuring out which patients will benefit from which programs is trickier. She is looking to us to provide some guidance, based on data mining, to figure out which patients are good candidates for which programs. Sonia's bottom line is that she wants to know whether or not something (a second heart attack) is likely to happen, and if so, how likely it is that it will or will not happen. **Logistic regression** is an excellent tool for predicting the likelihood of something happening or not.

DATA UNDERSTANDING

Sonia has access to the company's medical claims database. With this access, she is able to generate two data sets for us. This first is a list of people who have suffered heart attacks, with an attribute indicating whether or not they have had more than one; and the second is a list of those who have had a first heart attack, but not a second. The former data set, comprised of 138 observations, will serve as our training data; while the latter, comprised of 690 peoples' data, will be for scoring. Sonia's hope is to help this latter group of people avoid becoming second heart attack victims. In compiling the two data sets we have defined the following attributes:

- **Age**: The age in years of the person, rounded to the nearest whole year.
- **Marital_Status**: The person's current marital status, indicated by a coded number: 0–Single, never married; 1–Married; 2–Divorced; 3–Widowed.
- **Gender**: The person's gender: 0 for female; 1 for male.
- **Weight_Category**: The person's weight categorized into one of three levels: 0 for normal weight range; 1 for overweight; and 2 for obese.
- **Cholesterol**: The person's cholesterol level, as recorded at the time of their treatment for their most recent heart attack (their *only* heart attack, in the case of those individuals in the scoring data set.)

- **Stress_Management**: A binary attribute indicating whether or not the person has previously attended a stress management course: 0 for no; 1 for yes.

- **Trait_Anxiety**: A score on a scale of 0 to 100 measuring the level of each person's natural stress levels and abilities to cope with stress. A short time after each person in each of the two data sets had recovered from their first heart attack, they were administered a standard test of natural anxiety. Their scores are tabulated and recorded in this attribute along five point increments. A score of 0 would indicate that the person never feels anxiety, pressure or stress in any situation, while a score of 100 would indicate that the person lives in a constant state of being overwhelmed and unable to deal with his or her circumstances.

- **2nd_Heart_Attack**: This attribute exists only in the training data set. It will be our label, the prediction or target attribute. In the training data set, the attribute is set to 'yes' for individuals who have suffered second heart attacks, and 'no' for those who have not.

DATA PREPARATION

Two data sets have been prepared and are available for you to download from the companion web site. These are labeled Chapter09DataSet_Training.csv, and Chapter09DataSet_Scoring.csv. If you would like to follow along with this chapter's example, download these two datasets now, and complete the following steps:

1) Begin the process of importing the training data set first. For the most part, the process will be the same as what you have done in past chapters, but for logistic regression, there are a few subtle differences. Be sure to set the first row as the attribute names. On the fourth step, when setting data types and attribute roles, you will need to make at least one change. Be sure to set the 2nd_Heart_Attack data type to 'nominal', rather than binominal. Even though it is a yes/no field, and RapidMiner will default it to binominal because of that, the Logistic Regression operator we'll be using in our modeling phase expects the label to be nominal. RapidMiner does not offer binominal-to-nominal or integer-to-nominal operators, so we need to be sure to set this target attribute to the needed data type of 'nominal' as we import it. This is shown in Figure 9-1:

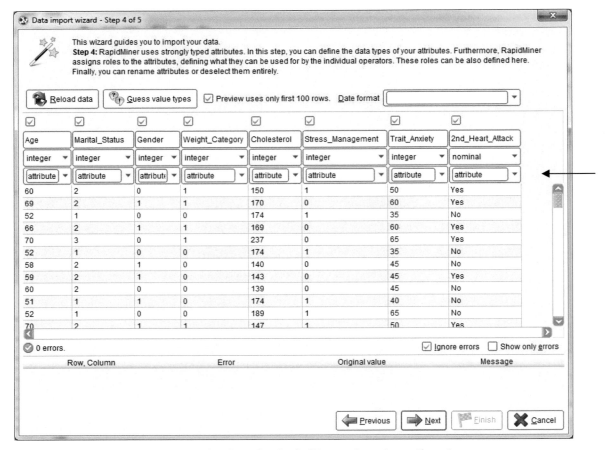

Figure 9-1. Setting the 2nd_Heart_Attack attribute's

data type to 'nominal' during import.

2) At this time you can also change the 2nd_Heart_Attack attribute's role to 'label', if you wish. We have not done this in Figure 9-1, and subsequently we will be adding a Set Role operator to our stream as we continue our data preparation.

3) Complete the data import process for the training data, then drag and drop the data set into a new, blank main process. Rename the data set's Retrieve operator as Training.

4) Import the scoring data set now. Be sure the data type for all attributes is 'integer'. This should be the default, but may not be, so double check. Since the 2nd_Heart_Attack attribute is not included in the scoring data set, you don't need to worry about changing it as you did in step 1. Complete the import process, drag and drop the scoring data set into your main process and rename this data set's Retrieve operator to be Scoring. Your model should now appear similar to Figure 9-2.

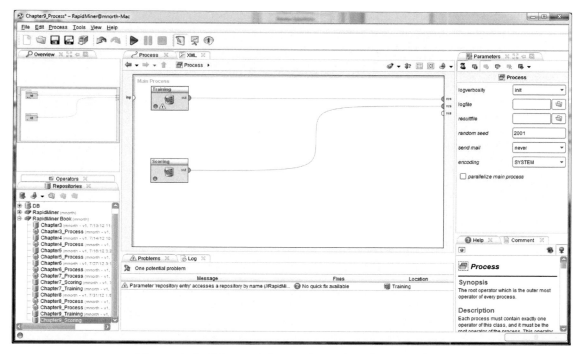

Figure 9-2. The training and scoring data sets in a

new main process window in RapidMiner.

5) Run the model and compare the ranges for all attributes between the scoring and training
result set tabs (Figures 9-3 and 9-4, respectively). You should find that the ranges are the
same. As was the case with Linear Regression, the scoring values must all fall within the
lower and upper bounds set by the corresponding values in the training data set. We can
see in Figures 9-3 and 9-4 that this is the case, so our data are very clean, they were
prepared during extraction from Sonia's source database, and we will not need to do
further data preparation in order to filter out observations with inconsistent values or
modify missing values.

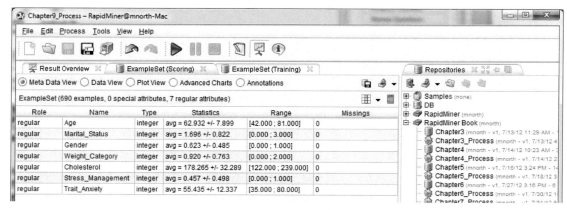

Figure 9-3. Meta data for the scoring data set

(note absence of 2nd_Heart_Attack attrtibute).

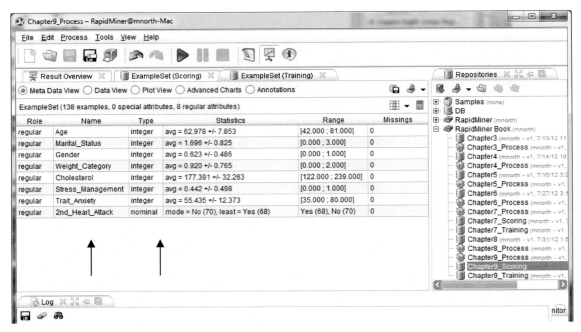

Figure 9-4. Meta data for the training data set (2nd_Heart_Attack attribute is present with 'nominal' data type.) Note that all scoring ranges fall within all training ranges.

6) Switch back to design perspective and add a Set Role operator to your training stream. Remember that if you designated 2nd_Heart_Attack to have a 'label' role during the import process, you won't need to add a Set Role operator at this time. We did not do this in the book example, so we need the operator to designate 2nd_Heart_Attack as our label, our target attribute:

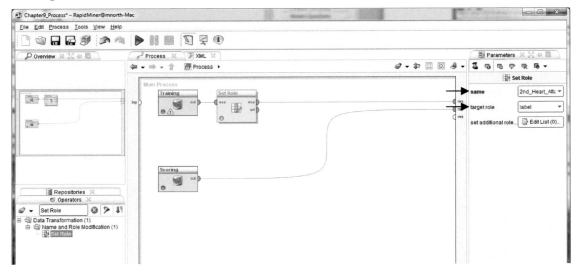

Figure 9-5. Configuring the 2nd_Heart_Attack attribute's role in preparation for logistic regression mining.

With the label attribute set, we are now prepared to begin…

MODELING

7) Using the search field in the Operators tab, locate the Logistic Regression operator. You will see that if you just search for the word 'logistic' (as has been done in Figure 9-6), there are several different logistic, and logistic regression operators available to you in RapidMiner. We will use the first one in this example, however, you are certainly encouraged to experiment with the others as you would like. Drag the Logistic Regression operator into your training stream.

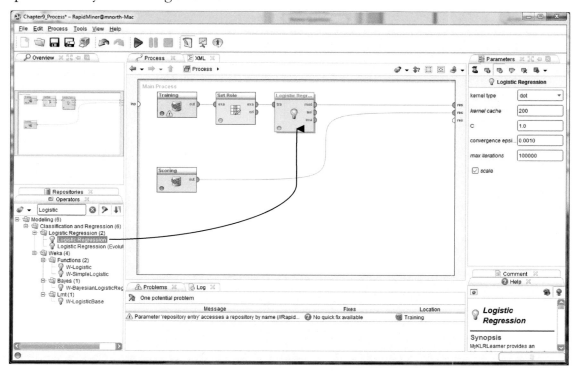

Figure 9-6. The Logistic Regression operator in our training stream.

8) The Logistic Regression operator will generate coefficients for each of our predictor attributes, in much the same way that the linear regression operator did. If you would like to see these, you can run your model now. The algebraic formula for logistic regression is different and a bit more complicated than the one for linear regression. We are no longer calculating the slope of a straight line, but rather, we are trying to determine the likelihood of an observation falling at a given point along a curvy and less well-defined imaginary line through a data set. The coefficients for logistic regression are used in that formula.

9) If you ran your model to see your coefficients, return now to design perspective. As you have done in our most recent few chapter examples, add an Apply Model operator to your stream, to bring the training and scoring data sets together. Remember that you may need to disconnect and reconnect some ports, as we did in Chapter 7 (step 13), in order to merge your two streams together. Be sure your *lab* and *mod* ports are both connected to *res* ports.

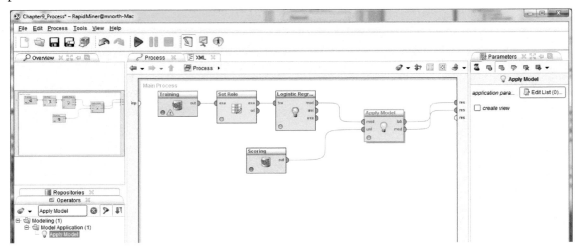

Figure 9-7. Applying the model to the scoring data set.

We are finished building the model. Run it now, and we will proceed to...

EVALUATION

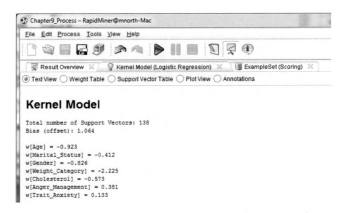

Figure 9-8. Coefficients for each predictor attribute.

The initial tab shown in results perspective is a list of our coefficients. These coefficients are used in the logistic regression algorithm to predict whether or not each person in our scoring data set

Chapter 9: Logistic Regression

will suffer a second heart attack, and if so, how confident we are that the prediction will come true. Switch to the Scoring results tab. We will look first at the meta data (Figure 9-9).

Role	Name	Type	Statistics	Range	Missings
confidence_Yes	confidence(Yes)	real	avg = 0.473 +/- 0.420	[0.000 ; 0.996]	0
confidence_No	confidence(No)	real	avg = 0.527 +/- 0.420	[0.004 ; 1.000]	0
prediction	prediction(2nd_Heart_Attack)	nominal	mode = No (357), least = Yes (333)	Yes (333), No (357)	0
regular	Age	integer	avg = 62.932 +/- 7.899	[42.000 ; 81.000]	0
regular	Marital_Status	integer	avg = 1.696 +/- 0.822	[0.000 ; 3.000]	0
regular	Gender	integer	avg = 0.623 +/- 0.485	[0.000 ; 1.000]	0
regular	Weight_Category	integer	avg = 0.920 +/- 0.763	[0.000 ; 2.000]	0
regular	Cholesterol	integer	avg = 178.265 +/- 32.289	[122.000 ; 239.000]	0
regular	Stress_Management	integer	avg = 0.457 +/- 0.498	[0.000 ; 1.000]	0
regular	Trait_Anxiety	integer	avg = 55.435 +/- 12.337	[35.000 ; 80.000]	0

Figure 9-9. Meta data for our scoring predictions.

We can see in this figure that RapidMiner has generated three new attributes for us: confidence(Yes), confidence(No), and prediction(2nd_Heart_Attack). In our Statistics column, we find that out of the 690 people represented, we're predicting that 357 *will not* suffer second heart attacks, and that 333 will. Sonia's hope is that she can engage these 333, and perhaps some of the 357 with low confidence levels on their 'No' prediction, in programs to improve their health, and thus their chances of avoiding another heart attack. Let's switch to Data View.

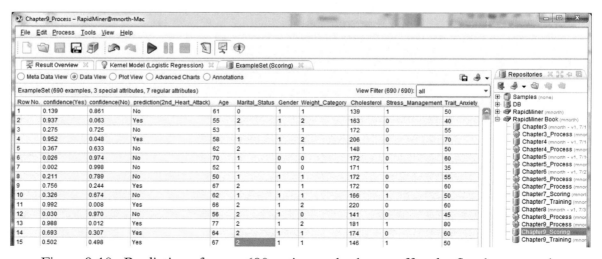

Figure 9-10. Predictions for our 690 patients who have suffered a first heart attack.

149

In Figure 9-10, we can see that each person has been given a predication of 'No' (they won't suffer a second heart attack), or 'Yes' (they will). It is critically important to remember at this point of our evaluation that if this were real, and not a textbook example, these would be real people, with names, families and lives. Yes, we are using data to evaluate their health, but we shouldn't treat these people like numbers. Hopefully our work and analysis will help our imaginary client Sonia in her efforts to serve these people better. When data mining, we should always keep the human element in mind, and we'll talk more about this in Chapter 14.

So we have these predictions that some people in our scoring data set are on the path to a second heart attack and others are not, but how confident are we in these predictions? The confidence(Yes) and confidence(No) attributes can help us answer that question. To start, let's just consider the person represented on Row 1. This is a single (never been married) 61 year old man. He has been classified as overweight, but has lower than average cholesterol (the mean shown in our meta data in Figure 9-9 is just over 178). He scored right in the middle on our trait anxiety test at 50, and has attended stress management class. With these personal attributes, compared with those in our training data, our model offers us an 86.1% level of confidence that the 'No' prediction is correct. This leaves us with 13.9% worth of doubt in our prediction. The 'No' and 'Yes' values will always total to 1, or in other words, 100%. For each person in the data set, their attributes are fed into the logistic regression model, and a prediction with confidence percentages is calculated.

Let's consider one other person as an example in Figure 9-10. Look at Row 11. This is a 66 year old man who's been divorced. He's above the average values in every attribute. While he's not as old as some in our data set, he is getting older, and he's obese. His cholesterol is among the highest in our data set, he scored higher than average on the trait anxiety test and hasn't been to a stress management class. We're predicting, with 99.2% confidence, that this man will suffer a second heart attack. The warning signs are all there, and Sonia can now see them fairly easily. With an understanding of how to read the output, Sonia can now proceed to…

DEPLOYMENT

In the context of the person represented on Row 11, it seems pretty obvious that Sonia should try to reach out to this gentleman right away, offering help in every aspect. She may want to help him find a weight loss support group, such as Overeaters Anonymous, provide information about dealing with divorce and/or stress, and encourage the person to work with his doctor to better regulate his cholesterol through diet and perhaps medication as well. There may be a number of the 690 individuals who fairly clearly need specific help. Click twice on the attribute name confidence(Yes). Clicking on a column heading (the attribute name) in RapidMiner results perspective will sort the data set by that attribute. Click it once to sort in ascending order, twice to re-sort in descending order, and a third time to return the data set to its original state. Figure 9-11 shows our results sorted in descending order on the confidence(Yes) attribute.

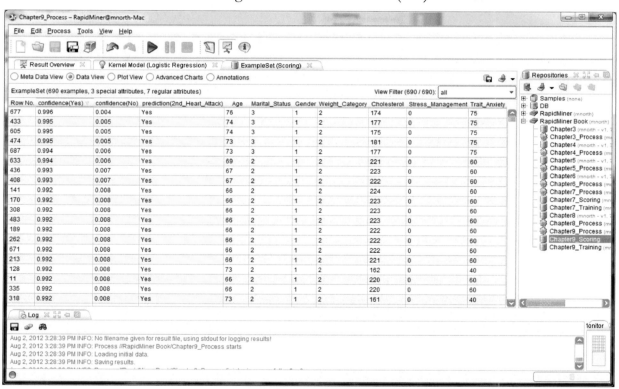

Figure 9-11. Results sorted by confidence(Yes) in descending order (two clicks on the attribute name).

If you were to count down from the first record (Row 667) to the point at which our confidence(Yes) value is 0.950, you would find that there are 140 individuals in the data set for whom we have a 95% or better confidence that they are at risk for heart attack recurrence (and that's not rounding up those who have a 0.949 in the 'Yes' column). So there are some who are fairly easy to spot. You might notice that many are divorced, but several are also widowed. Loss of a spouse by any means is difficult, so perhaps Sonia can begin by offering more programs to support those who fit this description. Most of these individuals are obese and have cholesterol levels over 200, and none have participated in stress management classes. Sonia has several opportunities to help these individuals, and she would probably offer these folks opportunities to participate in *several* programs, or create one program that offers a holistic approach to physical and mental well-being. Because there are a good number of these individuals who share so many high risk traits, this may be an excellent way to create support groups for them.

But there are also those individuals in the data set who maybe need help, but aren't quite as obvious, and perhaps only need help in one or two areas. Click confidence(yes) a third time to return the results data to its original state (sorted by Row No.). Now, scroll down until you find Row 95 (highlighted in Figure 9-12). Make a note of this person's attributes.

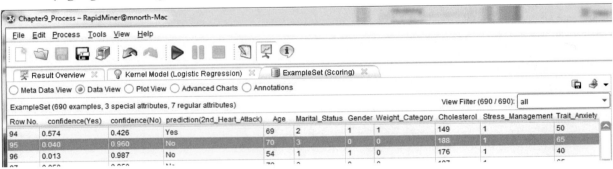

Figure 9-12. Examining the first of two similar individuals with different risk levels.

Next locate Row 554 (Figure 9-13).

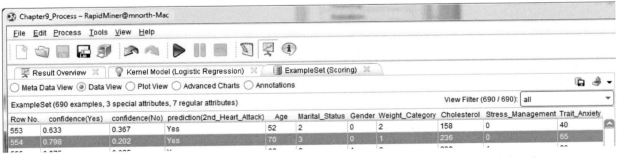

Figure 9-13. The second of two similar individuals with different risk levels.

The two people represented on rows 95 and 554 have a lot in common. First of all, they're both in this data set because they've suffered heart attacks. They are both 70 year old women who's husbands have died. Both have trait anxiety of 65 points. And yet we are predicting with 96%

certainty that the first will *not* suffer another heart attack, while predicting with almost 80% that the other *will*. Even their weight categories are similar, though being overweight certainly plays into the second woman's risk. But what is really evident in comparing thes two women is that the second woman has a cholesterol level that nearly touches the top of our range in this data set (the upper bound shown in Figure 9-9 is 239), and she hasn't been to stress management classes. Perhaps Sonia can use such comparisons to help this woman understand just how dramatically she can improve her chances of avoiding another heart attack. In essence, Sonia could say: "There are women who are a lot like you who have almost zero chance of suffering another heart attack. By lowering your cholesterol, learning to manage your stress, and perhaps getting your weight down closer to a normal level, you can almost eliminate your risk for another heart attack." Sonia could follow up by offering specific programs for this woman targeted specifically at cholesterol, weight or stress management.

CHAPTER SUMMARY

Logistic regression is an excellent way to predict whether or not something will happen, and how confident we are in such predictions. It takes a number of numeric attributes into account and then uses those through a training data set to predict the probable outcomes in a comparable scoring data set. Logistic regression uses a nominal target attribute (or label, in RapidMiner) to categorize observations in a scoring data set into their probable outcomes.

As with linear regression, the scoring data must have ranges that fall within their corresponding training data ranges. Without such bounds, it is unsafe and unwise to draw assumptions about observations in the scoring data set, since there are no comparable observations in the training data upon which to base your scoring assumptions. When used within these bounds however, logistic regression can help us quickly and easily predict the outcome of some phenomenon in a data set, and to determine how confident we can be in the accuracy of that prediction.

REVIEW QUESTIONS

1) What is the appropriate data type for independent variables (predictor attributes) in logistic regression? What about for the dependent variable (target or label attribute)?

2) Compare the predictions for Row 15 and 669 in the chapter's example model.

    a. What is the single difference between these two people, and how does it affect their predicted 2nd_Heart_Attack risk?

    b. Locate other 67 year old men in the results and compare them to the men on rows 15 and 669. How do they compare?

    c. Can you spot areas when the men represented on rows 15 and 669 could improve their chances of not suffering a second heart attack?

3) What is the difference between confidence(Yes) and confidence(No) in this chapter's example?

4) How can you set an attribute's role to be 'label' in RapidMiner without using the Set Role operator? What is one drawback to doing it that way?

EXERCISE

For this chapter's exercise, you will use logistic regression to try to predict whether or not young people you know will eventually graduate from college. Complete the following steps:

1) Open a new blank spreadsheet in OpenOffice Calc. At the bottom of the spreadsheet there will be three default tabs labeled Sheet1, Sheet2, Sheet3. Rename the first one Training and the second one Scoring. You can rename the tabs by double clicking on their labels. You can delete or ignore the third default sheet.

2) On the training sheet, starting in cell A1 and going across, create attribute labels for five attributes: Parent_Grad, Gender, Income_Level, Num_Siblings, and Graduated.

3) Copy each of these attribute names except Graduated into the Scoring sheet.

4) On the Training sheet, enter values for each of these attributes for several adults that you know who are at the age that they could have graduated from college by now. These could be family members, friends and neighbors, coworkers or fellow students, etc. Try to do at least 20 observations; 30 or more would be better. Enter husband and wife couples as two separate observations. Use the following to guide your data entry:

   a. For Parent_Grad, enter a 0 if neither of the person's parents graduated from college, a 1 if one parent did, and a 2 if both parents did. If the person's parents went on to earn graduate degress, you could experiment with making this attribute even more interesting by using it to hold the total number of college degrees by the person's parents. For example, if the person represented in the observation had a mother who earned a bachelor's, master's and doctorate, and a father who earned a bachelor's and a master's, you could enter a 5 in this attribute for that person.

   b. For Gender, enter 0 for female and 1 for male.

   c. For Income_Level, enter a 0 if the person lives in a household with an income level below what you would consider to be below average, a 1 for average, and a 2 for above average. You can estimate or generalize. Be sensitive to others when gathering your data—don't snoop too much or risk offending your data subjects.

   d. For Num_Siblings, enter the number of siblings the person has.

   e. For Graduated, put 'Yes' if the person has graduated from college and 'No' if they have not.

5) Once you've compiled your Training data set, switch to the Scoring sheet in OpenOffice Calc. Repeat the data entry process for at least 20 (more is better) young people between the ages of 0 and 18 that you know. You will use the training set to try to predict whether or not these young people will graduate from college, and if so, how confident you are in your prediction. Remember this is your scoring data, so you won't provide the Graduated attribute, you'll predict it shortly.

6) Use the File > Save As menu option in OpenOffice Calc to save your Training and Scoring sheets as CSV files.

7) Import your two CSV files into your RapidMiner respository. Be sure to give them descriptive names.

8) Drag your two data sets into a new process window. If you have prepared your data well in OpenOffice Calc, you shouldn't have any missing or inconsistent data to contend with, so data preparation should be minimal. Rename the two retrieve operators so you can tell the difference between your training and scoring data sets.

9) One necessary data preparation step is to add a Set Role operator and define the Graduated attribute as your label in your training data. Alternatively, you can set your Graduated attribute as the label during data import.

10) Add a Logistic Regression operator to your Training stream.

11) Apply your Logistic Regression model to your scoring data and run your model. Evaluate and report your results. Are your confidence percentages interesting? Surprising? Do the predicted Graduation values seem reasonable and consistent with your training data? Does any one independent variable (predictor attribute) seem to be a particularly good predictor of the dependent variable (label or prediction attribute)? If so, why do you think so?

Challenge Step!

12) Change your Logistic Regression operator to a different type of Logistic operator (for example, maybe try the Weka W-Logistic operator). Re-run your model. Consider doing some research to learn about the difference between algorithms underlying different logistic approaches. Compare your new results to the original Logistic Regression results and report any interesting findings or differences.

CHAPTER TEN:
DECISION TREES

CONTEXT AND PERSPECTIVE

Richard works for a large online retailer. His company is launching a next-generation eReader soon, and they want to maximize the effectiveness of their marketing. They have many customers, some of whom purchased one of the company's previous generation digital readers. Richard has noticed that certain types of people were the most anxious to get the previous generation device, while other folks seemed to content to wait to buy the electronic gadget later. He's wondering what makes some people motivated to buy something as soon as it comes out, while others are less driven to have the product.

Richard's employer helps to drive the sales of its new eReader by offering specific products and services for the eReader through its massive web site—for example, eReader owners can use the company's web site to buy digital magazines, newspapers, books, music, and so forth. The company also sells thousands of other types of media, such as traditional printed books and electronics of every kind. Richard believes that by mining the customers' data regarding general consumer behaviors on the web site, he'll be able to figure out which customers will buy the new eReader early, which ones will buy next, and which ones will buy later on. He hopes that by predicting when a customer will be ready to buy the next-gen eReader, he'll be able to time his target marketing to the people most ready to respond to advertisements and promotions.

LEARNING OBJECTIVES

After completing the reading and exercises in this chapter, you should be able to:
- Explain what decision trees are, how they are used and the benefits of using them.
- Recognize the necessary format for data in order to perform predictive decision tree mining.

- Develop a decision tree data mining model in RapidMiner using a training data set.

- Interpret the visual tree's nodes and leaves, and apply them to a scoring data set in order to deploy the model.

- Use different tree algorithms in order to increase the granularity of the tree's detail.

ORGANIZATIONAL UNDERSTANDING

Richard wants to be able to predict the timing of buying behaviors, but he also wants to understand how his customers' behaviors on his company's web site indicate the timing of their purchase of the new eReader. Richard has studied the classic diffusion theories that noted scholar and sociologist Everett Rogers first published in the 1960s. Rogers surmised that the adoption of a new technology or innovation tends to follow an 'S' shaped curve, with a smaller group of the most enterprising and innovative customers adopting the technology first, followed by larger groups of middle majority adopters, followed by smaller groups of late adopters (Figure 10-1).

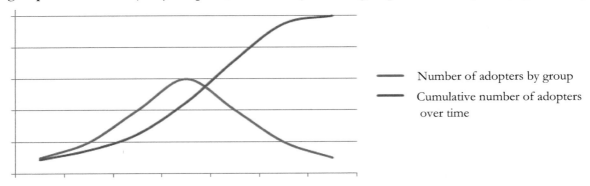

Figure 10-1. Everett Rogers' theory of adoption of new innovations.

Those at the front of the blue curve are the smaller group that are first to want and buy the technology. Most of us, the masses, fall within the middle 70-80% of people who eventually acquire the technology. The low end tail on the right side of the blue curve are the laggards, the ones who eventually adopt. Consider how DVD players and cell phones have followed this curve.

Understanding Rogers' theory, Richard believes that he can categorize his company's customers into one of four groups that will eventually buy the new eReader: Innovators, Early Adopters, Early Majority or Late Majority. These groups track with Rogers' social adoption theories on the diffusion of technological innovations, and also with Richard's informal observations about the speed of adoption of his company's previous generation product. He hopes that by watching the customers' activity on the company's web site, he can anticipate approximately when each person will be most likely to buy an eReader. He feels like data mining can help him figure out which activities are the best predictors of which category a customer will fall into. Knowing this, he can time his marketing to each customer to coincide with their likelihood of buying.

DATA UNDERSTANDING

Richard has engaged us to help him with his project. We have decided to use a **decision tree model in order to find good early predictors of buying behavior**. Because Richard's company does all of its business through its web site, there is a rich data set of information for each customer, including items they have just browsed for, and those they have actually purchased. He has prepared two data sets for us to use. The training data set contains the web site activities of customers who bought the company's previous generation reader, and the timing with which they bought their reader. The second is comprised of attributes of current customers which Richard hopes will buy the new eReader. He hopes to figure out which category of adopter each person in the scoring data set will fall into based on the profiles and buying timing of those people in the training data set.

In analyzing his data set, Richard has found that customers' activity in the areas of digital media and books, and their general activity with electronics for sale on his company's site, seem to have a lot in common with when a person buys an eReader. With this in mind, we have worked with Richard to compile data sets comprised of the following attributes:

- **User_ID**: A numeric, unique identifier assigned to each person who has an account on the company's web site.

- **Gender**: The customer's gender, as identified in their customer account. In this data set, it is recorded a 'M' for male and 'F' for Female. The Decision Tree operator can handle non-numeric data types.

- **Age**: The person's age at the time the data were extracted from the web site's database. This is calculated to the nearest year by taking the difference between the system date and the person's birthdate as recorded in their account.

- **Marital_Status**: The person's marital status as recorded in their account. People who indicated on their account that they are married are entered in the data set as 'M'. Since the web site does not distinguish single types of people, those who are divorced or widowed are included with those who have never been married (indicated in the data set as 'S').

- **Website_Activity**: This attribute is an indication of how active each customer is on the company's web site. Working with Richard, we used the web site database's information which records the duration of each customers visits to the web site to calculate how frequently, and for how long each time, the customers use the web site. This is then translated into one of three categories: Seldom, Regular, or Frequent.

- **Browsed_Electronics_12Mo**: This is simply a Yes/No column indicating whether or not the person browsed for electronic products on the company's web site in the past year.

- **Bought_Electronics_12Mo**: Another Yes/No column indicating whether or not they purchased an electronic item through Richard's company's web site in the past year.

- **Bought_Digital_Media_18Mo**: This attribute is a Yes/No field indicating whether or not the person has purchased some form of digital media (such as MP3 music) in the past year and a half. This attribute <u>does not</u> include digital book purchases.

- **Bought_Digital_Books**: Richard believes that as an indicator of buying behavior relative to the company's new eReader, this attribute will likely be the best indicator. Thus, this attribute has been set apart from the purchase of other types of digital media. Further, this attribute indicates whether or not the customer has *ever* bought a digital book, not just in the past year or so.

- **Payment_Method**: This attribute indicates how the person pays for their purchases. In cases where the person has paid in more than one way, the mode, or most frequent method of payment is used. There are four options:
  - Bank Transfer—payment via e-check or other form of wire transfer directly from the bank to the company.
  - Website Account—the customer has set up a credit card or permanent electronic funds transfer on their account so that purchases are directly charged through their account at the time of purchase.
  - Credit Card—the person enters a credit card number and authorization each time they purchase something through the site.
  - Monthly Billing—the person makes purchases periodically and receives a paper or electronic bill which they pay later either by mailing a check or through the company web site's payment system.

- **eReader_Adoption**: This attribute exists only in the training data set. It consists of data for customers who purchased the previous-gen eReader. Those who purchased within a week of the product's release are recorded in this attribute as 'Innovator'. Those who purchased after the first week but within the second or third weeks are entered as 'Early Adopter'. Those who purchased after three weeks but within the first two months are 'Early Majority'. Those who purchased after the first two months are 'Late Majority'. This attribute will serve as our label when we apply our training data to our scoring data.

With Richard's data and an understanding of what it means, we can now proceed to...

DATA PREPARATION

This chapter's example consists of two data sets: Chapter10DataSet_Training.csv and Chapter10DataSet_Scoring.csv. Download these from the companion web site now, then complete the following steps:

1) Import both data sets into your RapidMiner repository. You do not need to worry about attribute data types because the Decision Tree operator can handle all types of data. Be sure that you do designate the first row of each of the data sets as the attribute names as you import. Save them in the repository with descriptive names, so that you will be able to tell what they are.

2) Drag and drop both of the data sets into a new main process window. Rename the Retrieve objects as Training and Scoring respectively. Run your model to examine the data and familiarize yourself with the attributes.

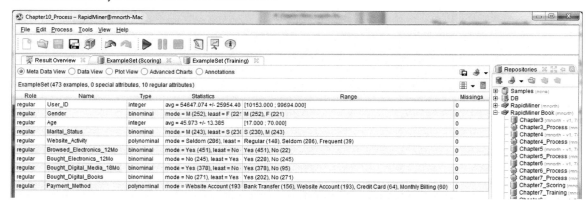

Figure 10-2. Meta data for the scoring data set.

3) Switch back to design perspective. While there are no missing or apparently inconsistent values in the data set, there is still some data preparation yet to do. First of all, the User_ID is an arbitrarily assigned value for each customer. The customer doesn't use this value for anything, it is simply a way to uniquely identify each customer in the data set. It is not something that relates to each person in any way that would correlate to, or be predictive of, their buying and technology adoption tendencies. As such, it should not be included in the model as an independent variable.

We can handle this attribute in one of two ways. First, we can remove the attribute using a Select Attributes operator, as was demonstrated back in Chapter 3. Alternatively, we can try a new way of handling a non-predictive attribute. This is accomplished using the Set Role operator. Using the search field in the Operators tab, find and add Set Role operators to both your training and scoring streams. In the Parameters area on the right hand side of the screen, set the role of the User_ID attribute to 'id'. This will leave the attribute in the data set throughout the model, but it won't consider the attribute as a predictor for the label attribute. Be sure to do this for both the training and scoring data sets, since the User_ID attribute is found in both of them (Figure 10-3).

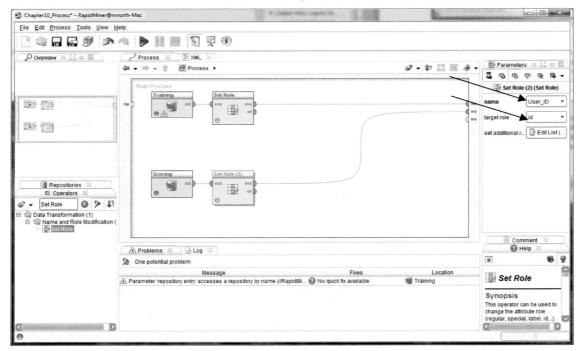

Figure 10-3. Setting the User_ID attribute to an 'id' role, so
it won't be considered in the predictive model.

4) One of the nice side-effects of setting an attribute's role to 'id' rather than removing it using a Select Attributes operator is that it makes each record easier to match back to individual people later, when viewing predictions in results perspective. Thinking back to some of our other predictive models in previous chapters (e.g. Discriminant Analysis), you could use such an approach to leave in peoples' names or ID numbers so that you could easily know who to contact during the deployment phase of data mining projects.

Before adding a Decision Tree operator, we still need to do another data preparation step. The Decision Tree operator, as with other predictive model operators we've used to this point in the text, expects the training stream to supply a 'label' attribute. For this example, we want to predict which adopter group Richard's next-gen eReader customers are likely to be in. So our label will be eReader_Adoption (Figure 10-4).

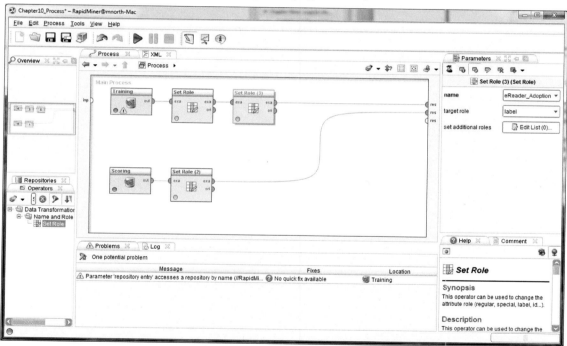

Figure 10-4. Setting the eReader_Adoption attribute as the label in our training stream.

5) Next, search in the Operators tab for 'Decision Tree'. Select the basic Decision Tree operator and add it to your training stream as it is in Figure 10-5.

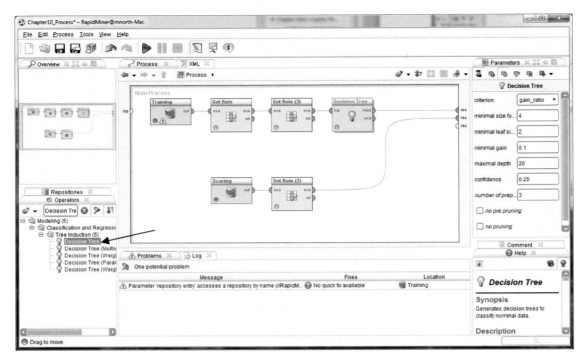

Figure 10-5. The Decision Tree operator added to our model.

6) Run the model and switch to the Tree (Decision Tree) tab in results perspective. You will see our preliminary tree (Figure 10-6).

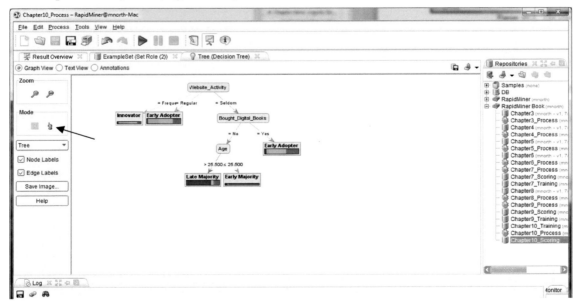

Figure 10-6. Decision tree results.

7) In Figure 10-6, we can see what are referred to as **nodes** and **leaves**. The nodes are the gray oval shapes. They are attributes which serve as good predictors for our label attribute. The leaves are the multicolored end points that show us the distribution of categories from

our label attribute that follow the branch of the tree to the point of that leaf. We can see in this tree that Website_Activity is our best predictor of whether or not a customer is going to adopt (buy) the company's new eReader. If the person's activity is frequent or regular, we see that they are likely to be an Innovator or Early Adopter, respectively. If however, they seldom use the web site, then whether or not they've bought digital books becomes the next best predictor of their eReader adoption category. If they have not bought digital books through the web site in the past, Age is another predictive attribute which forms a node, with younger folks adopting sooner than older ones. This is seen on the branches for the two leaves coming from the Age node in Figure 10-6. Those who seldom use the company's website, have never bought digital books on the site, and are older than 25 ½ are most likely to land in the Late Majority category, while those with the same profile but are under 25 ½ are bumped to the Early Majority prediction. In this example you can see how you read the nodes, leaves and branch labels as you move down through the tree.

Before returning to design perspective, take a minute to try some of the tools on the left hand side of the screen. The magnifying glasses can help you see your tree better, spreading out or compacting the nodes and leaves to enhance readability or to view more of a large tree at one time. Also, try using the 'hand' icon under Mode (see the arrow on Figure 10-6). This allows you to click and hold on individual leaves or nodes and drag them around to enhance your tree's readability. Finally, try hovering your mouse over one of the leaves in the tree. In Figure 10-7, we see a tool-tip hover box showing details of this leaf. Although our training data is going to predict that 'regular' web site users are going to be Early Adopters, the model is not 100% based on that prediction. In the hover, we read that in the training data set, 9 people who fit this profile are Late Adopters, 58 are Innovators, 75 are Early Adopters and 41 are Early Majority. When we get to Evaluation phase, we will see that this uncertainty in our data will translate into confidence percentages, similar to what we saw in Chapter 9 with logistic regression.

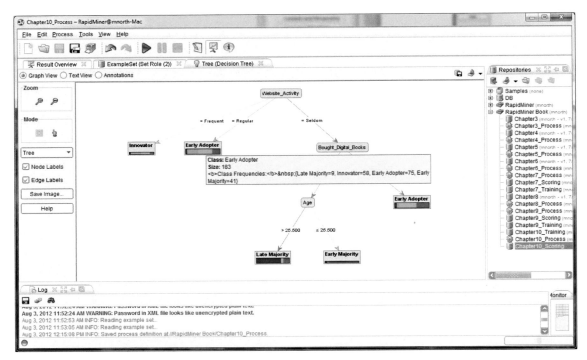

Figure 10-7. A tool-tip hover showing expanded leaf detail in our tree.

With our predictor attributes prepared, we are now ready to move on to...

MODELING

8) Return to design perspective. In the Operators tab search for and add an Apply Model operator, bringing your training and scoring streams together. Ensure that both the *lab* and *mod* ports are connected to *res* ports in order to generate our desired outputs (Figure 10-8).

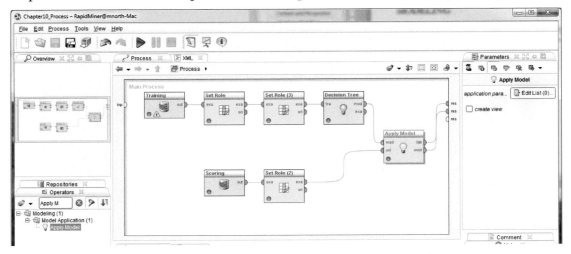

Figure 10-8. Applying the model to our scoring data, and outputting
label predictions (*lab*) and a decision tree model (*mod*).

9) Run the model. You will see familiar results—the tree remains the same as it was in Figure 10-6, for now. Click on the ExampleSet tab next to the Tree tab. Our tree has been applied to our scoring data. As was the case with logistic regression, confidence attributes have been created by RapidMiner, along with a prediction attribute.

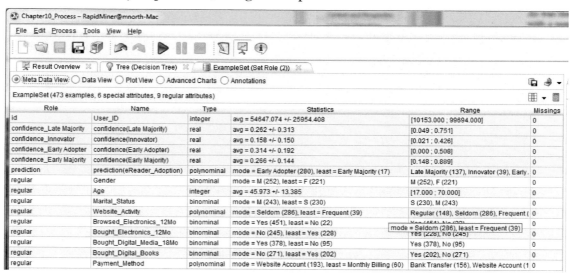

Figure 10-9. Meta data for scoring data set predictions.

10) Switch to Data View using the radio button. We see in Figure 10-10 the prediction for each customer's adoption group, along with confidence percentages for each prediction. Unlike the logistic regression example in the previous chapter, there are four confidence attributes, corresponding to the four possible values in the label (eReader_Adoption). We interpret these the same way that we did with the other models though—the percentages add to 100%, and the prediction is whichever category yielded the highest confidence percentage. RapidMiner is very (but not 100%) convinced that person 77373 (Row 14, Figure 10-10) is going to be a member of the early majority (88.9%). Despite some uncertainty, RapidMiner is completely sure that this person is _not_ going to be an early adopter (0%).

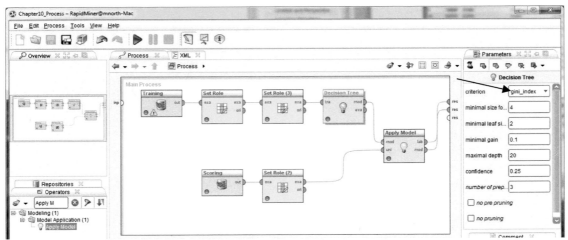

ExampleSet (473 examples, 6 special attributes, 9 regular attributes)

View Filter (473 / 473): all

Row No.	User_ID	confidence(Late Majority)	confidence(Innovator)	confidence(Early Adopter)	confidence(Early Majority)	prediction(eReader_Adoption)	Gender	Age	M:
1	56031	0.049	0.317	0.410	0.224	Early Adopter	M	57	S
2	25913	0.049	0.317	0.410	0.224	Early Adopter	F	51	M
3	19396	0.751	0.021	0.053	0.175	Late Majority	M	41	M
4	93666	0.049	0.317	0.410	0.224	Early Adopter	M	66	S
5	72282	0.751	0.021	0.053	0.175	Late Majority	F	31	S
6	64466	0.049	0.317	0.410	0.224	Early Adopter	M	68	M
7	76655	0.751	0.021	0.053	0.175	Late Majority	F	51	S
8	48465	0.074	0.426	0.352	0.148	Innovator	F	36	S
9	19889	0.049	0.317	0.410	0.224	Early Adopter	M	29	M
10	63570	0.074	0.426	0.352	0.148	Innovator	M	61	M
11	63239	0.049	0.317	0.410	0.224	Early Adopter	M	47	S
12	67603	0.049	0.317	0.410	0.224	Early Adopter	F	62	S
13	65685	0.049	0.317	0.410	0.224	Early Adopter	M	32	M
14	77373	0.083	0.028	0	0.889	Early Majority	M	17	M
15	54239	0.049	0.317	0.410	0.224	Early Adopter	M	36	S
16	55781	0.049	0.317	0.410	0.224	Early Adopter	M	58	S
17	19854	0.049	0.317	0.410	0.224	Early Adopter	F	62	M
18	27852	0.751	0.021	0.053	0.175	Late Majority	M	37	S

Figure 10-10. Predictions and their associated confidence percentages using our decision tree.

11) We've already begun to evaluate our model's results, but what if we feel like we'd like to see greater detail, or granularity in our model. Surely some of our other attributes are also predictive in nature. Remember that CRISP-DM is cyclical in nature, and that in some modeling techniques, especially those with less structured data, some back and forth trial-and-error can reveal more interesting patterns in data. Switch back to design perspective, click on the Decision Tree operator, and in the Parameters area, change the 'criterion' parameter to 'gini_index', as shown in Figure 10-11.

Figure 10-11. Constructing our decision tree model using the **gini_index** algorithm rather than the **gain_ratio** algorithm.

Now, re-run the model and we will move on to...

EVALUATION

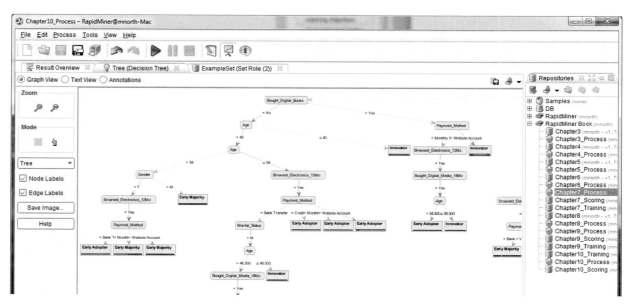

Figure 10-12. Tree resulting from a gini_index algorithm.

We see in this tree that there is much more detail, more granularity in using the Gini algorithm as our parameter for our decision tree. We could further modify the tree by going back to design view and changing the minimum number of items to form a node (size for split) or the minimum size for a leaf. Even accepting the defaults for those parameters though, we can see that the Gini algorithm alone is much more sensitive than is the Gain Ratio algorithm in identifying nodes and leaves. Take a minute to explore around this new tree model. You will find that it is extensive, and that you will to use both the Zoom and Mode tools to see it all. You should find that most of our other independent variables (predictor attributes) are now being used, and the granularity with which Richard can identify each customer's likely adoption category is much greater. How active the person is on Richard's employer's web site is still the single best predictor, but gender, and multiple levels of age have now also come into play. You will also find that a single attribute is sometimes used more than once in a single branch of the tree. Decision trees are a lot of fun to experiment with, and with a sensitive algorithm like Gini generating them, they can be tremendously interesting as well.

Switch to the ExampleSet tab in Data View. We see here (Figure 10-13) that changing our tree's underlying algorithm has, in some cases, also changed our confidence in the prediction.

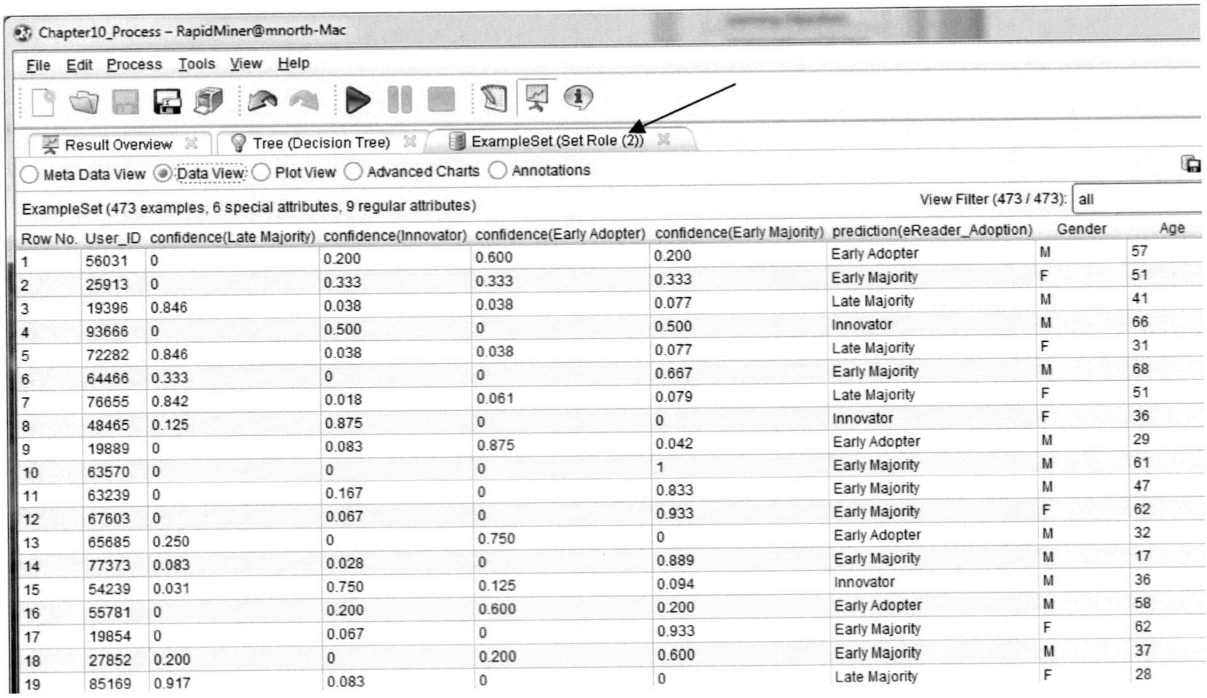

Row No.	User_ID	confidence(Late Majority)	confidence(Innovator)	confidence(Early Adopter)	confidence(Early Majority)	prediction(eReader_Adoption)	Gender	Age
1	56031	0	0.200	0.600	0.200	Early Adopter	M	57
2	25913	0	0.333	0.333	0.333	Early Majority	F	51
3	19396	0.846	0.038	0.038	0.077	Late Majority	M	41
4	93666	0	0.500	0	0.500	Innovator	M	66
5	72282	0.846	0.038	0.038	0.077	Late Majority	F	31
6	64466	0.333	0	0	0.667	Early Majority	M	68
7	76655	0.842	0.018	0.061	0.079	Late Majority	F	51
8	48465	0.125	0.875	0	0	Innovator	F	36
9	19889	0	0.083	0.875	0.042	Early Adopter	M	29
10	63570	0	0	0	1	Early Majority	M	61
11	63239	0	0.167	0	0.833	Early Majority	M	47
12	67603	0	0.067	0	0.933	Early Majority	F	62
13	65685	0.250	0	0.750	0	Early Adopter	M	32
14	77373	0.083	0.028	0	0.889	Early Majority	M	17
15	54239	0.031	0.750	0.125	0.094	Innovator	M	36
16	55781	0	0.200	0.600	0.200	Early Adopter	M	58
17	19854	0	0.067	0	0.933	Early Majority	F	62
18	27852	0.200	0	0.200	0.600	Early Majority	M	37
19	85169	0.917	0.083	0	0	Late Majority	F	28

Figure 10-13. New predictions and confidence percentages using Gini.

Let's take the person on Row 1 (ID 56031) as an example. In Figure 10-10, this person was calculated as having at least some percentage chance of landing in any one of the four adopter categories. Under the Gain Ratio algorithm, we were 41% sure he'd be an early adopter, but almost 32% sure he might also turn out to be an innovator. In other words, we feel confident he'll buy the eReader early on, but we're not sure how early. Maybe that matters to Richard, maybe not. He'll have to decide during the deployment phase. But perhaps using Gini, we can help him decide. In Figure 10-13, this same man is now shown to have a 60% chance of being an early adopter and only a 20% chance of being an innovator. The odds of him becoming part of the late majority crowd under the Gini model have dropped to zero. We know he will adopt (or at least we are *predicting* with 100% confidence that he will adopt), and that he will adopt early. While he may not be at the top of Richard's list when deployment rolls around, he'll probably be higher than he otherwise would have been under gain_ratio. Note that while Gini has changed some of our predictions, it hasn't affected all of them. Re-check person ID 77373 briefly. There is no difference in this person's predictions under either algorithm—RapidMiner is quite certain in its predictions for this young man. Sometimes the level of confidence in a prediction through a decision tree is so high that a more sensitive underlying algorithm won't alter an observation's prediction values at all.

DEPLOYMENT

Richard's original desire was to be able to figure out which customers he could expect to buy the new eReader and on what time schedule, based on the company's last release of a high-profile digital reader. The decision tree has enabled him to predict that and to determine how reliable the predictions are. He's also been able to determine which attributes are the most predictive of eReader adoption, and to find greater granularity in his model by using gini_index as his tree's underlying algorithm.

But how will he use this new found knowledge? The simplest and most direct answer is that he now has a list of customers and their probable adoption timings for the next-gen eReader. These customers are identifiable by the User_ID that was retained in the results perspective data but not used as a predictor in the model. He can segment these customers and begin a process of target marketing that is timely and relevant to each individual. Those who are most likely to purchase immediately (predicted innovators) can be contacted and encouraged to go ahead and buy as soon as the new product comes out. They may even want the option to pre-order the new device. Those who are less likely (predicted early majority) might need some persuasion, perhaps a free digital book or two with eReader purchase or a discount on digital music playable on the new eReader. The least likely (predicted late majority), can be marketed to passively, or perhaps not at all if marketing budgets are tight and those dollars need to be spent incentivizing the most likely customers to buy. On the other hand, perhaps very little marketing is needed to the predicted innovators, since they are predicted to be the most likely to buy the eReader in the first place.

Further though, Richard now has a tree that shows him which attributes matter most in determining the likelihood of buying for each group. New marketing campaigns can use this information to focus more on increasing web site activity level, or on connecting general electronics that are for sale on the company's web site with the eReaders and digital media more specifically. These types of cross-categorical promotions can be further honed to appeal to buyers of a specific gender or in a given age range. Richard has much that he can use in this rich data mining output as he works to promote the next-gen eReader.

CHAPTER SUMMARY

Decision trees are excellent predictive models when the target attribute is categorical in nature, and when the data set is of mixed types. Although this chapter's data sets did not contain any examples, decision trees are better than more statistics-based approaches at handling attributes that have missing or inconsistent values that are not handled—decision trees will work around such data and still generate usable results.

Decision trees are made of nodes and leaves (connected by labeled branch arrows), representing the best predictor attributes in a data set. These nodes and leaves lead to confidence percentages based on the actual attributes in the training data set, and can then be applied to similarly structured scoring data in order to generate predictions for the scoring observations. Decision trees tell us what is predicted, how confident we can be in the prediction, and *how we arrived at* the prediction. The 'how we arrived at' portion of a decision tree's output is shown in a graphical view of the tree.

REVIEW QUESTIONS

1) What characteristics of a data set's attributes might prompt you to choose a decision tree data mining methodology, rather than a logistic or linear regression approach? Why?

2) Run this chapter's model using the gain_ratio algorithm and make a note of three or four individuals' prediction and confidences. Then re-run the model under gini_index. Locate the people you noted. Did their prediction and/or confidences change? Look at their attribute values and compare them to the nodes and leaves in the decision tree. Explain why you think at least one person's prediction changed under Gini, based on that person's attributes and the tree's nodes.

3) What are confidence percentages used for, and why would they be important to consider, in addition to just considering the prediction attribute?

4) How do you keep an attribute, such as a person's name or ID number, that should not be considered predictive in a process's model, but is useful to have in the data mining results?

5) If your decision tree is large or hard to read, how can you adjust its visual layout to improve readability?

EXERCISE

For this chapter's exercise, you will make a decision tree to predict whether or not you, and others you know would have lived, died, or been lost if you had been on the Titanic. Complete the following steps.

1) Conduct an Internet search for passenger lists for the Titanic. The search term 'Titanic passenger list' in your favorite search engine will yield a number of web sites containing lists of passengers.

2) Select from the sources you find a sample of passengers. You do not need to construct a training data set of every passenger on the Titanic (unless you want to), but get at least 30, and preferably more. The more robust your training data set is, the more interesting your results will be.

3) In a spreadsheet in OpenOffice Calc, enter these passengers' data.

   a. Record attributes such as their name, age, gender, class of service they traveled in, race or nationality if known, or other attributes that may be available to you depending on the detail level of the data source you find.

   b. Be sure to have at least four attributes, preferably more. Remember that the passengers' names or ID numbers won't be predictive, so that attribute shouldn't be counted as one of your predictor attributes.

   c. Add to your data set whether the person lived (i.e. was rescued from a life boat or from the water), died (i.e. their body was recovered), or was lost (i.e. was on the Titanic's manifest but was never accounted for and therefore presumed dead after the ship's sinking). Call this attribute 'Survival_Result'.

   d. Save this spreadsheet as a CSV file and then import it into your RapidMiner repository. Set the Survival_Result attribute's role to be your label. Set other attributes which are not predictive, such as names, to not be considered in the decision tree model.

e. Add a Decision Tree operator to your stream.

4) In a new, blank spreadsheet in OpenOffice Calc, duplicate the attribute names from your training data set, with the exception of Survival_Result. You will predict this attribute using your decision tree.

5) Enter data for yourself and people that you know into this spreadsheet.

a. For some attributes, you may have to decide what to put. For example, the author acknowledges that based on how relentlessly he searches for the absolutely cheapest ticket when shopping for airfare, he almost certainly would have been in 3rd class if he had been on the Titanic. He further knows some people who very likely would have been in 1st class.

b. If you want to include some people in your data set but you don't know every single attribute for them, remember, decision trees can handle some missing values.

c. Save this spreadsheet as a CSV file and import it into your RapidMiner repository.

d. Drag this data set into your process and ensure that attributes that are not predictive, such as names, will not be included as predictors in the model.

6) Apply your decision tree model to your scoring data set.

7) Run your model using gain_ratio. Report your tree nodes, and discuss whether you and the people you know would have lived, died or been lost.

8) Re-run your model using gini_index. Report differences in your tree's structure. Discuss whether your chances for survival increase under Gini.

9) Experiment with changing leaf and split sizes, and other decision tree algorithm criteria, such as information_gain. Analyze and report your results.

CHAPTER ELEVEN:
NEURAL NETWORKS

CONTEXT AND PERSPECTIVE

Juan is a statistical performance analyst for a major professional athletic team. His team has been steadily improving over recent seasons, and heading into the coming season management believes that by adding between two and four excellent players, the team will have an outstanding shot at achieving the league championship. They have tasked Juan with identifying their best options from among a list of 59 experienced players that will be available to them. All of these players have experience, some have played professionally before and some have many years of experience as amateurs. None are to be ruled out without being assessed for their potential ability to add star power and productivity to the existing team. The executives Juan works for are anxious to get going on contacting the most promising prospects, so Juan needs to quickly evaluate these athletes' past performance and make recommendations based on his analysis.

LEARNING OBJECTIVES

After completing the reading and exercises in this chapter, you should be able to:

- Explain what a neural network is, how it is used and the benefits of using it.
- Recognize the necessary format for data in order to perform neural network data mining.
- Develop a neural network data mining model in RapidMiner using a training data set.
- Interpret the model's outputs and apply them to a scoring data set in order to deploy the model.

ORGANIZATIONAL UNDERSTANDING

Juan faces high expectations and has a delivery deadline to meet. He is a professional, he knows his business and knows how important the intangibles are in assessing athletic talent. He also knows that those intangibles are often manifest by athletes' past performance. He wants to mine a data set of all current players in the league in order to help find those prospects that can bring the most excitement, scoring and defense to the team in order to reach the league championship. While salary considerations are always a concern, management has indicated to Juan that their desire is to push for the championship in the upcoming season, and they are willing to do all they can financially to bring in the best two to four athletes Juan can identify. With his employers' objectives made clear to him, Juan is prepared to evaluate each of the 59 prospects' past statistical performance in order to help him formulate what his recommendations will be.

DATA UNDERSTANDING

Juan knows the business of athletic statistical analysis. He has seen how performance in one area, such as scoring, is often interconnected with other areas such as defense or fouls. The best athletes generally have strong connections between two or more performance areas, while more typical athletes may have a strength in one area but weaknesses in others. For example, good role players are often good defenders, but can't contribute much scoring to the team. Using league data and his knowledge of and experience with the players in the league, Juan prepares a training data set comprised of 263 observations and 19 attributes. The 59 prospective athletes Juan's team could acquire form the scoring data set, and he has the same attributes for each of these people. We will help Juan build a **neural network**, which is a data mining methodology that can predict categories or classifications in much the same way that decision trees do, but neural networks are better at finding the strength of connections between attributes, and it is those very connections that Juan is interested in. The attributes our neural network will evaluate are:

- **Player_Name**: This is the player's name. In our data preparation phase, we will set its role to 'id', since it is not predictive in any way, but is important to keep in our data set so that Juan can quickly make his recommendations without having to match the data back to the players' names later. (Note that the names in this chapter's data sets were created using a random name generator. They are fictitious and any similarity to real persons is unintended and purely conincidental.)

- **Position_ID**: For the sport Juan's team plays, there are 12 possible positions. Each one is represented as an integer from 0 to 11 in the data sets.

- **Shots**: This the total number of shots, or scoring opportunities each player took in their most recent season.

- **Makes**: This is the number times the athlete scored when shooting during the most recent season.

- **Personal_Points**: This is the number of points the athlete personally scored during the most recent season.

- **Total_Points**: This is the total number of points the athlete contributed to scoring in the most recent season. In the sport Juan's team plays, this statistic is recorded for each point an athlete contributes to scoring. In other words, each time an athlete scores a personal point, their total points increase by one, and every time an athlete contributes to a teammate scoring, their total points increase by one as well.

- **Assists**: This is a defensive statistic indicating the number of times the athlete helped his team get the ball away from the opposing team during the most recent season.

- **Concessions**: This is the number of times the athlete's play directly caused the opposing team to concede an offensive advantage during the most recent season.

- **Blocks**: This is the number of times the athlete directly and independently blocked the opposing team's shot during the most recent season.

- **Block_Assists**: This is the number of times an athlete collaborated with a teammate to block the opposing team's shot during the most recent season. If recorded as a block assist, two or more players must have been involved. If only one player blocked the shot, it is recorded as a block. Since the playing surface is large and the players are spread out, it is much more likely for an athlete to record a block than for two or more to record block assists.

- **Fouls**: This is the number of times, in the most recent season, that the athlete committed a foul. Since fouling the other team gives them an advantage, the lower this number, the better the athlete's performance for his own team.

- **Years_Pro**: In the training data set, this is the number of years the athlete has played at the professional level. In the scoring data set, this is the number of year experience the athlete has, including years as a professional if any, and years in organized, competitive amateur leagues.

- **Career_Shots**: This is the same as the Shots attribute, except it is cumulative for the athlete's entire career. All career attributes are an attempt to assess the person's ability to perform consistently over time.

- **Career_Makes**: This is the same as the Makes attribute, except it is cumulative for the athlete's entire career.

- **Career_PP**: This is the same as the Personal Points attribute, except it is cumulative for the athlete's entire career.

- **Career_TP**: This is the same as the Total Points attribute, except it is cumulative for the athlete's entire career.

- **Career_Assists**: This is the same as the Career Assists attribute, except it is cumulative for the athlete's entire career.

- **Career_Con**: This is the same as the Career Concessions attribute, except it is cumulative for the athlete's entire career.

- **Team_Value**: This is a categorical attribute summarizing the athlete's value to his team. It is present only in the training data, as it will serve as our label to predict a Team_Value for each observation in the scoring data set. There are four categories:

  - Role Player: This is an athlete who is good enough to play at the professional level, and may be really good in one area, but is not excellent overall.

  - Contributor: This is an athlete who contributes across several categories of defense and offense and can be counted on to regularly help the team win.

  - Franchise Player: This is an athlete whose skills are so broad, strong and consistent that the team will want to hang on to them for a long time. These players are of such a talent level that they can form the foundation of a really good, competitive team.

  - Superstar: This is that rare individual who gifts are so superior that they make a difference in every game. Most teams in the league will have one such player, but teams with two or three always contend for the league title.

Juan's data are ready and we understand the attributes available to us. We can now proceed to…

DATA PREPARATION

Access the book's companion web site and download two files: Chapter11DataSet_Training.csv and Chapter11DataSet_Scoring.csv. These files contain the 263 current professional athletes and the 59 prospects respectively. Complete the following steps:

1) Import both Chapter 11 data sets into your RapidMiner repository. Be sure to designate the first row as attribute names. You can accept the defaults for data types. Save them

with descriptive names, then drag them and drop them into a new main process window. Be sure to rename the retrieve objects as Training and Scoring.

2) Add three Set Role operators; two to your training stream and one to your scoring stream. Use the first in the training stream to set the Player_Name attribute's role to 'id', so it will not be included in the neural network's prediction calculations. Do the same for the Set Role attribute in the scoring stream. Finally, use the second Set Role attribute in the training stream to set the Team_Value attribute as the 'label' for our model. When you are finished with steps 1 and 2, your process should look like Figure 11-1.

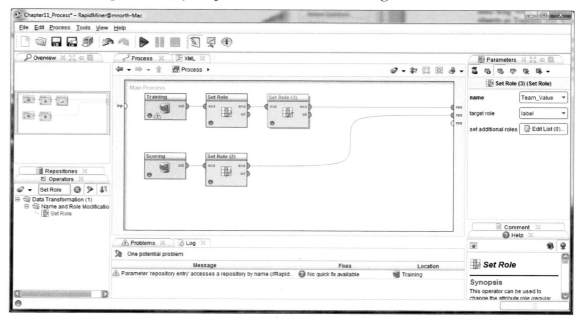

Figure 11-1. Data preparation for neural network analysis.

3) Go ahead and run the model. Use the meta data view for each of the two data sets to familiarize yourself with the data. Ensure that your special attributes have their roles set as they should, in accordance with the parameters you configured in step 2 (see Figures 11-2 and 11-3 which show meta data).

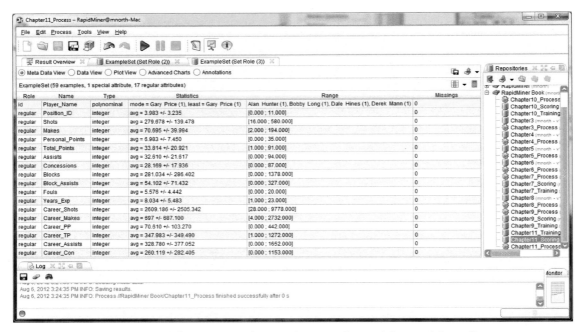

Figure 11-2. The scoring data set's meta data with special attribute
Player_Name designated as an 'id'.

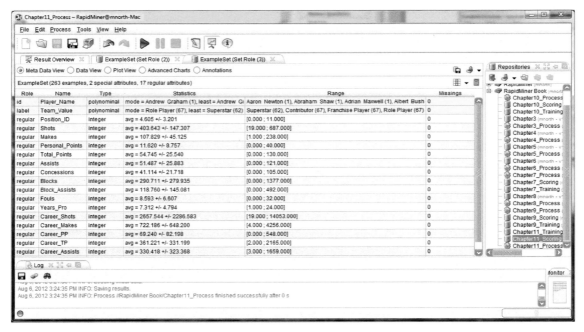

Figure 11-3. The training data set with two special attributes:
Player_Name ('id') and Team_Value ('label').

4) As you review the data sets, note that these two have one characteristic that is unique from prior example data sets: the ranges for the scoring data sets are not within the ranges for the training data set. Neural network algorithms, including the one used in RapidMiner,

often employ a concept called **fuzzy logic**, which is an inferential, probability-based approach to data comparisons allowing us to *infer*, based on probabilities, the strength of the relationship between attributes in our data sets. This gives us added flexibility over some of the other predictive data mining techniques previously shown in this book. Having reviewed the data sets' meta data, return to design perspective so that we can continue with...

MODELING

5) Using the search field on the Operators tab, locate the Neural Net operator and add it to your training stream. Use Apply Model to apply your neural network to your scoring data set. Be sure both the *mod* and *lab* ports are connected to *res* ports (Figure 11-4).

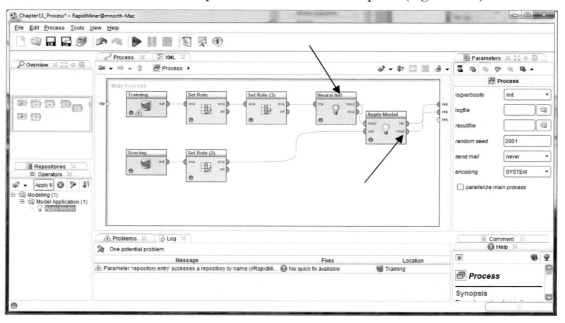

Figure 11-4. Generating a neural network model and applying it to our scoring data set.

Run the model again. In results perspective, you will find both a graphical model and our predictions. At this stage we can begin our...

EVALUATION

Neural networks use what is called a 'hidden layer' to compare all attributes in a data set to all other attributes. The circles in the neural network graph are nodes, and the lines between nodes are called neurons. The thicker and darker the neuron is between nodes, the strong the affinity between the nodes. The graph begins on the left, with one node for each predictor attribute. These can be clicked on to reveal the attribute name that each left-hand node represents. The hidden layer performs the comparison between all attributes, and the column of nodes on the right represent the four possible values in our predicted (label) attribute: Role_Player, Contributor, Franchise Player, or Superstar.

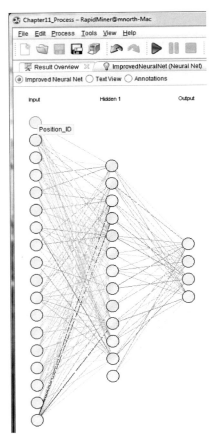

Figure 11-5. A graphical view of our neural network showing different strength neurons and the four nodes for each of the possible Team_Value categories.

Switch to the ExampleSet tab in results perspective. Again, as with past predictive models, we can see that four new special attributes have been generated by RapidMiner. Each of our 59 athlete prospects have a prediction as to their Team_Value category, with accompanying confidence percentages.

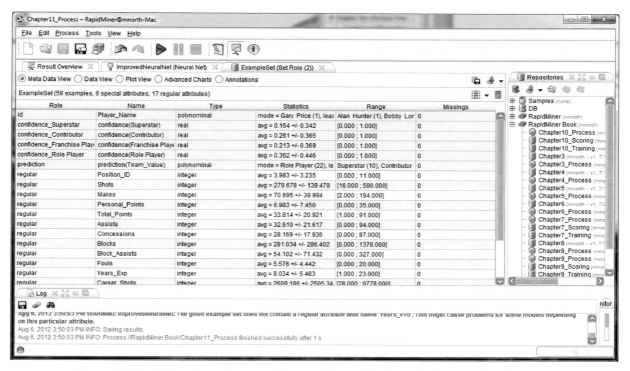

Figure 11-6. Meta data for neural network predictions in the scoring data set.

Change to Data View using the radio button. By now the results of this type of predictive data mining model should look fairly familiar to you.

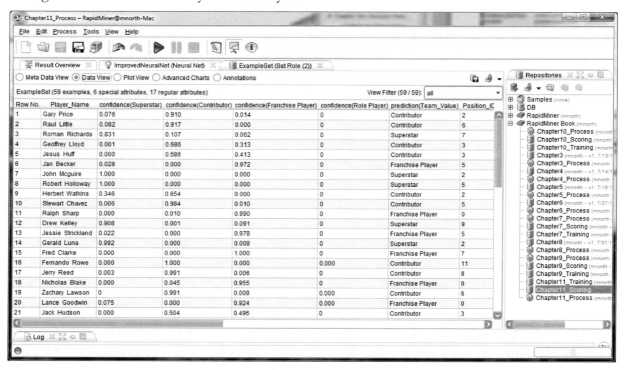

Figure 11-7. Predictions and confidences for our neural net model.

All 59 prospects are now predicitvely categorized. We know how confident RapidMiner is based on our training data, and Juan can now proceed to...

DEPLOYMENT

Juan wanted to quickly and easily assess these 59 prospects based on their past performance. He can deploy his model by responding to management with several different outputs from our neural network. First, he can click twice on the prediction(Team_Value) column heading to bring all of the Superstars to the top. (Superstar is the last of our values in alphabetical order, so it is first in reverse alphabetical order).

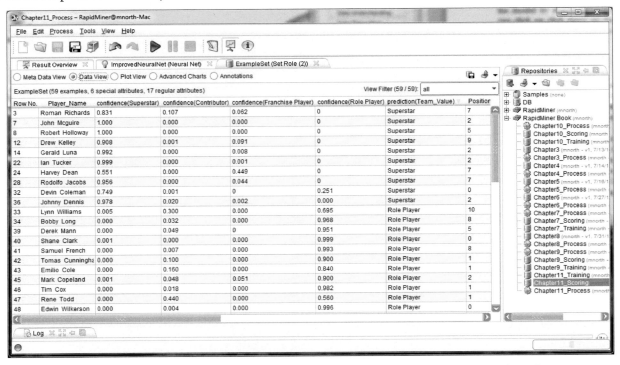

Figure 11-8. The scoring data set's predicted values, with Superstars sorted to the top.

The ten athletes with superstar potential are now shown at the top. Furthermore, the confidence for two of them, John Mcguire and Robert Holloway have confidence(Superstar) percentages of 100%. Juan may want to go ahead and quickly recommend that management take a hard look at these two athletes. Gerald Luna and Ian Tucker are extremely close as well, with only slight probabilities of being Franchise Players instead of Superstars. Even Franchise Players are athletes with huge potential upsides, so the risk of pursuing either of these two players is minimal. There are a couple of others with predicted superstar status and confidences above 90%, so Juan has a solid list of players to work from.

But Juan knows that these players are likely already on the radar screen for many other teams in the league as well. Perhaps he should look at a few potential alternatives, that aren't quite as obvious to everyone. Juan might be able to score a real win by thinking creatively, and his savvy and experience has told him that sometimes the best player acquisitions aren't always the most obvious ones. Click on confidence(Franchise_Player) twice.

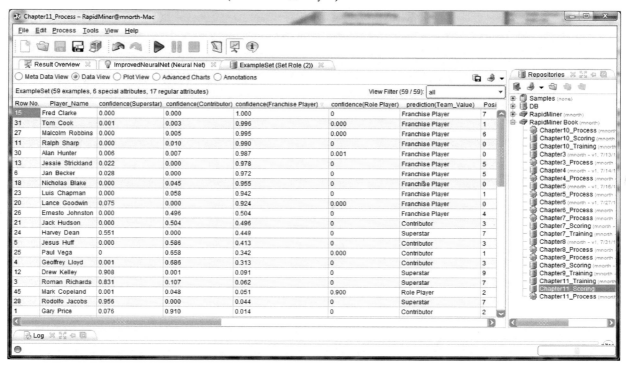

Figure 11-9. The scoring data set's predicted values, with highest Franchise_Player confidences sorted to the top.

There are 11 predicted Franchise Players in the list of 59 prospects. Perhaps Juan could suggest to management that a solid, long-term building block player could be Fred Clarke. Clarke may be easier to persuade to come to the team because fewer teams may already be in contact with him, and he may be less expensive in terms of salary than most of the superstars will be. This makes sense, but there may be an even better player to pursue. Consider Lance Goodwin on Row 20. Goodwin is predicted to be a Franchise Player, so Juan knows he can play—consistently and at a high level. He would be a solid and long term acquisition for any team. But add to this Goodwin's confidence percentage in the Superstar column. Our neural network is predicting that there is almost an 8% chance that Goodwin will rise to the level of Superstar. With 10 years of experience, Goodwin may be poised to reach the pinnacle of his career within the next season or two. Although he was not the first or most obvious choice in the data set, Goodwin certainly appears to be an athlete worth taking a hard look at. He may just be the final piece to the puzzle of bringing Juan's franchise the championship at the end of next season.

Of course Juan must continue to use his expertise, experience and evaluation of other factors not represented in the data sets, to make his final recommendations. For example, while all 59 prospects have some number of years experience, what if their performance statistics have all been amassed against inferior competition? It may not be representative of their ability to perform at the professional level. While the model and its predictions have given Juan a lot to think about, he must still use his experience to make good recommendations to management.

CHAPTER SUMMARY

Neural networks try to mimic the human brain by using artificial 'neurons' to compare attributes to one another and look for strong connections. By taking in attribute values, processing them, and generating nodes connected by neurons, this data mining model can offer predictions and confidence percentages, even amid uncertainty in some data. Neural networks are not as limited regarding value ranges as some other methodologies.

In their graphical representation, neural nets are drawn using nodes and neurons. The thicker or darker the line between nodes, the stronger the connection represented by that neuron. Stronger neurons equate to a stronger ability by that attribute to predict. Although the graphical view can be difficult to read, which can often happen when there are a larger number of attributes, the computer is able to read the network and apply the model to scoring data in order to make predictions. Confidence percentages can further inform the value of an observation's prediction, as was illustrated with our hypothetical athlete Lance Goodwin in this chapter. Between the prediction and confidence percentages, we can use neural networks to find interesting observations that may not be obvious, but still represent good opportunities to answer questions or solve problems.

REVIEW QUESTIONS

1) Where do neural networks get their name? What characteristics of the model make it 'neural'?

2) Find another observation in this chapter's example that is interesting but not obvious, similar to the Lance Goodwin observation. Why is the observation you found interesting? Why is it less obvious than some?

3) How should confidence percentages be used in conjunction with a neural network's predictions?

4) Why might a data miner prefer a neural network over a decision tree?

5) If you want to see a node's details in a RapidMiner graph of a neural network, what can you do?

EXERCISE

For this chapter's exercise, you will create a neural network to predict risk levels for loan applicants at a bank. Complete the following steps.

1) Access the companion web site for this text. Locate and download the training data set labeled Chapter11Exercise_TrainingData.csv. *Applicant_ID, Credit_Score, Late_payment, months_in_job, Debt_income, Loan_amt, liquid_assets, amn_Credit Credit_Risk*

2) Import the training data set into your RapidMiner repository and name it descriptively. Drag and drop the data set into a new, blank main process.

3) Set the Credit_Risk attribute as your label. Remember that Applicant_ID is not predictive.

4) Add a Neural Net operator to your model.

5) Create your own scoring data set using the attributes in the training data set as a guide. Enter at least 20 observations. You can enter data for people that you know (you may have to estimate some of their attribute values, e.g. their credit score), or you can simply test different values for each of the attributes. For example, you might choose to enter four consecutive observations with the same values in all attributes except for the credit score, where you might increment each observation's credit score by 100 from 400 up to 800.

6) Import your scoring data set and apply your model to it.

7) Run your model and review your predictions for each of your scoring observations. Report your results, including any interesting or unexpected results.

Challege Step!

8) See if you can experiment with different lower bounds for each attribute to find the point at which a person will be predicted in the 'DO NOT LEND' category. Use a combination of Declare Missing Values and Replace Missing Values operators to try different thresholds on various attributes. Report your results.

CHAPTER TWELVE:
TEXT MINING

CONTEXT AND PERSPECTIVE

Gillian is a historian and archivist at a national museum in the Unites States. She has recently curated an exhibit on the Federalist Papers. The Federalist Papers are a series of dozens of essays that were written and published in the late 1700's. The essays were published in two different newspapers in the state of New York over the course of about one year, and they were released anonymously under the author name 'Publius'. Their intent was to educate the American people about the new nation's proposed constitution, and to advocate in favor of its ratification. No one really knew at the time if 'Publius' was one individual or many, but several individuals familiar with the authors and framers of the constitution had spotted some patterns in vocabulary and sentence structure that seemed familiar to sections of the U. S. constitution. Years later, after Alexander Hamilton died in the year 1804, some notes were discovered that revealed that he (Hamilton), James Madison and John Jay had been the authors of the papers. The notes indicated specific authors for some papers, but not for others. Specifically, John Jay was revealed to be the author for papers 3, 4 and 5; Madison for paper 14; and Hamilton for paper 17. Paper 18 had no author named, but there was evidence that Hamilton and Madison worked on that one together.

LEARNING OBJECTIVES

After completing the reading and exercises in this chapter, you should be able to:

- Explain what text mining is, how it is used and the benefits of using it.
- Recognize the various formats that text can be in, in order to perform text mining.
- Connect to and import text as a data source for a text mining model.
- Develop a text mining model in RapidMiner including common text-parsing operators such as **tokenization**, **stop word** filtering, **n-gram** construction, **stemming**, etc.

- Apply other data mining models to text mining results in order to predict or classify based on textual analysis.

ORGANIZATIONAL UNDERSTANDING

Gillian would like to analyze paper 18's content in the context of the other papers with known authors, to see if she can generate some evidence that the suspected collaboration between Hamilton and Madison is in fact a likely scenario. She feels like **text mining** might be a good method to analyze the text in a structured way, and has enlisted our help. Having studied all of the Federalist Papers and other writings by the three statesmen who wrote them, Gillian feels confident that paper 18 is a collaboration that John Jay *did not* contribute to—his vocabulary and grammatical structure was quite different from those of Hamilton and Madison, even when all three wrote on the same topic, as they had with the Federalist Papers. She would like to look for word and phrase choice frequencies and present the outcome as part of her exhibit on the papers. We will help Gillian by constructing a text mining model using the text from the Federalist Papers and some standard text mining methodologies.

DATA UNDERSTANDING

Gillian's data set is simple: we will include the full text of Federalist Papers number 5 (Jay), 14 (Madison), 17 (Hamilton), and 18 (suspected collaboration between Madison and Hamilton). The Federalist Papers are available through a number of sources: they have been re-published in book form, they are available on a number of different web sites, and their text is archived in many libraries throughout the world. For this chapter's exercise, the text of these four papers has been added to the book's companion web site. There are four files for you to download:

- Chapter12_Federalist05_Jay.txt
- Chapter12_Federalist14_Madison.txt
- Chapter12_Federalist17_Hamilton.txt
- Chapter12_Federalist18_Collaboration.txt.

Please download these now, but do not import them into a RapidMiner repository. The process of handling textual data in RapidMiner is a bit different than what we have done in past chapters. With these four papers' text available to us, we can move directly into the CRISP-DM phase of…

DATA PREPARATION

The text mining module of RapidMiner is an optional add-in. When you installed RapidMiner (way back in Step 4 of the 'Preparing RapidMiner...' section of Chapter 3), we mentioned that you might want to include the Text Processing component. Whether you did or did not at that time, we will need it for this chapter's example, so we can add it now. Even if you did add it earlier, it might be a good idea to complete all of the steps below to ensure your Text Processing add-in is up-to-date.

1) Open RapidMiner to a new, blank process. From the application menu, select Help > Update RapidMiner...

Figure 12-1: Updating RapidMiner add-ins.

2) Your computer will need to be connected to the Internet, so that it can check Rapid-I's servers to see if any updates are available. Once the connection has been established and the software has checked for available updates, you will see a window similar to Figure 12-2. Locate Text Processing in the list (it should be about fourth from the top). If it is grayed out, that means that the add-in is installed and up-to-date on your computer. If it is not installed, or not up to the current version, it will be orange. You can double click the

small square to the left of the Text Processing icon (the circle with 'ABC' in it). Then click the Install button to add or update the module. When it is finished, the window will disappear and you will be back to your main RapidMiner window.

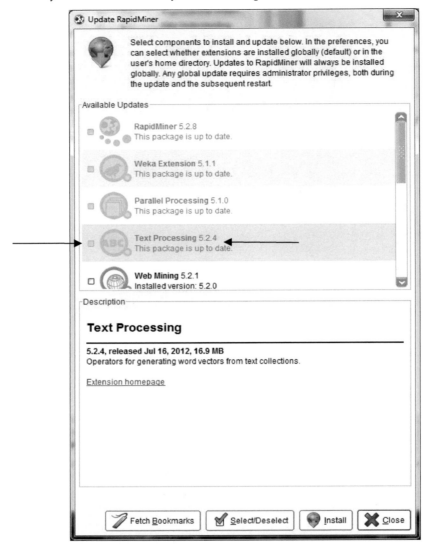

Figure 12-2. Adding/updating the RapidMiner Text Processing add-in.

3) In the Operators tab in the lower left hand area of your RapidMiner window, locate and expand the Text Processing operators folder by clicking on the + sign next to it.

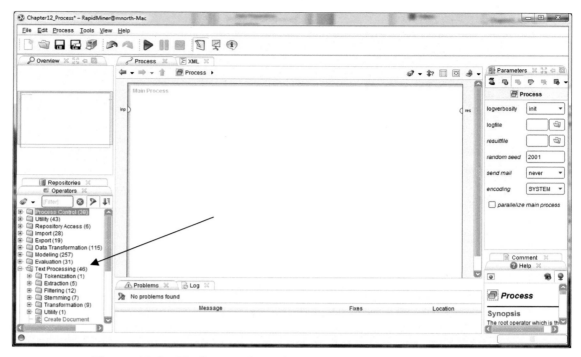

Figure 12-3. Finding tools in the Text Processing operator area.

4) Within the Text Processing menu tree, there is an operator called Read Document. Drag this operator and drop it into your main process window. Right click on it and rename it 'Paper 5', as shown in Figure 12-4.

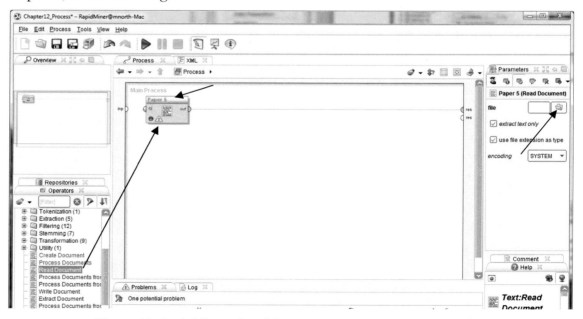

Figure 12-4. Adding a Read Document operator to our model.

5) In the Parameters area of the RapidMiner window (right hand side), note that you must specify a 'file' that RapidMiner can read. Click on the folder icon to the right of the file parameter to browse for our first text file.

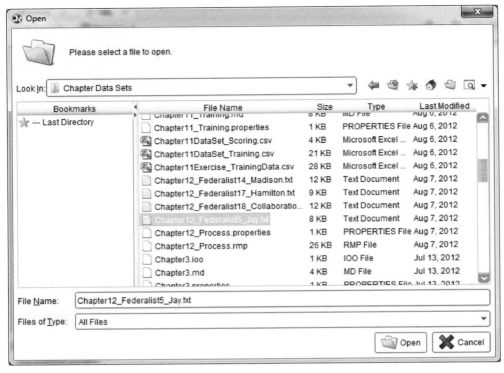

Figure 12-5. Locating the John Jay Federalist Paper (No. 5).

6) In this case, we have saved the text files containing the papers' text in a folder called Chapter Data Sets. We have browsed to this folder, and highlighted the John Jay paper. We can click Open to connect our RapidMiner operator to this text file. This will return us to our main process window in RapidMiner. Repeat steps 4 and 5 three more times, each time connecting one of the other papers, preferably in numerical order, to a Read Document operator in RapidMiner. Use care to ensure that you connect the right operator to the right text file, so that you can keep the text of each paper straight with the operator that's handling it. Once finished, your model should look like Figure 12-6.

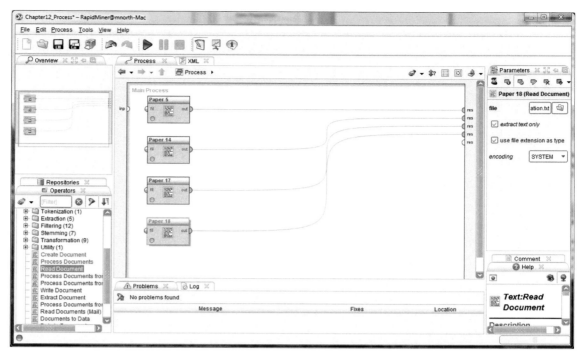

Figure 12-6. All four Federalist Paper text files are now connected in RapidMiner.

7) Go ahead and run the model. You will see that each of the four papers have been read into RapidMiner and can be reviewed in results perspective. After reviewing the text, return to design perspective.

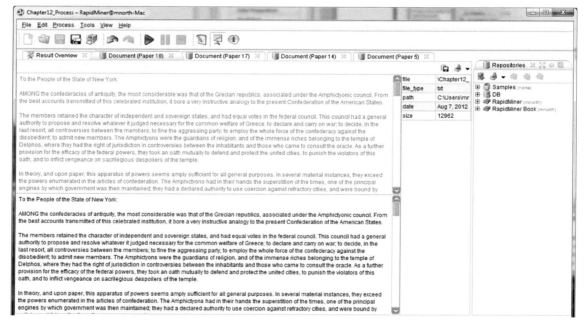

Figure 12-7. Reviewing the suspected collaboration paper (no. 18) in results perspective.

8) We now have our four essays available in RapidMiner. Reading the papers is not enough however. Gillian's goal is to analyze the papers. For this, we will use a Process Documents operator. It is located just above the Read Document operator in the Text Processing menu tree. Drag this operator into your process and drop it into the Paper 5 stream. There will be an empty *doc* port on the bottom left hand side of the Process Documents operator. Disconnect your Paper 14's *out* port from its *res* port and connect it to the open *doc* port instead. Remember that you can rearrange port connections by clicking on the first, then clicking on the second. You will get a warning message asking you to confirm the disconnect/reconnect action each time you do this. Repeat this process until all four documents are feeding into the Process Documents operator, as is the case in Figure 12-8.

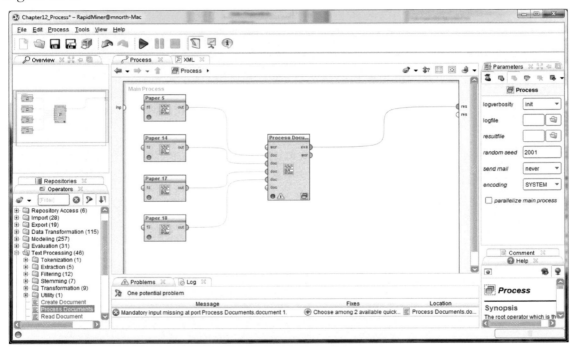

Figure 12-8. All four Federalist Papers feeding into a single document processor.

9) Next, double click on the Process Documents operator. This will take us into a sub-process window.

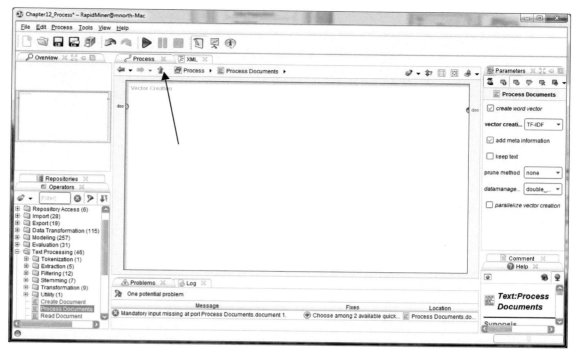

Figure 12-9. A view inside the sub-process of our Process Documents operator.

10) Note that the blue up arrow in the process toolbar is now illuminated, where previously it has been grayed out. This will allow us to return to our main process, once we have constructed our **sub-process**. Within the sub-process though, there are a few things we *need* to do, and a couple we can choose to do, in order to mine our text. Use the search field in the Operators tab to locate an operator called **Tokenize**. It is under the Text Processing menu in the Tokenization folder. When mining text, the words in the text must be grouped together and counted. Without some numeric structure, the computer cannot assess the meaning of the words. The Tokenize operator performs this function for us. Drag it into the sub-process window (labeled 'Vector Creation' in the upper left hand corner). The *doc* ports from the left hand side of the screen to the operator, and from the operator to the right hand side of the screen, should all be connected by splines, as illustrated in Figure 12-10.

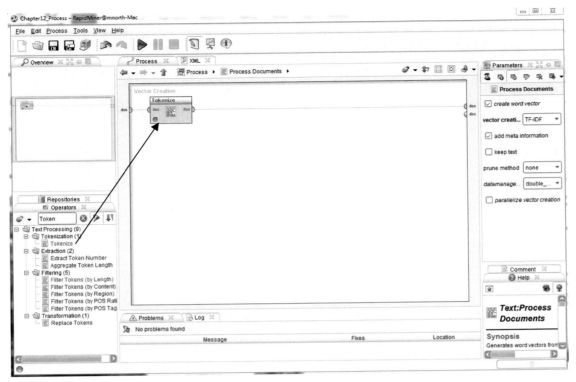

Figure 12-10. Adding tokenization to the text mining model's sub-process.

11) Run the model and briefly review the output. You will see that each word from our four input documents is now an attribute in our data set. We also have a few new special attributes, created by RapidMiner.

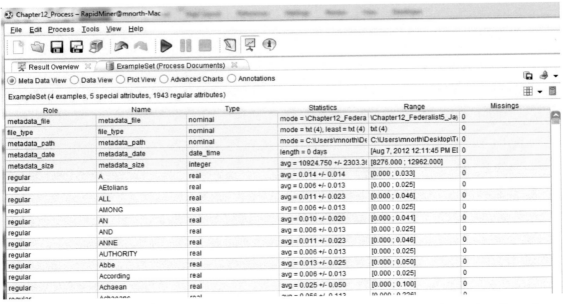

Figure 12-11. A view of the words from our input documents as tokens (attributes).

12) Switch back to design perspective. You will see that we return to the sub-process from where we ran the model. We've put the words from our documents into attributes through tokenization, but further processing is needed to make sense of the value of the words in relation to one another. For one thing, there are some words in our data set that really don't mean much. These are necessary conjunctions and articles that make the text readable in English, but that won't tell us much about meaning or authorship. We should remove these words. In the Operators search field, look for the word 'Stop'. These types of words are called **stopwords**, and RapidMiner has built-in dictionaries in several languages to find and filter these out. Add the Filter Stopwords (English) operator to the sub-process stream.

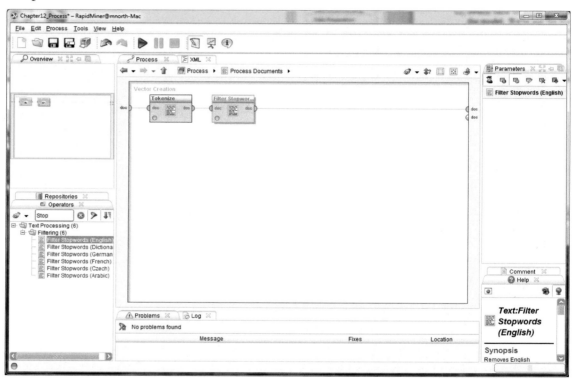

Figure 12-12. Removing stopwords such as 'and', 'or', 'the', etc. from our model.

13) In some instances, letters that are uppercase will not match with the same letters in lowercase. When text mining, this could be a problem because 'Data' might be interpreted different from 'data'. This is known as **Case Sensitivity**. We can address this matter by adding a **Transform Cases** operator to our sub-process stream. Search for this operator in the Operators tab and drag it into your stream, as shown in Figure 12-13.

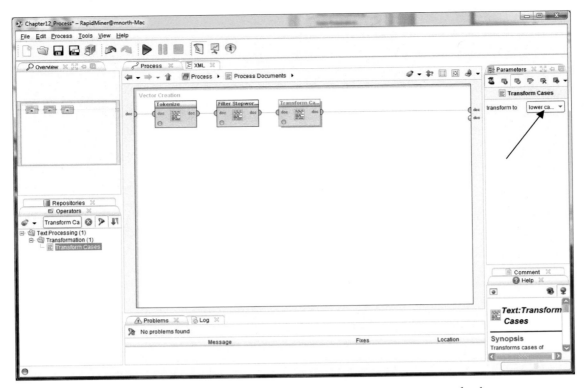

Figure 12-13. Setting all tokens (word attributes) from our text to be lowercase.

At this point, we have a model that is capable of mining and displaying to us the words that are most frequent in our text documents. This will be interesting for us to review, but there are a few more operators that you should know about in addition to the ones we are using here. These are highlighted by black arrows in Figure 12-14, and discussed below.

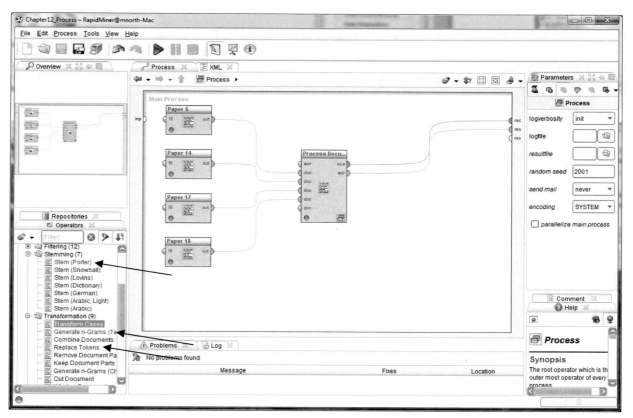

Figure 12-14. Additional text mining operators of interest.

- **Stemming**: In text mining, stemming means finding terms that share a common root and combining them to mean essentially the same thing. For example, 'America', 'American', 'Americans', are all like terms and effectively refer to the same thing. By stemming (you can see there are a number of stemming operators using different algorithms for you to choose from), RapidMiner can reduce all instances of these word variations to a common form, such as 'Americ', or perhaps 'America', and have all instances represented in a single attribute.

- **Generate n-Grams**: In text mining, an n-gram is a phrase or combination of words that may take on meaning that is different from, or greater than the meaning of each word individually. When creating n-grams, the *n* is simply the maximum number of terms you want RapidMiner to consider grouping together. Take for example the token 'death'. This word by itself is strong, evoking strong emotion. But now consider the meaning, strength and emotion if you were to add a Generate n-Grams operator to your model with a size of 2 (this is set in the parameters area of the n-gram operator). Depending on your input text, you might find the token 'death_penalty'. This certainly has a more specific meaning and evokes different and even stronger emotions than just the token 'death'. What if we increased the n-gram size to 3? We might find a token 'death_penalty_execution'. Again, more specific meaning and perhaps stronger emotion is attached. Understand that these example gram tokens would only be created by RapidMiner if the two or three words in each of them were found together, and in close proximity to one another in the input text. Generating grams can be an excellent way to bring a more granular analysis to your text mining activities.

- **Replace Tokens**: This is similar to replacing missing or inconsistent values in more structured data. This operator can come in handy once you've tokenized your text input. Suppose for example that you had the tokens 'nation', 'country', and 'homeland' in your data set but you wanted to treat all of them as one token. You could use this operator to change both 'country' and 'homeland' to 'nation', and all instances of any of the three terms (or their stems if you also use stemming) would subsequently be combined into a single token.

These are a just a few of the other operators in the Text Processing area that can be nice additions to a text mining model. There are many others, and you may experiment with these at your leisure. For now though, we will proceed to...

MODELING

Click the blue up arrow to move from your sub-process back to your main process window.

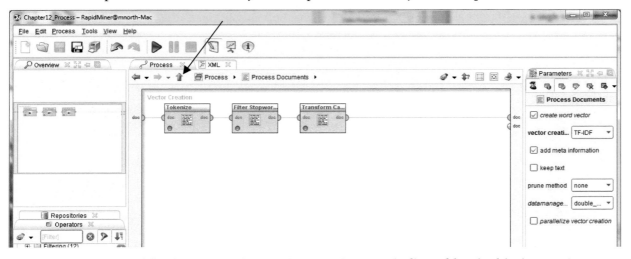

Figure 12-15. The 'Return to Parent Operator' arrow (indicated by the black arrow).

In the main process window, ensure that both the *exa* and *wor* ports on the Process Documents operator are connected to *res* ports as shown in Figure 12-16.

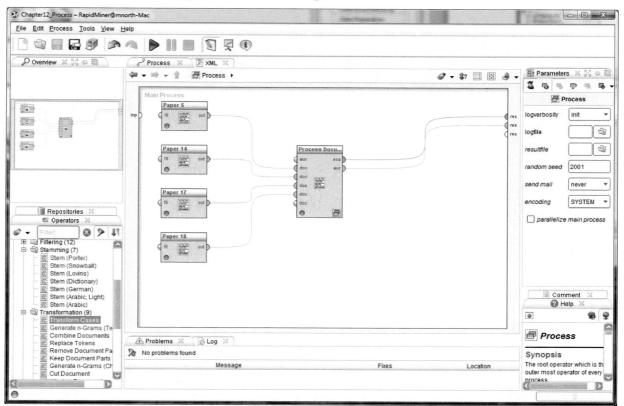

Figure 12-16. The Federalist Papers text mining model.

The *exa* port will generate a tab in results perspective showing the words (tokens) from our documents as attributes, with the attributes' relative strength in each of the four documents indicated by a decimal coefficient. The *wor* port will create a tab in results perspective that shows the words as tokens with the total number of occurrences, and the number of documents each token appeared in. Although we will do a bit more modeling in this chapter's example, at this point we will go ahead and proceed to…

EVALUATION

Let's run our model again. We can see the WordList tab in results perspective, showing our tokens and their frequencies in the input documents.

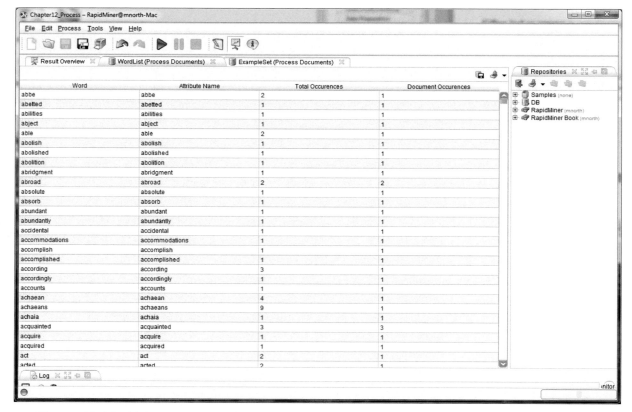

Figure 12-17. Tokens generated from Federalist Papers 5, 14, 17 and 18, with frequencies.

There are many tokens, which is not surprising considering the length of each essay we have fed into the model. In Figure 12-17, we can see that some of our tokens appear in multiple documents. Consider the word (or token) 'acquainted'. This term shows up one time each in three of the four documents. How can we tell? The Total Occurrences for this token shows as 3, and the Document Occurrences shows as 3, so it must be in each of three documents one time. (Note that even a cursory review of these tokens reveals some stemming opportunities—for example 'accomplish' and 'accomplished' or 'according' and 'accordingly'.) Click on the Total Occurrences column twice to bring the most common terms to the top.

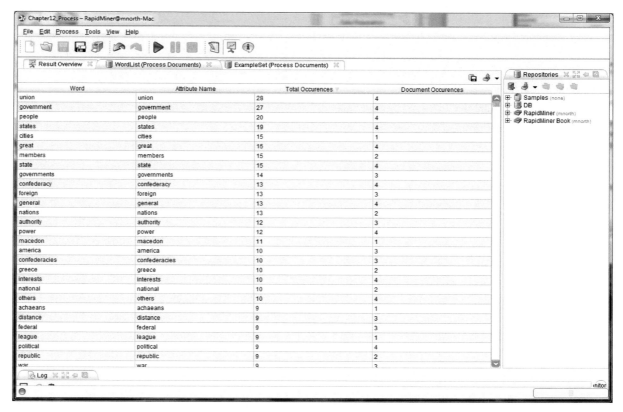

Word	Attribute Name	Total Occurences	Document Occurences
union	union	28	4
government	government	27	4
people	people	20	4
states	states	19	4
cities	cities	15	1
great	great	15	4
members	members	15	2
state	state	15	4
governments	governments	14	3
confederacy	confederacy	13	4
foreign	foreign	13	3
general	general	13	4
nations	nations	13	2
authority	authority	12	3
power	power	12	4
macedon	macedon	11	1
america	america	10	3
confederacies	confederacies	10	3
greece	greece	10	2
interests	interests	10	4
national	national	10	2
others	others	10	4
achaeans	achaeans	9	1
distance	distance	9	3
federal	federal	9	3
league	league	9	1
political	political	9	4
republic	republic	9	2
war	war	9	3

Figure 12-18. Our tokens re-sorted from highest to lowest total occurrences.

Here we see powerful words that all of the authors have relied upon extensively. The Federalist Papers were written to argue in favor of the adoption of a new constitution, and these tokens reflect that agenda. Not only were these terms frequently used across all four documents, the vocabulary reflects the objective of writing and publishing the essays in the first place. Note again here that there is an opportunity to benefit from stemming ('government', 'governments'). Also, some n-grams would be interesting and informative. The term 'great' is both common and frequent, but in what context? Could it be that an n-gram operator might yield the term 'great_nation', which bears much more meaning than just the word 'great'? Feel free to experiment by re-modeling and re-evaluating.

These results in and of themselves are interesting, but we haven't gotten to the heart of Gillian's question, which was: Is it likely that Federalist Paper 18 was indeed a collaboration between Hamilton and Madison? Think back through this book and about what you have learned thus far. We have seen many data mining methodologies that help us to check for affinity or group classifications. Let's attempt to apply one of these to our text mining model to see if it will reveal more about the authors of these papers. Complete the following steps:

1) Switch back to design perspective. Locate the k-Means operator and drop it into your stream between the *exa* port on Process Documents and the *res* port (Figure 12-19).

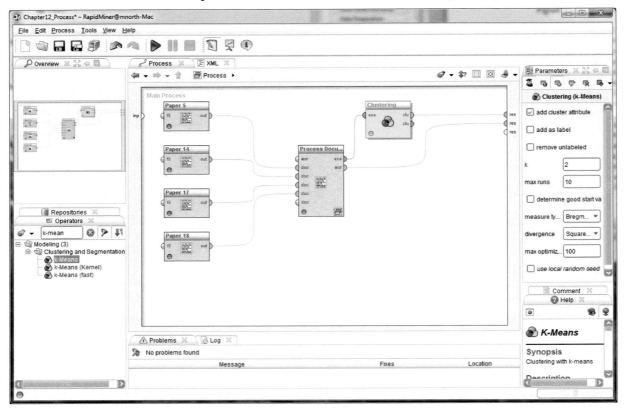

Figure 12-19. Clustering our documents using their token frequncies as means.

2) For this model we will accept the default *k* of 2, since we want to group Hamilton's and Madison's writings together, and keep Jay's separate. We'd hope to get a Hamilton/Madison cluster, with paper 18 in that one, and a Jay cluster with only his paper in there. Run the model and then click on the Cluster Model tab.

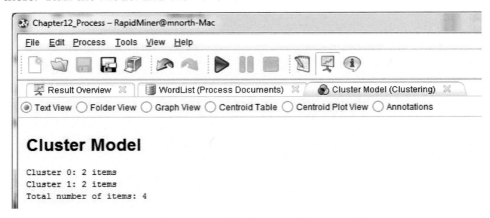

Figure 12-20. Cluster results for our four text documents.

3) Unfortunately, it looks like at least one of our four documents ended up associated with John Jay's paper (no. 5). This probably happened for two reasons: (1) We are using the k-Means methodology and means in general tend to try to find a middle with equal parts on both sides; and (2) Jay *was* writing on the same topic as were Hamilton and Madison. Thus, there is going to be much similarity across the essays, so the means will more easily balance even if Jay didn't contribute to paper 18. The topic alone will cause enough similarity that paper 18 could be grouped with Jay, especially when the operator we've chosen is trying to find equal balance. We can see how the four papers have been clustered by clicking on the Folder View radio button and expanding both of the folder menu trees.

Figure 12-21. Examining the document clusters.

4) We can see that the first two papers and the last two papers were grouped together. This can be a bit confusing because RapidMiner has renumbered the documents from 1 to 4, in the order that we added them to our model. In the book's example, we added them in numerical order: 5, 14, 17, and then 18. So paper 5 corresponds to document 1, paper 14 corresponds to document 2, and so forth. If we can't remember the order in which we added the papers to the model, we can click on the little white page icon to the left of the document number to view the document's details:

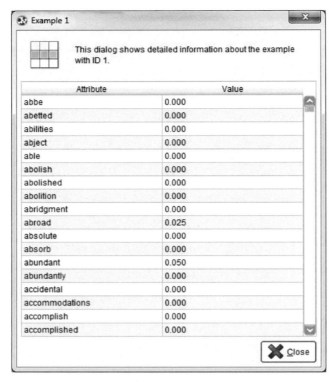

Figure 12-22. Details of document 1.0 in RapidMiner.

5) Click on the Value column heading twice. This will bring the file path for the document toward the top, as shown in Figure 12-23.

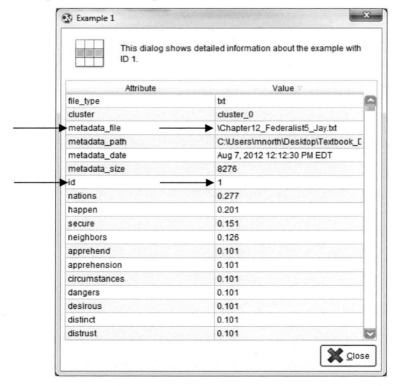

Figure 12-23. Document 1's values in reverse sort order.

6) We can see by looking at the first several attributes that for document ID 1, the file is Chapter12_Federalist05_Jay.txt. Thus if we can't remember that we added paper 5 first, resulting in RapidMiner labeling it document 1, we can check it in the document details. This little trick works when you have used the Read Document operator, as the document being read becomes the value for the metadata_file attribute, however when using some other operators, such as the Create Document operator, it doesn't work, as you will see momentarily. Since we added our papers in numerical order in this chapter's example, we do not necessarily need to view and sort the details for each of the documents, but you may if you wish. Knowing that documents 1 and 2 are Jay (no. 5) and Madison (no. 14), and documents 3 and 4 are Hamilton (no. 17) and suspected collaboration (no. 18), we can be encouraged by what we see in this model. It appears that Hamilton *does* have something to do with Federalist Paper 18, but we don't know about Madison yet because Madison was grouped with Jay, probably as a result of the previously discussed mean balancing that k-means clustering is prone to do.

7) Perhaps we can address this by better training our model to recognize Jay's writing. Using your favorite search engine, search the Internet for the text of Federalist Paper No. 3. Gillian knows that this paper's authorship has been connected to John Jay. We will use the text to train our model to better recognize Jay's writing. If paper 18 was written by, or even contributed to by Jay, perhaps we will find that it gets clustered with Jay's papers 3 and 5 when we add paper 3 to the model. In this case, Hamilton and Madison should get clustered together. If on the other hand paper 18 was *not* written or contributed to by Jay, paper 18 should gravitate toward Hamilton (no. 17) and/or Madison (no. 14), so long as Jay was consistent in his writing between papers 3 and 5. Copy the text of paper 3 by highlighting it in whichever web site you found (it is available on a number of sites). Then in design perspective in RapidMiner, locate the Create Document operator and drag it into your process (Figure 12-23).

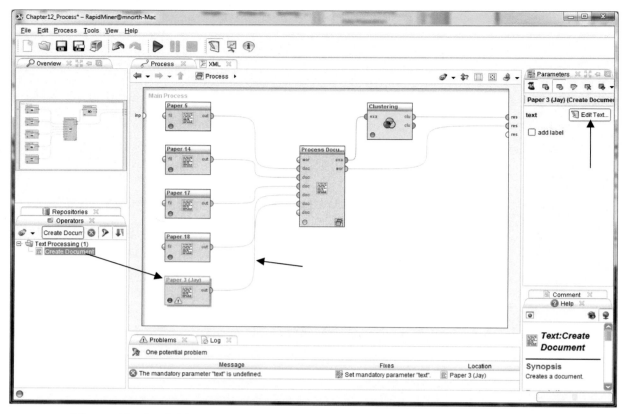

Figure 12-23. Adding a Create Document operator to our text mining model.

8) Be sure the Create Document operator's *out* port is connected to one of the Process Document operator's *doc* ports. It will likely connect itself to a *res* port, so you'll have to reconnect it to the Process Documents operator. Let's rename this operator 'Paper 3 (Jay)'. Then click on the Edit Text button in the Parameters area on the right hand side of the screen. You will see a window like Figure 12-24.

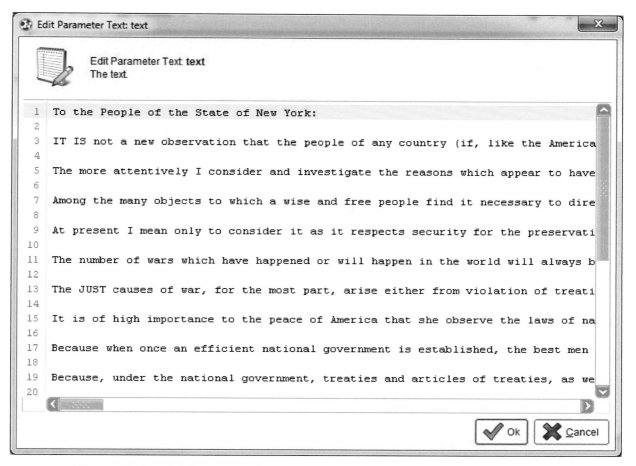

Figure 12-24. Adding a text document through a Create Document operator.

9) Paste the text of Federalist Paper 3 into the Edit Parameter Text window and then click OK. We now have five documents to be processed and run through our k-Means model. RapidMiner will assign document ID 5 to this new document, since it was the fifth one we added to our main process. Let's run the model to see how our documents are grouped now.

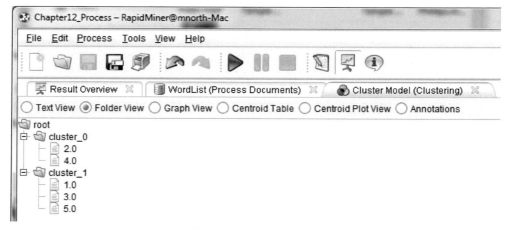

Figure 12-25. New clusters identified by RapidMiner with the addition of another of Jay's papers.

10) On the Cluster Model tab in results perspective, with the cluster menu trees expanded, we now see that documents 2 and 4 (papers 14 (Madison) and 18 (collaboration)) are grouped together, while the two of Jay's papers (documents 1 (paper 5) and 5 (paper 3)) are grouped with Hamilton's paper (document 3; paper 17). This is very encouraging because the suspected collaboration paper (no. 18) has now been associated with both Madison's and Hamilton's writing, but not with Jay's. Let's give our model one more of Jay's papers to further train it in Jay's writing style, and see if we can find further evidence that paper 18 is most strongly connected to Madison and Hamilton. Repeat steps 7 through 9, only this time, find the text of Federalist Paper 4 (also written by John Jay) and paste it into a new Create Document operator.

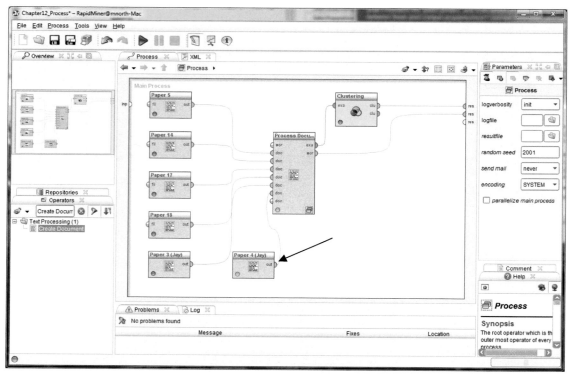

Figure 12-26. The addition of another Create Document operator containing the text of Federalist Paper 4 by John Jay.

11) Be sure to rename the second Create Document operator descriptively, as we have done in Figure 12-26. When you have used the Edit Text button to paste the text for Federalist Paper 4 into your model and have ensured that your ports are all connected correctly, run the model one last time and we will proceed to…

DEPLOYMENT

Gillian had an interest in investigating the similarities and differences between several of the Federalist Papers in order to lend credence to the belief that Alexander Hamilton and James Madison collaborated on paper 18.

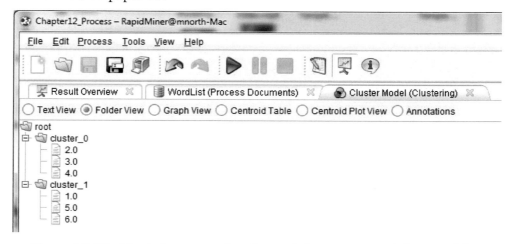

Figure 12-27. Final cluster results after training our text mining model to recognize John Jay's writing style.

Gillian now has the evidence she had hoped to find. As we continued to train our model in John Jay's writing style, we have found that he indeed was consistent from paper 3 to 4 to 5, as RapidMiner found these documents to be the most similar and subsequently clustered them together in cluster_1. At the same time, RapidMiner consistently found paper 18, the suspected collaboration between Hamilton and Madison to be associated with one, then the other, and finally both of them together. Gillian could further strengthen her model by adding additional papers from all three authors, or she could go ahead and add what we've already found to her exhibit at the museum.

CHAPTER SUMMARY

Text mining is a powerful way of analyzing data in an unstructured format such as in paragraphs of text. Text can be fed into a model in different ways, and then that text can be broken down into tokens. Once tokenized, words can be further manipulated to address matters such as case sensitivity, phrases or word groupings, and word stems. The results of these analyses can reveal the frequency and commonality of strong words or grams across groups of documents. This can reveal trends in the text, such as what topics are most important to author(s), or what message should be taken away from the text when reading the documents.

Further, once the documents' tokens are organized into attributes, the documents can be modeled, just as other, more structured data sets can be modeled. Multiple documents can be handled by a single Process Document operator in RapidMiner, which will apply the same set of tokenization and token handlers to all documents at once through the sub-process stream. After a model has been applied to a set of documents, additional documents can be added to the stream, passed through the document processor, and run through the model to yield more well-trained and specific results.

REVIEW QUESTIONS

1) What are some of the benefits of text mining as opposed to the other models you've learned in this book?

2) How are some ways that text-based data is imported into RapidMiner?

3) What is a sub-process and when do you use one in RapidMiner?

4) Define the following terms: token, stem, n-gram, case-sensitive.

5) How does tokenization enable the application of data mining models to text-based data?

6) How do you view a k-Means cluster's details?

EXERCISE

For this chapter's exercise, you will mine text for common complaints against a company or industry. Complete the following steps.

1) Using your favorite search engine, locate a web site or discussion forum on the Internet where people have posted complaints, criticisms or pleas for help regarding a company or an industry (e.g. airlines, utility companies, insurance companies, etc.).

2) Copy and paste at least ten of these posts or comments into a text editor, saving each one as its own text document with a unique name.

3) Open a new, blank process in RapidMiner, and using the Read Documents operator, connect to each of your ten (or more) text documents containing the customer complaints you found.

4) Process these documents in RapidMiner. Be sure you tokenize and use other handlers in your sub-process as you deem appropriate/necessary. Experiment with grams and stems.

5) Use a k-Means cluster to group your documents into two, three or more clusters. Output your word list as well.

6) Report the following:

   a. Based on your word list, what seem to be the most common complaints or issues in your documents? Why do you think that is? What evidence can you give to support your claim?

   b. Based on your word list, are there some terms or phrases that show up in all, or at least most of your documents? Why do you think these are so common?

   c. Based on your clusters, what groups did you get? What are the common themes in each of your clusters? Is this surprising? Why or why not?

   d. How might a customer service manager use your model to address the common concerns or issues you found?

Challenge Step!

7) Using your knowledge from past chapters, removed the k-Means clustering operator, and try to apply a different data mining methodology such as association rules or decision trees to your text documents. Report your results.

SECTION THREE: SPECIAL CONSIDERATIONS IN DATA MINING

CHAPTER THIRTEEN:
EVALUATION AND DEPLOYMENT

HOW FAR WE'VE COME

The purpose of this book, which was explained in Chapter 1, is to introduce non-experts and non-computer scientists to some of the methods and tools of data mining. Certainly there have been a number of processes, tools, operators, data manipulation techniques, etc., demonstrated in this book, but perhaps the most important lesson to take away from this broad treatment of data mining is that the field has become huge, complex, and dynamic. You have learned about the CRISP-DM process, and had it shown to you numerous times as you have seen data mining models that classified, predicted and did both. You have seen a number of data processing tools and techniques, and as you have done this, you have hopefully noticed thy myriad other operators in RapidMiner that we did not use or discuss. Although you may be feeling like you're getting good at data mining (and we hope you do), please recognize that there is a world of data mining that this book has *not* touched on—so there is still much for you to learn.

This chapter and the next will discuss some cautions that should be taken before putting any real-world data mining results into practice. This chapter will demonstrate a method for using RapidMiner to conduct some validation for data mining models; while Chapter 14 will discuss the choices you will make as a data miner, and some ways to guide those choices in good directions. Remember from Chapter 1 that CRISP-DM is cyclical—you should always be learning from the work you are doing, and feeding what you've learned from your work back into your next data mining activity.

For example, suppose you used a Replace Missing Values operator in a data mining model to set all missing values in a data set to the average for each attribute. Suppose further that you used results of that data mining model in making decisions for your company, and that those decisions turned out to be less than ideal. What if you traced those decisions back to your data mining activities and found that by using the average, you made some general assumptions that weren't really very realistic. Perhaps you don't need to throw out the data mining model entirely, but for the next run of that model you should be sure to change it to either remove observations with missing values, or use a more appropriate replacement value based upon what you have learned. Even if you used your data mining results and had excellent outcomes, remember that your business is constantly moving, and through the day-to-day operations of your organization, you are gathering more data. Be sure to add this data to training data sets, compare actual outcomes to predictions, and tune your data mining models in accordance with your experience and the expertise you are developing. Consider Sarah, our hypothetical sales manager from Chapters 4 and 8. Certainly now that we've helped her predict heating oil usage by home through a linear regression model, Sarah can track these homes' *actual* heating oil orders to see how well their actual use matches our predictions. Once these customers have established several months or years of actual heating oil consumption, their data can be fed into Sarah's model's training data set, helping it to be even more accurate in its predictions.

One of the benefits of connecting RapidMiner to a database or data warehouse, rather than importing data via a file (CSV, etc.) is that data can be added to the data sets in real time and fed straight into the RapidMiner models. If you were to acquire some new training data, as Sarah could in the scenario just proposed in the previous paragraph, it could be immediately incorporated into the RapidMiner model if the data were in a connected database. With a CSV file, the new training data would have to be added into the file, and then re-imported into the RapidMiner repository.

As we tune and hone our models, they perform better for us. In addition to using our growing expertise and adding more training data, there are some built-in ways that we can check a model's performance in RapidMiner.

LEARNING OBJECTIVES

After completing the reading and exercises in this chapter, you should be able to:

- Explain what cross-validation is, and discuss its role in the Evaluation and Deployment phases of CRISP-DM.
- Define false positives and explain why their existence is not all bad in data mining.
- Perform a cross-validation on a training data set in RapidMiner.

• Interpret and discuss the results of cross-validation matrix.

CROSS-VALIDATION

Cross-validation is the process of checking for the likelihood of false positives in predictive models in RapidMiner. Most data mining software products will have operators for cross-validation and for other forms of false positive detection. A **false positive** is when a value is predicted incorrectly. We will give one example here, using the decision tree we built for our hypothetical client Richard, back in Chapter 10. Complete the following steps:

1) Open RapidMiner and start a new, blank data mining process.
2) Go to the Repositories tab and locate the Chapter 10 training data set. This was the one that had attributes regarding peoples' buying habits on Richard's employer's web site, along with their category of eReader adoption. Drag this data set into your main process window. You can rename it if you would like. In Figure 13-1, we have renamed it eReader Train.

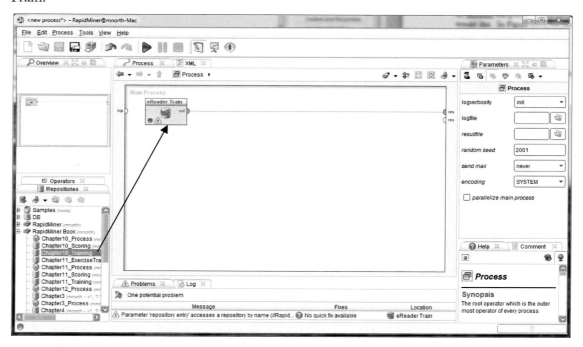

Figure 13-1. Adding the Chapter 10 training data to a new model in order to cross-validate its predictive capabilities.

3) Add a Set Role operator to the stream. We'll learn a new trick here with this operator. Set the User_ID attribute to be 'id'. We know we still need to set eReader_Adoption to be

'label' (the thing we want to predict). Back in Chapter 10, we did this by adding another Set Role operator, but this time, click on the 'set additional roles: Edit List' button in the Parameters area. This is indicated by the black arrow in Figure 13-2.

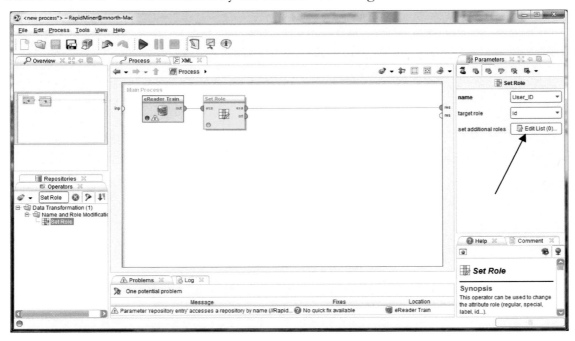

Figure 13-2. Setting multiple roles with a single Set Role operator.

4) In the resulting pop-up window, set the name field to be eReader_Adoption and the target role field to be label. (Note that we could use the Add Entry button to use this single Set Role operator to handle role assignments for many attributes all at once.)

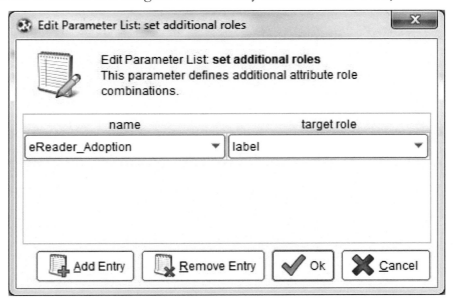

Figure 13-3. Setting additional roles by editing the parameters

of a single Set Role operator.

5) When we used this data set previously, we added our Decision Tree operator at this point. This time, we will use the search field in the Operators tab to find x-Validation operators. There are four of them, but we will use the basic cross-validation operator in this example:

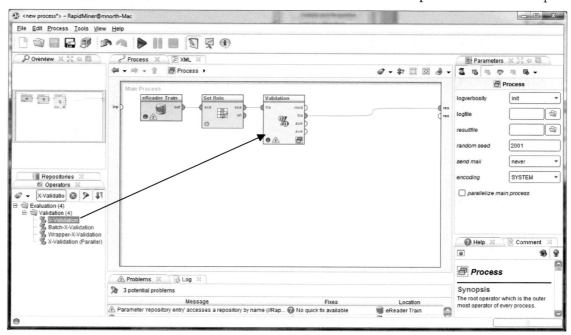

Figure 13-4. Adding a cross-validation operator to our stream.

6) The cross-validation operator requires a two-part sub-process. In the first part of the sub-process, we will add our Decision Tree operator to build a model, and in the second part we will apply our model and check its performance. Double click the Validation operator to enter the sub-process window.

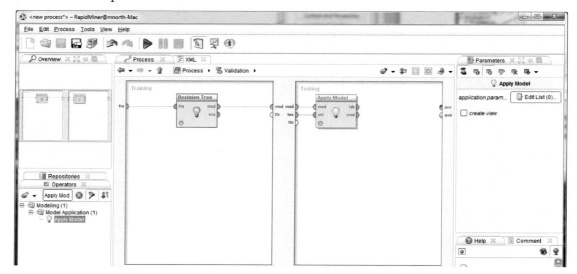

Figure 13-5. Modeling and applying the model in the cross-validation sub-process.

7) In Figure 13-5, add the Decision Tree operator in the Training side of the cross-validation sub-process, and the Apply Model operator on the Testing side. Leave the Decision Tree's operator as gain_ratio for now. The splines depicted here are automatically drawn when you drag these operators into these two areas. If for any reason you do not have these splines configured in this way, connect the ports as shown so that your sub-process matches Figure 13-5. We must now complete the Testing portion of the sub-process. In the Operators search field, search for an operator called 'Performance'. There are a number of these. We will use the first onw: Performance (Classification). The reason for this is that a decision tree predicts a classification in an attribute—in our example, the adopter class (innovator, early adopter, etc.).

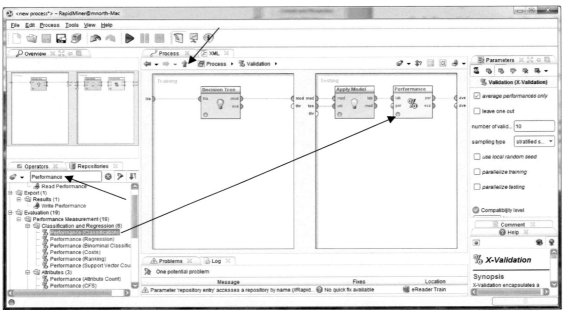

Figure 13-6. The configuration of the cross-validation sub-process.

8) Once your sub-process is configured, click the blue up arrow to return to the main process. Connect the *mod, tra* and *ave* ports to *res* ports as shown in Figure 13-7. The *mod* port will generate the visual depiction of our decision tree, the *tra* port will create the training data set's attribute table, and the *avg* port will calculate a True Positive table showing the training data set's ability to predict accurately.

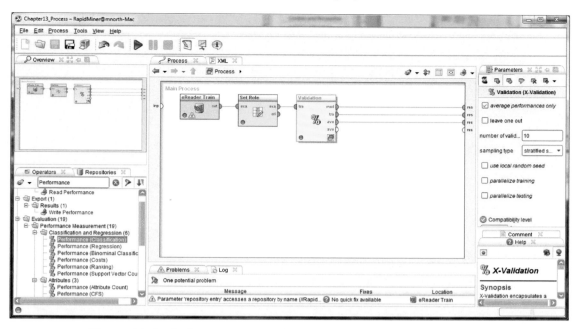

Figure 13-7. Splines to create the three desired outputs from our cross-validated Decision Tree data mining model.

9) Run the model. The ExampleSet (*tra* port) and Tree (*mod* port) tabs will be familiar to you. The PerformanceVector (*avg* port) is new, and in the context of Evaluation and Deployment, this tab is the most interesting to us. We see that using this training data set and Decision Tree algorithm (gain_ratio), RapidMiner calculates a 54% accuracy rate for this model. This overall accuracy rate reflects the class precision rates for each possible value in our eReader_Adoption attribute. For pred. Late Majority as an example, the class precision (or true positive rate) is 69.8%, leaving us with a 30.2% false positive rate for this value. If all of the possible eReader_Adoption values had true positive class precisions of 69.8%, then our model's overall accuracy would be 69.8% as well, but they don't—some are lower, and so when they are weighted and averaged, our model's overall accuracy is only 54%.

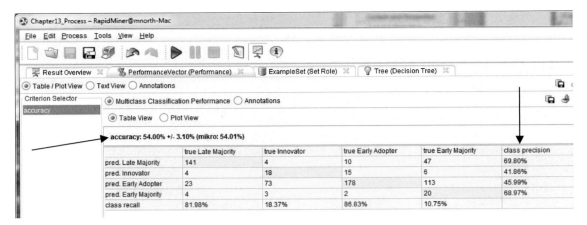

Figure 13-8. Evaluating the predictive quality of our decision tree model.

10) An overall accuracy of 54% might seem alarming, and even individual class precisions in the 40-60% range might seem discouraging, but remember, life is unpredictable, or at least inconsistent, so 100% true positives are probably a pipe dream. The probability of false positives shouldn't even be that surprising to us, because back in Chapter 10, we evaluated our Confidence Percentage attributes, and we knew back then that most of our observations had partial confidences in the predicted value. In Figure 10-10, person 77373 had some chance of landing in any one of three of the four possible adopter categories—of course there is a chance of a false positive! But that doesn't render our model useless, and perhaps we can improve it. Return to design perspective and double click on the Validation operator to re-open the sub-process. Click on the Decision Tree operator to change its criterion parameter to use gini_index as its underlying algorithm.

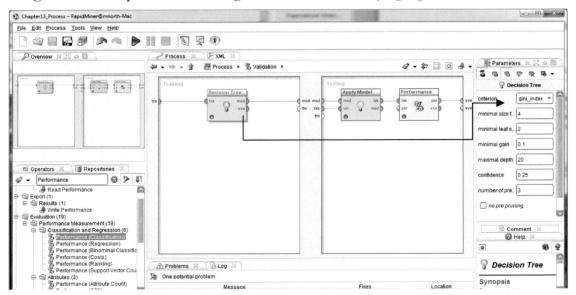

Figure 13-9. Changing the Decision Tree operator to use Gini.

11) Re-run the model. You do not need to switch back to the main process to re-run the model. You may if you wish, but you can stay in sub-process view and run it too. When you return from results perspective to design perspective, you will see whichever design window you were last in. When you re-run the model, you will see a new performance matrix, showing the model's predictive power using Gini as the underlying algorithm.

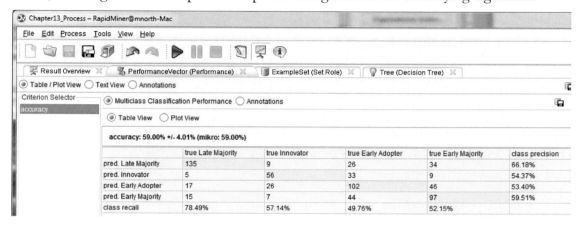

Figure 13-10. New cross-validation performance results based on the gini_index decision tree model.

We see in Figure 13-10 that our model's ability to predict is significantly improved if we use Gini for our decision tree model. This should also not come as a great surprise. We knew from Chapter 10 that the granularity in our tree's detail under Gini was much greater. Greater detail in the predictive tree *should* result in a more reliably predictive model. Feeding more and better training data into the training data set would likely raise this model's reliability even more.

CHAPTER SUMMARY: THE VALUE OF EXPERIENCE

So now we have seen one way to statistically evaluate a model's reliability. You have seen that there are a number of cross-validation and performance operators that you can use to check a training data set's ability to perform. But the bottom line is that there is no substitute for experience and expertise. Use subject matter experts to review your data mining results. Ask them to give you feedback on your model's output. Run pilot tests and use focus groups to try out your model's predictions before rolling them out organization-wide. Do not be offended if someone questions or challenges the reliability of your model's results—be humble enough to take their questions as an opportunity to validate and strengthen your model. Remember that 'pride goeth before the fall'! Data mining is a process. If you present your data mining results and recommendations as infallible, you are not participating in the cyclical nature of CRISP-DM, and you'll likely end up looking foolish sooner or later. CRISP-DM is such a good process precisely because of its ability to help us investigate data, learn from our investigation, and then do it again from a more informed position. Evaluation and Deployment are the two steps in the process where we establish that more informed position.

REVIEW QUESTIONS

1) What is cross-validation and why should you do it?

2) What is a false positive and why might one be generated?

3) Why would false positives not negate all value for a data mining model?

4) How does a model's overall performance percentage relate to the target attribute's (label's) individual performance percentages?

5) How can changing a data mining methodology's underlying algorithm affect a model's cross-validation performance percentages?

EXERCISE

For this chapter's exercise, you will create a cross-validation model for your Chapter 10 exercise training data set. Complete the following steps.

1) Open RapidMiner to a new, blank process and add the training data set you created for your Chapter 10 exercise (the Titanic survival data set).

2) Set roles as necessary.

3) Apply a cross-validation operator to the data set.

4) Configure your sub-process using gain_ratio for the Decision Tree operator's algorithm. Apply the model and run it through a Performance (Classification) operator.

5) Report your training data set's ability to predict.

6) Change your Decision Tree operator's algorthim to gini_index and re-run your model.

7) Report your results in the context of any changes that occurred in your training data set's ability to predict.

Challenge Step!

8) Change your Decision Tree operator's algorithm to one of the other options, such as information_schema, and report your results again, comparative to gain_ratio and gini_index.

Extra Challenge Step!

9) Repeat steps 1-7 for the linear regression training data set (Chapter 8). You will need to use a slightly different Performance operator. Report your results. If you would like, repeat step 8 for your Chapter 8 exercise training data set and report your results.

CHAPTER FOURTEEN:
DATA MINING ETHICS

WHY DATA MINING ETHICS?

It has been said that when you are teaching someone something, you should leave the thing that you want them to remember most to the very end. It will be the last thing they remember hearing from you, the thing they take with them as they depart from your instruction. It is in harmony with this philosophy that the chapter on data mining ethics has been left to the end of this book. Please don't misconstrue this chapter's placement as an afterthought. It is here at the end so you'll take it with you and remember it. It is believed that especially if you make a big deal out of it, the last thing you share with your audience will end up being what they remember from your teaching, so here is our effort at making a big deal about data mining ethics:

FIGURE 14-1. This Just In:
<u>BEING AN ETHICAL DATA MINER IS IMPORTANT</u>

In all seriousness, when we are dealing with data, those data represent peoples' lives. In this book alone, we have touched on peoples' buying behaviors, ownership of creative works, and even serious health issues. Imagine the ethical ramifications of using a decision tree to predict the risk levels of juvenile delinquents as just one example. You'd be profiling, potentially branding these youth, so any attempt to do so must be done ethically. But what does this mean? **Ethics** is the set of moral codes, above and beyond the legally required minimums, that an individual uses to make right and respectful decisions. When mining data, questions of an ethical nature will invariably arise. Simply because it is legal to gather and mine certain data does not make it ethical.

Because of these serious matters, there are some in the world who fear, shun and even fight against data mining. These types of reactions have led some data mining advocates and leaders to respond with attempts to defend and explain data mining technologies. One such response came in the year 2003. The Association for Computing Machinery (ACM) is the world's foremost professional organization for computing professionals in all disciplines. This includes the ACM Special Interest Group for Knowledge Discovery and Data Mining (SIGKDD). At that time, a number of criticisms and calls against data mining were occurring, mostly driven by concerns over citizens' privacy as the United States government increased its use of data mining in anti-terrorism activities in the years following the September 11th terrorist attacks. Certainly any time a government increases its scrutiny of its own citizens and those of other countries, it can be unsettling; however the leaders of ACM SIGKDD were likewise unsettled by the blame being placed on data mining itself. These leaders felt that the tool should be separated from the way it was being used. In response, the executive committee of ACM SIGKDD, a group that included such pioneers as Gregory Piatetsky-Shapiro, Usama Fayyad, Jiawei Han, and others, penned an open letter titled *"Data Mining" is NOT Against Civil Liberties*. (The two-page text of their letter is easily available on the Internet and you are encouraged to read and consider it). Their objective in writing this letter was not to defend government, or any data mining programs, but rather, to help individuals see that there is a large difference between a technology and the choices people make in the ways they use that technology.

In truth, every technology will have its detractors. It may seem a silly example, but consider a chair as a technology. It is a tool, invented by mankind to serve a purpose: sitting. If it is ergonomically designed and made of the right materials, it can facilitate very comfortable sitting. If it is fancy enough, it may exclude certain socio-economic classes from being able to own it. If pointed into a corner and associated with misbehavior, it becomes an object for punishment. If equipped with restraining straps and voltage high enough to take someone's life, it becomes a politicized object of controversy. If picked up and used to strike another person it becomes a weapon; and yet, it is still a chair. So it is with essentially all technologies—all tools invented by mankind to do work. It is not the tool, but the choices we make in how to use it, that create and answer the questions of ethics.

This is not a simple proposition. Every one of us have a different moral compass. Each is guided by a different set of values and influenced by a unique set of backgrounds, experiences and forces. No one set of ethical guidelines is completely right or completely wrong. However, there are ways for each of us to reflectively evaluate, at least for our own, and hopefully for our organizations' purposes, what our ethical parameters will be for each data mining activity we undertake. In order to aid in this process, we offer here a series of...

ETHICAL FRAMEWORKS AND SUGGESTIONS

- The brilliant legal scholar Lawrence Lessig has offered four mechanisms whereby we can frame and contain computing activities within reasonable bounds. These are:
  - **Laws**: These are statutes, enacted by a government and enforced by the same. If these are violated, they carry with them a prescribed punishment, adjudicated by a judge or a jury. Adherence to laws as a mechanism for right behavior represents the basest form of ethical decision making, because at this level, a person is merely doing what they have to do to stay out of trouble. Lessig suggests that while we often look to laws first as a method to enforce good behavior, there are other more reasonable and perhaps more effective methods.
  - **Markets**: Here Lessig suggests an economic solution to guiding behavior. If bad behavior is not profitable or would not enable an organization to stay in business, then bad behavior will not be prevalent. There are many ways that market forces, such as a good reputation for high quality products, excellent customer service, reliability, etc., can help guide good actions.
  - **Code**: In computing disciplines, code is a powerful guide of behavior, because it can be written to allow some actions while stopping others. If we feel that although it would not be illegal for members of a web site to access one another's accounts,

but that it would be unethical, we can write code to require usernames and passwords, making it more difficult for users to get into each other's personal information. Further, we can write a code of conduct, usually referred to as an Acceptable Use Policy, which dictates what users can and cannot do. The policy is not a law, that is, it is not enacted or enforced by a government, but it is an agreement to abide by certain rules or risk losing the privilege of using the site's services.

- **Social Norms**: This form of determining what is ethical is based on what is acceptable in our society. As we look around us, interact with our friends, family, neighbors, and associates, ethical bounds can be established by what is acceptable to these people. Often, if we would be embarrassed, humiliated or otherwise shamed by our behavior, if we find ourselves wanting to hide what we're doing from others, we have a strong indication that our activity is not ethical. We can also contribute to the establishment of social norms as ethical guides by making our own expectations of what is acceptable clear to others.

- **Organizational Standard Operating Procedures**: Ethical standards can often be established by creating a set of acceptable practices for your organization. Such an effort should be undertaken by company leadership, with input from a broad cross-section of employees. These should be well-documented and communicated to employees, and reviewed regularly. Checks and balances can be built into work processes to help ensure that workers are adhering to established procedures.

- **Professional Code of Conduct**: Similar to organizational operating standards, professional codes of conduct can help to establish boundaries of ethical conduct. The aforementioned Association for Computing Machinery maintains a Code of Ethics and Professional Conduct that is an excellent resource for computing professionals seeking guidance (http://www.acm.org/about/code-of-ethics). Other organizations also have codes of conduct that could be consulted in order to frame ethical decision making in data mining.

- **Immanuel Kant's Categorical Imperative**: Immanuel Kant was a German philosopher and anthropologist who lived in the 1700's. Among his extensive writings on ethical morality, Kant's Categorical Imperative is perhaps his most famous. This maxim states that if a given action cannot ethically be taken by anyone in a certain situation, then it should not be taken at all. In data mining, we could use this philosophy to determine: Would it be ethical for any business to collect and mine these data? What would be the outcome if every business mined data in this way? If the answers to such questions are negative and appear to be unethical, then we should not undertake the data mining project either.

- **Rene Descartes' Rule of Change**: Rene Descartes was a French philosopher and mathematician who like Kant, wrote extensively about moral decision making. His rule of change reflects his mathematical background. It states that if an act cannot be taken repeatedly, it is not ethical to do that act even once. Again to apply this to data mining, we can ask: Can I collect and mine these data on an ongoing basis without causing problems for myself, my organization, our customers or others? If you cannot do it repeatedly, according to Decartes, then you shouldn't do it at all.

There are a few other ways that are not quite as specifically defined that you can use to seek out ethical boundaries. There is the old adage known as the Golden Rule, which dictates that we should treat others the way we hope they would treat us. There are also philosophies that help us to consider how our actions might be perceived by others and how they might make them feel. Some ethical frameworks are built around actions that will bring the greatest good to the largest number of people.

CONCLUSION

We can protect privacy by aggregating data, anonymizing observations through removal of names and personally identifiable information, and by storing it in secure and protected environments. When you are busy working with numbers, attributes and observations, it can be easy to forget about the people behind the data. We should be cautious when data mining models might brand a person as a certain risk. Be sensitive to peoples' feelings and rights. When appropriate, ask for the their permission to gather and use data about them. Don't rationalize a justification for your data mining project—ensure that you're doing fair and just work that will help and benefit others.

Regardless of the mechanism you use to determine your ethical boundaries, our hope is that you will always keep ethical behavior in mind when mining data. Remember the personal side of what you are doing. As we began this book, we talked about the desire to introduce the subject of data mining to a new, non-traditional audience. We hope you are gaining confidence in your data mining skills, and that your creativity is helping you to envision your own data mining solutions to real-world problems you might be facing. Go exploring both within RapidMiner and through other tools for ways to find unexpected and interesting patterns in your data. The purpose of this book from the outset was to be a beginner's guide, a way to get started in data mining—even if you don't have a background in computer science or data analysis. Hopefully through the chapter examples and exercises, you've learned a lot and are well on your way to becoming an accomplished, and ethical, data miner. You've learned enough to be dangerous...don't be. Apply what you've learned to use data as a powerful and beneficial advantage. And so as we close this book, let us do so as we began it: Let's start digging!

GLOSSARY AND INDEX

This glossary contains key words, bolded throughout the text, and their definitions as they are used for the purposes of this book. The page number listed is not the only page where the term is found, but it is the page where the term is introduced or where it is primarily defined and discussed.

Antecedent: In an association rules data mining model, the antecedent is the attribute which precedes the consequent in an identified rule. Attribute order makes a difference when calculating the confidence percentage, so identifying which attribute comes first is necessary even if the reciprocal of the association is also a rule. (Page 85)

Archived Data: Data which have been copied out of a live production database and into a data warehouse or other permanent system where they can be accessed and analyzed, but not by primary operational business systems. (Page 18)

Association Rules: A data mining methodology which compares attributes in a data set across all observations to identify areas where two or more attributes are frequently found together. If their frequency of coexistence is high enough throughout the data set, the association of those attributes can be said to be a rule. (Page 74)

Attribute: In columnar data, an attribute is one column. It is named in the data so that it can be referred to by a model and used in data mining. The term attribute is sometimes interchanged with the terms 'field', 'variable', or 'column'. (Page 16)

Average: The arithmetic mean, calculated by summing all values and dividing by the count of the values. (Pages 47, 77)

Binomial: A data type for any set of values that is limited to one of two numeric options. (Page 80)

Binominal: In RapidMiner, the data type binominal is used instead of binomial, enabling both numerical and character-based sets of values that are limited to one of two options. (Page 80)

Business Understanding: See Organizational Understanding. (Page 6)

Case: See Observation. (Page 16)

Case Sensitive: A situation where a computer program recognizes the uppercase version of a letter or word as being different from the lowercase version of the same letter or word. (Page 199)

Classification: One of the two main goals of conducting data mining activities, with the other being prediction. Classification creates groupings in a data set based on the similarity of the observations' attributes. Some data mining methodologies, such as decision trees, can predict an observation's classification. (Page 9)

Code: Code is the result of a computer worker's work. It is a set of instructions, typed in a specific grammar and syntax, that a computer can understand and execute. According to Lawrence Lessig, it is one of four methods humans can use to set and control boundaries for behavior when interacting with computer systems. (Page 233)

Coefficient: In data mining, a coefficient is a value that is calculated based on the values in a data set that can be used as a multiplier or as an indicator of the relative strength of some attribute or component in a data mining model. (Page 63)

Column: See Attribute. (Page 16)

Comma Separated Values (CSV): A common text-based format for data sets where the divisions between attributes (columns of data) are indicated by commas. If commas occur naturally in some of the values in the data set, a CSV file will misunderstand these to be attribute separators, leading to misalignment of attributes. (Page 35)

Conclusion: See Consequent. (Page 85)

Confidence (Alpha) Level: A value, usually 5% or 0.05, used to test for statistical significance in some data mining methods. If statistical significance is found, a data miner can say that there is a 95% likelihood that a calculated or predicted value is not a false positive. (Page 132)

Confidence Percent: In predictive data mining, this is the percent of calculated confidence that the model has calculated for one or more possible predicted values. It is a measure for the likelihood of false positives in predictions. Regardless of the number of possible predicted values, their collective confidence percentages will always total to 100%. (Page 84)

Consequent: In an association rules data mining model, the consequent is the attribute which results from the antecedent in an identified rule. If an association rule were characterized as "If *this*, then *that*", the consequent would be *that*—in other words, the outcome. (Page 85)

Correlation: A statistical measure of the strength of affinity, based on the similarity of observational values, of the attributes in a data set. These can be positive (as one attribute's values go up *or* down, so too does the correlated attribute's values); or negative (correlated attributes' values move in opposite directions). Correlations are indicated by coefficients which fall on a scale between -1 (complete negative correlation) and 1 (complete positive correlation), with 0 indicating no correlation at all between two attributes. (Page 59)

CRISP-DM: An acronym for Cross-Industry Standard Process for Data Mining. This process was jointly developed by several major multi-national corporations around the turn of the new millennium in order to standardize the approach to mining data. It is comprised of six cyclical steps: Business (Organizational) Understanding, Data Understanding, Data Preparation, Modeling, Evaluation, Deployment. (Page 5)

Cross-validation: A method of statistically evaluating a training data set for its likelihood of producing false positives in a predictive data mining model. (Page 221).

Data: Data are any arrangement and compilation of facts. Data may be structured (e.g. arranged in columns (attributes) and rows (observations)), or unstructured (e.g. paragraphs of text, computer log file). (Page 3)

Data Analysis: The process of examining data in a repeatable and structured way in order to extract meaning, patterns or messages from a set of data. (Page 3)

Data Mart: A location where data are stored for easy access by a broad range of people in an organization. Data in a data mart are generally archived data, enabling analysis in a setting that does not impact live operations. (Page 20)

Data Mining: A computational process of analyzing data sets, usually large in nature, using both statistical and logical methods, in order to uncover hidden, previously unknown, and interesting patterns that can inform organizational decision making. (Page 3)

Data Preparation: The third in the six steps of CRISP-DM. At this stage, the data miner ensures that the data to be mined are clean and ready for mining. This may include handling outliers or other inconsistent data, dealing with missing values, reducing attributes or observations, setting attribute roles for modeling, etc. (Page 8)

Data Set: Any compilation of data that is suitable for analysis. (Page 18)

Data Type: In a data set, each attribute is assigned a data type based on the kind of data stored in the attribute. There are many data types which can be generalized into one of three areas: Character (Text) based; Numeric; and Date/Time. Within these categories, RapidMiner has several data types. For example, in the Character area, RapidMiner has Polynominal, Binominal, etc.; and in the Numeric area it has Real, Integer, etc. (Page 39)

Data Understanding: The second in the six steps of CRISP-DM. At this stage, the data miner seeks out sources of data in the organization, and works to collect, compile, standardize, define and document the data. The data miner develops a comprehension of where the data have come from, how they were collected and what they mean. (Page 7)

Data Warehouse: A large-scale repository for archived data which are available for analysis. Data in a data warehouse are often stored in multiple formats (e.g. by week, month, quarter and year), facilitating large scale analyses at higher speeds. The data warehouse is populated by extracting data from operational systems so that analyses do not interfere with live business operations. (Page 18)

Database: A structured organization of facts that is organized such that the facts can be reliably and repeatedly accessed. The most common type of database is a relational database, in which facts (data) are arranged in tables of columns and rows. The data are then accessed using a query language, usually SQL (Structured Query Language), in order to extract meaning from the tables. (Page 16)

Decision Tree: A data mining methodology where leaves and nodes are generated to construct a predictive tree, whereby a data miner can see the attributes which are most predictive of each possible outcome in a target (label) attribute. (Pages 9, 159).

Denormalization: The process of removing relational organization from data, reintroducing redundancy into the data, but simultaneously eliminating the need for joins in a relational database, enabling faster querying. (Page 18)

Dependent Variable (Attribute): The attribute in a data set that is being acted upon by the other attributes. It is the thing we want to predict, the target, or label, attribute in a predictive model. (Page 108)

Deployment: The sixth and final of the six steps of CRISP-DM. At this stage, the data miner takes the results of data mining activities and puts them into practice in the organization. The data miner watches closely and collects data to determine if the deployment is successful and ethical. Deployment can happen in stages, such as through pilot programs before a full-scale roll out. (Page 10)

Descartes' Rule of Change: An ethical framework set forth by Rene Descartes which states that if an action cannot be taken repeatedly, it cannot be ethically taken even once. (Page 235)

Design Perspective: The view in RapidMiner where a data miner adds operators to a data mining stream, sets those operators' parameters, and runs the model. (Page 41)

Discriminant Analysis: A predictive data mining model which attempts to compare the values of all observations across all attributes and identify where natural breaks occur from one category to another, and then predict which category each observation in the data set will fall into. (Page 108)

Ethics: A set of moral codes or guidelines that an individual develops to guide his or her decision making in order to make fair and respectful decisions and engage in right actions. Ethical standards are higher than legally required minimums. (Page 232)

Evaluation: The fifth of the six steps of CRISP-DM. At this stage, the data miner reviews the results of the data mining model, interprets results and determines how useful they are. He or she may also conduct an investigation into false positives or other potentially misleading results. (Page 10)

False Positive: A predicted value that ends up not being correct. (Page 221)

Field: See Attribute (Page 16).

Frequency Pattern: A recurrence of the same, or similar, observations numerous times in a single data set. (Page 81)

Fuzzy Logic: A data mining concept often associated with neural networks where predictions are made using a training data set, even though some uncertainty exists regarding the data and a model's predictions. (Page 181)

Gain Ratio: One of several algorithms used to construct decision tree models. (Page 168)

Gini Index: An algorithm created by Corrodo Gini that can be used to generate decision tree models. (Page 168)

Heterogeneity: In statistical analysis, this is the amount of variety found in the values of an attribute. (Page 119)

Inconsistent Data: These are values in an attribute in a data set that are out-of-the-ordinary among the whole set of values in that attribute. They can be statistical outliers, or other values that simply don't make sense in the context of the 'normal' range of values for the attribute. They are generally replaced or remove during the Data Preparation phase of CRISP-DM. (Page 50)

Independent Variable (Attribute): These are attributes that act on the dependent attribute (the target, or label). They are used to help predict the label in a predictive model. (Pages 133)

Jittering: The process of adding a small, random decimal to discrete values in a data set so that when they are plotted in a scatter plot, they are slightly apart from one another, enabling the analyst to better see clustering and density. (Pages 17, 70)

Join: The process of connecting two or more tables in a relational database together so that their attributes can be accessed in a single query, such as in a view. (Page 17)

Kant's Categorical Imperative: An ethical framework proposed by Immanuel Kant which states that if *everyone* cannot ethically take some action, then *no one* can ethically take that action. (Page 234)

k-Means Clustering: A data mining methodology that uses the mean (average) values of the attributes in a data set to group each observation into a cluster of other observations whose values are most similar to the mean for that cluster. (Page 92)

Label: In RapidMiner, this is the role that must be set in order to use an attribute as the dependent, or target, attribute in a predictive model. (Page 108)

Laws: These are regulatory statutes which have associated consequences that are established and enforced by a governmental agency. According to Lawrence Lessig, these are one of the four methods for establishing boundaries to define and regulate social behavior. (Page 233)

Leaf: In a decision tree data mining model, this is the terminal end point of a branch, indicating the predicted outcome for observations whose values follow that branch of the tree. (Page 164)

Linear Regression: A predictive data mining method which uses the algebraic formula for calculating the slope of a line in order to predict where a given observation will likely fall along that line. (Page 128)

Logistic Regression: A predictive data mining method which uses a quadratic formula to predict one of a set of possible outcomes, along with a probability that the prediction will be the actual outcome. (Page 142)

Markets: A socio-economic construct in which peoples' buying, selling, and exchanging behaviors define the boundaries of acceptable or unacceptable behavior. Lawrence Lessig offers this as one of four methods for defining the parameters of appropriate behavior. (Page 233)

Mean: See Average. (Pages 47, 77)

Median: With the Mean and Mode, this is one of three generally used Measures of Central Tendency. It is an arithmetic way of defining what 'normal' looks like in a numeric attribute. It is calculated by rank ordering the values in an attribute and finding the one in the middle. If there are an even number of observations, the two in the middle are averaged to find the median. (Page 47)

Meta Data: These are facts that describe the observational values in an attribute. Meta data may include who collected the data, when, why, where, how, how often; and usually include some descriptive statistics such as the range, average, standard deviation, etc. (Page 42)

Missing Data: These are instances in an observation where one or more attributes does not have a value. It is not the same as zero, because zero is a value. Missing data are like Null values in a database, they are either unknown or undefined. These are usually replaced or removed during the Data Preparation phase of CRISP-DM. (Page 30)

Mode: With Mean and Median, this is one of three common Measures of Central Tendency. It is the value in an attribute which is the most common. It can be numerical or text. If an attribute contains two or more values that appear an equal number of times and more than any other values, then all are listed as the mode, and the attribute is said to be Bimodal or Multimodal. (Pages 42, 47)

Model: A computer-based representation of real-life events or activities, constructed upon the basis of data which represent those events. (Page 8)

Name (Attribute): This is the text descriptor of each attribute in a data set. In RapidMiner, the first row of an imported data set should be designated as the attribute name, so that these are not interpreted as the first observation in the data set. (Page 38)

Neural Network: A predictive data mining methodology which tries to mimic human brain processes by comparing the values of all attributes in a data set to one another through the use of a hidden layer of nodes. The frequencies with which the attribute values match, or are strongly similar, create neurons which become stronger at higher frequencies of similarity. (Page 176)

n-Gram: In text mining, this is a combination of words or word stems that represent a phrase that may have more meaning or significance that would the single word or stem. (Page 201)

Node: A terminal or mid-point in decision trees and neural networks where an attribute branches or forks away from other terminal or branches because the values represented at that point have become significantly different from all other values for that attribute. (Page 164)

Normalization: In a relational database, this is the process of breaking data out into multiple related tables in order to reduce redundancy and eliminate multivalued dependencies. (Page 18)

Null: The absence of a value in a database. The value is unrecorded, unknown, or undefined. See Missing Values. (Page 30)

Observation: A row of data in a data set. It consists of the value assigned to each attribute for one record in the data set. It is sometimes called a tuple in database language. (Page 16)

Online Analytical Processing (OLAP): A database concept where data are collected and organized in a way that facilitates analysis, rather than practical, daily operational work. Evaluating data in a data warehouse is an example of OLAP. The underlying structure that collects and holds the data makes analysis faster, but would slow down transactional work. (Page 18)

Online Transaction Processing (OLTP): A database concept where data are collected and organized in a way that facilitates fast and repeated transactions, rather than broader analytical work. Scanning items being purchased at a cash register is an example of OLTP. The underlying structure that collects and holds the data makes transactions faster, but would slow down analysis. (Page 17)

Operational Data: Data which are generated as a result of day-to-day work (e.g. the entry of work orders for an electrical service company). (Page 19)

Operator: In RapidMiner, an operator is any one of more than 100 tools that can be added to a data mining stream in order to perform some function. Functions range from adding a data set, to setting an attribute's role, to applying a modeling algorithm. Operators are connected into a stream by way of ports connected by splines. (Page 34, 41)

Organizational Data: These are data which are collected by an organization, often in aggregate or summary format, in order to address a specific question, tell a story, or answer a specific question. They may be constructed from Operational Data, or added to through other means such as surveys, questionnaires or tests. (Page 19)

Organizational Understanding: The first step in the CRISP-DM process, usually referred to as Business Understanding, where the data miner develops an understanding of an organization's goals, objectives, questions, and anticipated outcomes relative to data mining tasks. The data miner must understand *why* the data mining task is being undertaken before proceeding to gather and understand data. (Page 6)

Parameters: In RapidMiner, these are the settings that control values and thresholds that an operator will use to perform its job. These may be the attribute name and role in a Set Role operator, or the algorithm the data miner desires to use in a model operator. (Page 44)

Port: The input or output required for an operator to perform its function in RapidMiner. These are connected to one another using splines. (Page 41)

Prediction: The target, or label, or dependent attribute that is generated by a predictive model, usually for a scoring data set in a model. (Page 8)

Premise: See Antecedent. (Page 85)

Privacy: The concept describing a person's right to be let alone; to have information about them kept away from those who should not, or do not need to, see it. A data miner must always respect and safeguard the privacy of individuals represented in the data he or she mines. (Page 20)

Professional Code of Conduct: A helpful guide or documented set of parameters by which an individual in a given profession agrees to abide. These are usually written by a board or panel of experts and adopted formally by a professional organization. (Page 234)

Query: A method of structuring a question, usually using code, that can be submitted to, interpreted, and answered by a computer. (Page 17)

Record: See Observation. (Page 16)

Relational Database: A computerized repository, comprised of entities that relate to one another through keys. The most basic and elemental entity in a relational database is the table, and tables are made up of attributes. One or more of these attributes serves as a key that can be matched (or related) to a corresponding attribute in another table, creating the relational effect which reduces data redundancy and eliminates multivalued dependencies. (Page 16)

Repository: In RapidMiner, this is the place where imported data sets are stored so that they are accessible for modeling. (Page 34)

Results Perspective: The view in RapidMiner that is seen when a model has been run. It is usually comprised of two or more tabs which show meta data, data in a spreadsheet-like view, and predictions and model outcomes (including graphical representations where applicable). (Page 41)

Role (Attribute): In a data mining model, each attribute must be assigned a role. The role is the part the attribute plays in the model. It is usually equated to serving as an independent variable (regular), or dependent variable (label). (Page 39)

Row: See Observation. (Page 16)

Sample: A subset of an entire data set, selected randomly or in a structured way. This usually reduces a data set down, allowing models to be run faster, especially during development and proof-of-concept work on a model. (Page 49)

Scoring Data: A data set with the same attributes as a training data set in a predictive model, with the exception of the label. The training data set, with the label defined, is used to create a predictive model, and that model is then applied to a scoring data set possessing the same attributes in order to predict the label for each scoring observation. (Page 108)

Social Norms: These are the sets of behaviors and actions that are generally tolerated and found to be acceptable in a society. According to Lawrence Lessig, these are one of four methods of defining and regulating appropriate behavior. (Page 233)

Spline: In RapidMiner, these lines connect the ports between operators, creating the stream of a data mining model. (Page 41)

Standard Deviation: One of the most common statistical measures of how dispersed the values in an attribute are. This measure can help determine whether or not there are outliers (a common type of inconsistent data) in a data set. (Page 77)

Standard Operating Procedures: These are organizational guidelines that are documented and shared with employees which help to define the boundaries for appropriate and acceptable behavior in the business setting. They are usually created and formally adopted by a group of leaders in the organization, with input from key stakeholders in the organization. (Page 234)

Statistical Significance: In statistically-based data mining activities, this is the measure of whether or not the model has yielded any results that are mathematically reliable enough to be used. Any model lacking statistical significance should not be used in operational decision making. (Page 133)

Stemming: In text mining, this is the process of reducing like-terms down into a single, common token (e.g. country, countries, country's, countryman, etc. → countr). (Page 201)

Stopwords: In text mining, these are small words that are necessary for grammatical correctness, but which carry little meaning or power in the message of the text being mined. These are often articles, prepositions or conjuntions, such as 'a', 'the', 'and', etc., and are usually removed in the Process Document operator's sub-process. (Page 199)

Stream: This is the string of operators in a data mining model, connected through the operators' ports via splines, that represents all actions that will be taken on a data set in order to mine it. (Page 41)

Structured Query Language (SQL): The set of codes, reserved keywords and syntax defined by the American National Standards Institute used to create, manage and use relational databases. (Page 17)

Sub-process: In RapidMiner, this is a stream of operators set up to apply a series of actions to all inputs connected to the parent operator. (Page 197)

Support Percent: In an association rule data mining model, this is the percent of the time that when the antecedent is found in an observation, the consequent is also found. Since this is calculated as the number of times the two are found together divided by the total number of they *could have* been found together, the Support Percent is the same for reciprocal rules. (Page 84)

Table: In data collection, a table is a grid of columns and rows, where in general, the columns are individual attributes in the data set, and the rows are observations across those attributes. Tables are the most elemental entity in relational databases. (Page 16)

Target Attribute: See Label; Dependent Variable. (Page 108)

Technology: Any tool or process invented by mankind to do or improve work. (Page 11)

Text Mining: The process of data mining unstructured text-based data such as essays, news articles, speech transcripts, etc. to discover patterns of word or phrase usage to reveal deeper or previously unrecognized meaning. (Page 190)

Token (Tokenize): In text mining, this is the process of turning words in the input document(s) into attributes that can be mined. (Page 197)

Training Data: In a predictive model, this data set already has the label, or dependent variable defined, so that it can be used to create a model which can be applied to a scoring data set in order to generate predictions for the latter. (Page 108)

Tuple: See Observation. (Page 16)

Variable: See Attribute. (Page 16)

View: A type of pseudo-table in a relational database which is actually a named, stored query. This query runs against one or more tables, retrieving a defined number of attributes that can then be referenced as if they were in a table in the database. Views can limit users' ability to see attributes to only those that are relevant and/or approved for those users to see. They can also speed up the query process because although they may contain joins, the key columns for the joins can be indexed and cached, making the view's query run faster than it would if it were not stored as a view. Views can be useful in data mining as data miners can be given read-only access to the view, upon which they can build data mining models, without having to have broader administrative rights on the database itself. (Page 27)

ABOUT THE AUTHOR

Dr. Matthew North is Associate Professor of Computing and Information Studies at Washington & Jefferson College in Washington, Pennsylvania, USA. He has taught data management and data mining for more than a decade, and previously worked in industry as a data miner, most recently at eBay.com. He continues to consult with various organizations on data mining projects as well.

Dr. North holds a Bachelor of Arts degree in Latin American History and Portuguese from Brigham Young University; a Master of Science in Business Information Systems from Utah State University; and a Doctorate in Technology Education from West Virginia University. He is the author of the book *Life Lessons & Leadership* (Agami Press, 2011), and numerous papers and articles on technology and pedagogy. His dissertation, on the topic of teaching models and learning styles in introductory data mining courses, earned him a New Faculty Fellows award from the Center for Advancement of Scholarship on Engineering Education (CASEE); and in 2010, he was awarded the Ben Bauman Award for Excellence by the International Association for Computer Information Systems (IACIS). He lives with his wife, Joanne, and their three daughters in southwestern Pennsylvania.

To contact Dr. North regarding this text, consulting or training opportunities, or for speaking engagements, please access this book's companion web site at:

https://sites.google.com/site/dataminingforthemasses/